Open Secrets

Open Secrets

ISRAELI NUCLEAR AND FOREIGN POLICIES

Israel Shahak

Pluto Press
LONDON • CHICAGO, ILLINOIS

First published 1997 by Pluto Press
345 Archway Road, London N6 5AA
and 1436 West Randolph
Chicago, Illinois 60607, USA

Reprinted 1997

British Library Cataloguing in Publication Data
A catalogue record for this book is available
from the British Library

ISBN 0 7453 1152 0 hbk

Library of Congress Cataloging in Publication Data
Shahak, Israel
   Open secrets: Israeli nuclear and foreign policies/Israel
Shahak.
      pp.   cm.
   Includes bibliographical references and index.
   ISBN 0–7453–1152–0 (hbk)
      1. Israel—Foreign relations. 2. Israel and the diaspora.
   3. Jews—United States—Attitudes towards Israel. I. Title.
   DS119.6.S49   1997
   327.5694–dc20
                                            96–34397
                                                CIP

Printed in Great Britain

Dedicated to the memory of Witold Jedlicki
without whose help this book could
not have been written

Contents

Foreword by Christopher Hitchens

I should like to begin – very probably to the ire of the author of these pages – by introducing the writer as well as the subject. Dr Israel Shahak has been for many decades a beloved guide, in the superior sense of that term, to the city of Jerusalem, to the culture of a multi-historical Palestine, to the politics of a multi-national state and to the archaeology of a multi-layered civilization. I am only one of many writers and visitors to have drawn upon an immense and uncovenanted reward, merely by acquaintance with a man who has decided to act and to live and to think as if we already dwelt in a reasoned community.

One can summarize the biographical headings without capturing the point. Nevertheless – born in the doomed Eastern European diaspora, unlucky by the obverse of what Helmut Kohl so crassly called (of his own complacent case) 'the grace of late birth'. Condemned as a boy to witness the clearance and then the destruction of his people and much of his family. Embracing Palestine as a refuge and home, and then deciding (by degrees, naturally) that the entire answer to the ancient conundrum of racialism and bigotry and fanaticism had not been discovered by the messianic. I think we can already see the difference between this kind of 'multi' and the soft-centred and innocuous versions that are so freely offered by those in the West who fear only intolerance and 'insensitivity' and who, under this sanitizing rubric, promote the phoney rhetoric of consensus.

On occasion, when I have telephoned him to discover the latest developments within Israeli society, Shahak has unaffectedly said, 'There are encouraging signs of polarization'. For most of our domesticated intellectuals, such a statement is absurd on its face. What, after all, can be more desirable than consensus? Yet Shahak, in his lonely analysis, has accomplished a synthesis that will forever mystify and evade our practitioners of pseudo-realism and 'accord'. Some decades ago, he foresaw a gruesome unity between the ultra-nationalists (who had been mostly secular) and the ultra-clerical (who had been mostly indifferent to the project of territorial acquisition). Now, for those Israeli Jews who seek an accommodation with their Palestinian Arab neighbours, and for those Israeli Jews who do not wish to live in a fully theocratic state, the alarm has begun to toll. Those who desire an Arab-free land, and those who wish for an exclusive and rabbinically-determined culture for Jews, have made common cause. The prophet of this confrontation (I trust he will overlook the first of these expressions) is Dr Shahak. And this explains the hatred which he attracts from the certified peaceniks. Shall I soon forget an evening in Washington DC, not long after the disaster and atrocity of Lebanon in the summer of 1982? A gathering of anxious and well-meaning liberals had been assembled, to hear General Matti Peled. As a uniformed figure, he was naturally considered acceptable and impregnable. He uttered some 'Peace Now' platitudes and consoled the audience. And then I asked him about Shahak's interpretation and he became contorted with rage: 'Madman ... delinquent ... extremist ...'. Here was the ticket to the status of OK dissident. (And now I ask myself: Whatever *did* happen to Matti, the one-time hero of Gaza and darling of the peace-loving diaspora?)

The following pages do not answer that now-irrelevant question. What the following pages do is to show a mind at work. And also a society at work – that Israeli Jewish society that is so seldom scrutinized in the West. In order to explain the reluctance or incapacity of our mainstream gurus to spend any time on this topic, we might have to postulate the hitherto unthinkable, the self-hating Gentile. How else to explain the refusal to engage with the way the Israeli elite actually thinks? The late I. F. Stone once said that it was easier to publish criticism of Zionism in the Israeli press than in the American. He didn't guess the half of it. In the public prints, in official reports and in semi-official interviews, the mentality of the ruling order gradually discloses itself. Very often, even if only because it must seek justification, the disclosure is authentic and requires a certain integrity. And Dr Shahak is there, at the elbow or the shoulder, keeping notes and taking names. Possibly you desire to know the real nature of Israeli nuclear doctrine. Then turn to page 37. In the case of a war with Syria, which city north of Damascus would first be obliterated? See page 76. Does it matter what Ariel Sharon thinks about Israel as a regional superpower? Don't make your mind up until you have scanned page 32 (I might add that these were written with unusual prescience at a time when many Panglossians believed that the Sharon factor was a thing of the past.) Have you ever heard yourself uttering the cretinous liberal mantra 'Think globally, act locally'? Read on, if you wish to understand how a truly serious regime will put such a slogan into reverse.

Shahak was unusual if not unique in his criticism of the 'Oslo accords' because he understood at once that the agreement was *not* local. It was, instead, a holding action, designed to keep the Palestinians in baulk while trumpeting a settlement as the admission card for international acceptance. In an especially luminous passage, he shows how the degraded Arafat dialectic operated even to the disadvantage of his Labor Party sponsors. Rendered effectually impotent by the 'accords', the great leader had no currency except the rhetoric of religious redemption. And in his fervid but empty periods about holy Jerusalem, he was able to frighten Israeli voters without threatening them, and thus to help consummate the return of the Jabotinsky/Stern faction – though this time draped in a *haredi* garb. By seeing this without sentiment, and by scorning those who had helped bring it to pass, Shahak earned again the right to sound the alarm against those who would coerce Jews in the analogous way. There is quite literally no other critic or commentator who can claim this non-sectarian privilege.

Those who will murder and repress Arabs for the sake of a pure land will also murder and repress Jews. This has already been proved, and proved at the expense not just of Israeli peace-marchers but even at the expense of a master of cynical statecraft like Yitzhak Rabin. Nobody warned of this contingency, to my knowledge, except Yehoshua Leibowicz – then editor of the *Encyclopaedia Hebraica* – and Israel Shahak. For Shahak in particular, the past is not another country but potentially the same one writ large. In his considered view, the emancipation of the Jews by the Enlightenment was not merely their emancipation from Christian anti-Semitism, it was also their liberation from a ghetto priesthood and from imposed scriptural control. Viewed through this optic, the reassertion of Orthodoxy is retrograde for Jews and calamitous for those non-Jews who might get in the way (by, say, chancing to live in the wrong place) of their heaven-determined project.

If I have a criticism of these pages (and I have several) it would be this: the strict insistence upon certifiable truth sometimes overlooks the ironies. Thus, Shahak tells us a good deal about the sordid errand-boy tasks performed by Israel for its American patron, everywhere from Zaire to El Salvador. But was not Zionism supposed to free the Jews from dependence upon the *goyim?* Again it is often said, and not entirely without evidence, that Israel is 'the only democracy in the Middle East'. How does this boast actually work upon the mentality of those who operate censorship, carry out beatings and curfews, enforce 'emergency laws' and preserve official secrecy? Our author is often sarcastic at the expense of such procedures. He was one of the very first to suggest, by a very intricate and exact process of induction from available evidence, that there must have been something more than negligence involved in the extraordinary laxity of Shabak, the over-praised security services, during the last rally attended by Prime Minister Rabin. But one would like to learn still more of those who, so to speak, 'live the contradiction'.

Perhaps I am asking too much. In a fine essay on religio-racial state ideology, Shahak drives home the elementary point that people with a decided world-view very often *actually mean what they say*. For tenderly-nurtured New York liberals, it might come as a bit of a shock that American cash is raised, tax-deductibly at that, so that Jewish-only roads may be built to connect Jewish-only towns. Any irony here will be at the expense of those who do not choose to see it. Mr Shimon Peres, the beau ideal of those liberal New York congregations, allows modestly but furtively that, yes, it was indeed he who 'fathered' the Israeli nuclear programme. But will he still claim the credit when Dimona turns into Chernobyl? Or when it is used as the threat for another 'Masada'? The logic of politics is pitiless – else why does Mr Peres even as I write look like a dog being washed? And why does Mr Arafat, the harried municipal underling of their agreement, look more and more like the Grand Mufti – a title which needs the word 'grand' to cover its nudity and its reminiscence of the servile role of the ancient Palestinian 'notable'?

Shahak can afford to speak as he finds, because he long ago discerned that revealed religion is man-made. In this book, you will have the pleasure of reading an equal-opportunity sceptic: disdainful alike of the supernatural claims of Maronites, Muslims, Druze and Orthodox of all stripes, shades and beard-lengths. Much depends upon the outcome of his critique and his honest inquiry. He may be seen as the outcrop of a secular and assimilated past, of the sort which gave Jewish genius its greatest efflorescence in the work of Marx and Freud and Einstein, and of those who grew up to criticize them in their turn. He may also be viewed as a descendant of Spinoza; of free thinking more or less for its own sake and of the consolations of philosophy for the isolated individual. Such speculations might be designed to embarrass him. It remains the case that he has kept alive the candle of reason and humanism, in a neighbourhood which always threatens it with the snuff, and at a time when this poor candle is all we have.

Preface

Netanyahu and Israel's Strategies

In my view the significance of Netanyahu's political victory, as far as Israeli strategies are concerned, is limited. Israeli long-range plans are decided upon by army generals, intelligence seniors and high officials. The government and the Prime Minister only rarely initiate policy. In all wars started by Israel, its government has been informed of decisions to attack when troops were already in position. Under such conditions, the government simply approves the decisions made, long before, by others. It is these 'others' who I mainly quote in this book.

There is much greater agreement on foreign policy among all parties, 'left' and 'right', than is supposed by observers outside Israel. Let me consider the career of Avraham Tamir, now one of the three members of the 'planning committee' advising Netanyahu on strategy. Tamir began in the 1970s as an expert to Labor Chief-of-Staff Gur; under Sharon he was chief planner of the 1982 invasion of Lebanon; in 1984 he became the director general of the Prime Minister's office under Peres; then he joined the 'left' Meretz party and, in early 1996, he joined Likud. Now he advises Netanyahu on Syria. Tamir's career (recorded in the Hebrew press) reveals a stability of strategic aims.

By comparison, phrases are of very limited significance. Netanyahu once said that Arafat was 'worse than Hitler' (Orna Kadosh, *Maariv*, 26 March 1993). On 3 October 1996, Avinoam Bar Yosef reported in the same paper that Netanyahu told Arafat: 'you are my partner and friend'. One may be sure that the principles of Israeli strategy, reported in this book, have not altered because of such changes in mere phraseology.

Israel Shahak
Jerusalem, October 1996

Introduction

I know that many books have been published in English about Israel and its policies. I also know that many books have been published in English about Arab–Israeli conflict. Omitting the merely apologetic presentations of Israel and its policies among them, to which I will not refer, there are in my view a number of systematic errors prevalent in most of those books (or at least in those I have seen). It is my intention to begin a process of rectification of those errors. However, instead of criticizing my predecessors I will try to explain what I am trying to do, and thus, I hope, the novelty of my approach will be apparent.

I would like to explain here the general assumptions (to be illustrated in the book itself) on which my approach is based. I think that the aims of the State of Israel (and its predecessor the Zionist Movement) at any given period of time have to be understood according to what the Israeli leaders say to their followers, and now especially by what they say to the Israeli Jewish elite. They cannot be understood according to what they they say to the outside world. The official declarations of any state are often intended to deceive, but the leaders of any state with relatively free elections must say what their real intentions are, to their followers, or to serious commentators of the press (who are mainly in general agreement with the establishment). This tendency must be especially strong in a state (like Israel) whose army is composed of its own citizens and dependent on their willingness to fight. This means that on the issues of Israeli foreign policy, what is said, especially by Israeli generals or commentators with good connections to those generals, to the Hebrew press, will reveal to some extent real Israeli policies.

In this respect it should be recalled that the strength of the State of Israel resides first of all in its armed forces which are comprised of citizens, some of whom (especially if of the upper class) serve as volunteers in elite units. It is because it enlists all its Jewish citizens in its army that Israel can manage to employ relatively large forces in relation to its population. True, Israel discriminates against all non-Jews, which in practice means against all its Arab citizens, most of whom are not called to serve in the Army, and may serve only if they volunteer. Nevertheless, the Jewish citizens of Israel who are the majority comprise the Army and Israeli policies must be

1

explained to them. Maybe some of them only need persuasion via
the television, but some need more. The Israeli Jewish elite, who
take a great interest in politics and also fulfil an enormous role in
the Army, require serious persuasion – through information,
explanation and even a debate carried out in the Hebrew press.

The latter stages of the Lebanese War have shown that when
Israeli Jewish society is deeply divided about the political aims of
the Israeli government, the Israeli Army fights badly. Other Israeli
wars have shown that when Israeli Jewish society agrees with the
political aims of the Israeli government, the Israeli Army fights well.
The invasion of Lebanon in June 1982 (supported initially by a great
majority of Israeli Jews) has illustrated two other important political
facts. First, it was possible to predict, several months ahead of the
actual invasion, that Israel would soon invade Lebanon: indeed, I
had predicted the invasion using only information taken from such
open sources as the Hebrew press. Second, the necessary process
of convincing Israeli Jewish society of the need to invade Lebanon,
carried out quite openly, allowed people, including opponents of
Israeli policies, to predict those policies. This is in my view even
more true now. This is also the reason why this book, which not
only tries to analyse past Israeli policies and the principles on
which they are based, but tries to predict their future trend, opens
with a chapter describing the nature of the Hebrew press, the
military censorship imposed on it and the increasingly successful
ways that the press has developed to struggle against and to
circumvent the limitations imposed on it. The book is, in many ways,
a description of the Israeli Jewish media, and especially of the
media as a social force.

Although this book deals with the principles on which the policies
of Israel are founded, especially as developed in the 1990s, and with
their probable results, it does not treat them as static but tries to
describe the constant development of those policies in time. It is
based on my 'reports' about Israeli policies, as they could be
understood from the Hebrew press at a given time, which I used
to send to my friends living outside Israel. I felt that such reports,
which I have discontinued, were essential, since my interpretation
of Israeli policies, based on what was being said within Israel, was
radically different from the interpretation of most of the Middle
Eastern 'experts', especially 'experts' of the Western media. The
latter, I am inclined to think, base their 'expertise' on the official
declarations about Israeli intentions as addressed to foreigners. In
this book, I don't intend to engage in controversy or fault-finding.
However, let me emphasize at once that the 'wish for peace', so
often assumed as the Israeli aim, is not in my view a principle of
Israeli policy, while the wish to extend Israeli domination and

influence is. The confirmation of these assertions will be found in this book.

Let me summarize here some principles on which, in my view, Israeli policies are based. In the first place they are regional in their extent; their subject is the entire Middle East from Morocco to Pakistan, and in addition they have an important global aspect, especially prominent in the 1990s. You will find in this book much evidence that Israel is quite involved in South Korea, Kenya and Estonia, countries which are surely not part of the Middle East! However, I consider that Israeli policies outside the Middle East are subordinated to Israeli regional aims. They can be described as having two intertwined aims: hegemony-seeking and the support of the 'stability' of most of the now-existing regimes in the Middle East, with the notable exception of Iran, and (only for a relatively short period, now ended) of Iraq. Although Israeli policies directed toward the overthrow of the Iranian regime (now a chief Israeli aim) are being justified, especially in the US with claptrap about 'fighting Islamic fundamentalism' for the supposed benefit of the West, this explanation, tamely accepted by many US 'experts', is in my view obviously incorrect. First, as is known to everybody who follows the Hebrew press, Israel has for years supported Hamas and other Islamic fundamentalist organizations against the PLO, when it thought that such support would serve its interest. Second, the most fundamentalist Islamic state in the Middle East is Saudi Arabia, which Israel, in spite of some frictions, is certainly not opposing. Therefore, the real reason for the Israeli enmity to Iran, which may yet lead to an Israeli assault on it is, in my view, quite simple: Israel's hegemonic aspirations. A state aspiring to hegemony in an area cannot tolerate other strong states in that area. Iran, which has defied the US for nearly twenty years, and which may be attempting to break the Israeli monopoly of nuclear weapons in the Middle East, is definitely a strong state. Those hegemonic aspirations were also the main reason why Israel instigated the triple alliance of France, Britain and Israel which invaded Egypt in 1956. Egypt was then in the process of becoming a strong state, too strong for Israeli regional intentions. Everything else is and was just propaganda, needed, by the way, not so much for Israeli domestic purposes as for foreign consumption.

It is also apparent now that Israel, especially Israel latterly ruled by Shimon Peres, does not desire just a peaceful economic development of the Middle East. After all, Peres is on the record in this book, stating that Israel does not want peace with Iran under any terms. Israeli policies of 'coalition building' against Iran, amply documented here in Part II, may yet lead to war, but if they do, such a war will be undoubtedly represented for the benefit of the Western media as 'War for the Peace of the Middle East', just as the invasion of Lebanon in 1982 was officially called by Israel 'War for the Peace of Galilee'.

The assumption that the main Israeli policy is to achieve a hegemony over the entire Middle East leads to other conclusions unpalatable to the 'experts', in this case also to Palestinian and other Arab 'experts'. In the first place it follows that although the Palestinians are the first victims of Israeli policies, and the people who have most suffered from them; still, the most important part of Israeli policies is not concerned with the Palestinians. Therefore, even a real peace (not to speak about the Oslo Accords, criticized here in Part V) between Israel and the Palestinians will not lead to peace in the Middle East. On the contrary, although there is an Israeli wish to keep the Palestinians quiet under a form of Israeli control, this control is intended to promote its real policies, for example, its wish to topple the Iranian regime, more effectually. Accordingly, except for an analysis of the Oslo Accords, this book will not deal with Israeli policies towards the Palestinians about which much has been written already. It will deal instead with the more general problems of what are the Israeli policies towards all the states (not only Arab states) of the Middle East, about which very little has been written.

I will give a very recent example, not discussed in this book, as an illustration of my reasons for adopting this approach. On 31 January 1996, Ze'ev Shiff, an important Hebrew press strategic commentator, also well-known for his good connections with the Israeli Army and Intelligence, reported from Qatar in the most prestigious Hebrew paper, *Haaretz*, that the establishment in the near future of 'an Israeli nuclear umbrella for the Gulf' is possible and is, indeed, supported by some strategists of Kuwait, Qatar and Oman. Shiff quotes a Kuwaiti strategy expert, Sammy Faraj, who came to meet him in Qatar and told him that provided Israel makes peace with Syria, it should be included in an alliance which 'would secure the peace in the Gulf' by its nuclear weapons. The reason given by Faraj and tacitly accepted by Shiff for establishing such an alliance is that 'Israel is the only state in the Middle East which has power for reacting quickly'. Even more important in Faraj's view is the 'Israeli nuclear deterrence' to be employed for securing the peace in the Gulf. Surely those weighty reasons for possible developments, should be discussed but, except in the Hebrew press, are not – they have very little to do with the oppression of the Palestinians by Israel! Rather, that oppression is only the first step toward the establishment of Israel as the nuclear power in the Gulf; supposedly to secure the Gulf States, really to acquire a hegemony over them.

Let me point out again that such Israeli intervention in the Gulf may lead to a war – even a war in which nuclear weapons will be used – against Iran from which untold calamities will ensue. Although I personally abhor the Iranian regime, its nature and its crimes, I am of the opinion that an aggressive war against Iran (especially if initiated or organized by Israel), with the object of changing the regime of that country from the outside and by force, will make a bad situation much worse, and not only in Iran. For example, I regard the death sentence issued from Iran against Salman Rushdie as a wicked crime. Nevertheless, assaulting Iran may bring Rushdie's life into greater danger than at present. The Iranian regime should be changed only by the Iranian people.

Another point follows from this basic assumption. The Israeli aims of establishing a hegemony are totally unconnected with the 'corruption of Arab culture' or other fantastic aims routinely attributed to Israel by so many Arab papers, and with even more fantastic aims attributed to Israel by some Arab intellectuals who should know better. However reprehensible, Israeli aims, which I of course oppose, are the ordinary aims of a state which wants to increase its power. Israel is not the first (or the last) state in the modern period which has tried to establish a hegemony over an area. The characteristic quality of modern hegemonies is indifference to culture and pursuit of power; the chief aims of modern imperialism are profits, especially such as can be acquired by trade carried out on terms favourable to a hegemonic state. Thus, the reader will find here in Part III information on the huge Israeli trade with Arab states which flourished even during the Arab boycott and was obviously tolerated or encouraged by some Arab regimes years before Oslo. The discussion of this trade includes a discussion of 'trade' in drugs, the first of its kind. But there is no discussion of 'cultural corruption' of Arab culture or other favourite inventions of Arab press, which in my view are not included in the real aims of Israeli policy.

Finally, something will be said in this book about one of the most important means of carrying out the Israeli hegemonic policies, which to my knowledge has not been adequately discussed: namely the Israeli influence over the US policies carried out through what is called 'the Jewish lobby' in the US. While the whole of Part IV is dedicated to this topic, this influence, discussed in the terms of the Hebrew press, appears in other sections as well. It may be that the Hebrew press exaggerates this issue (although in my view it does not exaggerate very much), but its view that rulers of many states now court the Israeli Prime Minister because of his great influence on US policies is, especially under Clinton, surely correct. (Clinton was called recently 'the real Israeli Ambassador in Washington' by an important Hebrew press commentator.) True, this influence is not absolute, but it is very great, and therefore it has to be known in detail and discussed. In my view, no better instrument exists than the Hebrew press, which devotes much space to this issue, for knowing the extent of Israeli influence over US policies. Let me add here an important point, not discussed in this book. Israel can influence the US not only because of the existence of 'the Jewish lobby', (helped by Christian fundamentalists), but also because Israel is, in itself, a strong state. No doubt, a great part of its current strength derives from US support, but it can also be argued that this support would not have been given in the first place (at least in its present size) had Israel not been strong to begin with.

Finally, let me say something about what I consider to be the 'reasons' which make Israel desire to acquire a hegemony in the Middle East and, in general, to conduct the policies it actually conducts. First, in my view the very act of 'looking for specific reasons' for political behaviour, in which some modern sociologists and pundits of political science delight, is a suspicious form of activity. It is a return to the modes of operation of the Aristotelian science which tried to assign a 'reason' for everything. In modern science, as it has been since Galileo, scientific laws are generalizations (capable of falsification) which have been found to predict observations and and have no other 'reason' for their validity. What is the 'reason' for the Law of Gravitation or for the Second Law of Thermodynamics? There is no reason except that they happen to predict what is actually observed. In the same way, until the last few decades of recorded human history it would be difficult to find a state which didn't desire to expand and increase its power and to establish hegemony over as large an area as it could. Even now, a great majority of states have this desire, which they disguise as 'establishing peace' or 'defending' it or some other propaganda phrase. After all, as Gibbon said, the Romans pretended that they established their empire solely in the aim of self-defence; all other empires or hegemonic states, west or east, were no better in their pretensions. Thus, while I regard it as a proven fact that the aim of Israeli policies is to establish a hegemony over the Middle East, if someone asked me why Israel behaves in this way a part of my answer would be that this behaviour is 'natural' to all or most states, as experience has shown. The question of why such behaviour is 'natural' to most states we must leave until the time when our knowledge of human nature is greater. At present we cannot even begin to answer it, and therefore, for the purpose of political analysis, it is enough if we observe that one can establish, by what I regard as the best evidence available, that Israel behaves as most states do as they try to establish a hegemony. It is more important to observe that Israel's efforts to establish a hegemony are, slowly, being crowned with success; its true aims are not suspected, and other, fantastic aims are being attributed to it. Who would have anticipated that some Gulf states would desire 'an Israeli nuclear umbrella for the Gulf'?

But Israeli policies, especially as they affect the Palestinians also have an ideological aspect, discussed in Chapter 14. The Israeli official ideology, openly admitted within the country itself, is widely misunderstood outside, since, as in the case of foreign policy, no attention is paid to what the Israeli establishment says to Israeli Jews about its intentions and policies. Briefly, discrimination, amounting to a form of apartheid, but one based on religion not on race, is inherent in the character of Israel as 'a Jewish state'. On this point, there exists outside Israel a grave misunderstanding about its policies. Israel discriminates not only against Arabs, or only against Palestinians, as it incorrectly supposed (especially amongst the Arabs) outside Israel, but against all non-Jews, including its best non-Jewish friends. It follows from that official attitude which Israel tries to inculcate among all its Jewish citizens that Israel must regard even its best non-Jewish friends as its potential enemies. A political conclusion follows from that ideological attitude: there exists in Israeli policies a latent (and often a not-so-latent) hostility toward its present allies. Thus, the Israeli claim that its hegemony is intended to be exercised for the benefit of the West (by itself an absurd claim, if one considers the 'normal' behaviour of states) cannot possibly be true in the case of a state which officially defines itself as 'a Jewish state' and, as a point of principle, discriminates against all non-Jews. A hegemony exercised by such a state must be, much more than a hegemony exercised by the 'usual' empires, solely intended for the benefit of Jews. The pattern of Israeli rule in the Conquered Territories, which, as generally admitted in the Hebrew press, was much worse than any imperial rule of the twentieth century, supports this idea. It is for this reason that I don't like to discuss Israeli policies in terms of 'settler states', or 'colonial rule', since I regard Israeli policies as being much worse than those applied by other colonial regimes. It can be further presumed that Peres' 'New Middle East', if established (even under Netanyahu), would be a much worse form of hegemonic exploitation of the Middle East than those employed by the former imperial regimes.

The only way of avoiding Israeli hegemony and generally of avoiding the increase of Israeli power in the Middle East (which in my view will be also a disaster for Israeli Jews) is a detailed knowledge of Israeli policies and the way they are presented to the Israeli Jews. Slogan-mongering, or endless quoting of the Balfour Declaration only aggravates the situation. As Francis Bacon, one of the founders of modern science said, 'Knowledge is power.' This dictum is as valid in politics as in anything else. One can add that lack of knowledge is weakness. No political struggle, just or unjust, can be waged from a position of wilful weakness. The aim of this book is to add detailed knowledge for those, of whatever nation (including Jews) who don't like the prospect of an Israeli hegemony being established over the Middle East.

Note: Since this book was written as a series of individual reports a date indicating when each report was written accompanies the title of each chapter. The short prefaces to each chapter were, however, written in February 1996.

A note on the Hebrew press

Since I am constantly quoting the Hebrew newspapers in this book, let me say something about each of them. As of February 1996, four national Hebrew papers are published in Israel. All of them are 'quality papers', avoiding the more lurid forms of sex and crime reporting, and publishing (especially on Fridays and the eves of Jewish holidays) long and thoughtful articles and interviews with the leaders of the state. There are also a host of local Friday papers, often of as high a quality as the national papers. The four national Hebrew papers are discussed below.

Haaretz ('The Land') – Regarded as the most prestigious, serious and informative of the Hebrew papers, it is, for those very reasons, read only by the Israeli Jewish elite and has a more or less steady circulation. It used to support the views of the Israeli centre, and as such was more moderate than other papers, but lately it has tended to support (critically, however) the views of the two left Zionist parties: Labor and Meretz ('Energy'). Because it employs good journalists having good connections with the government in power, its news and views must be treated seriously. On the other hand, for that very reason and because of its unbridled support for the Israeli economic elite, its views must be 'corrected' by the other papers. Haaretz is owned and published by the Schoken family.

Davar ('Matter') – For years Davar had been the official paper of the Israeli trade union movement (the Histadrut) and really of the Israeli Labor party. It was, quite justifiably, regarded as dull, but became more open to other views than it used be. However, its circulation declined all the time, and it finally ceased publication in March 1996.

Yediot Ahronot ('Last News') – The paper with the largest circulation, *Yediot Ahronot* sells more copies than all the other papers together. It tends to include all views in the framework of Zionism. Back in the late 1960s it was the first Hebrew paper to publish articles seriously critical of the Israeli establishment and its 'sacred cows', and not only on issues of human rights (which all papers published). For example, before October 1973 it not only published articles by radical writers which predicted the War and put the blame for its outbreak on the Israeli government, but also published articles (by Boaz Evron) in which the Holocaust appeared as a part of a more general Nazi plan to colonize Europe, especially eastern Europe, directed against Israeli Jewish dogma that Nazism was uniquely anti-Jewish. I consider it the best Hebrew paper which appears now.

Maariv ('Evening tide') – The second largest Hebrew paper, *Maariv* originally tended to support the right-wing parties, but now its position is not very different from that of *Yediot Ahronot*. It is especially prominent in its critique of the Army, including past Israeli war crimes. Originally they both were evening papers and are sometimes referred to as such, but for a long time both have appeared in the early morning like the other papers. They still retain, however, a more popular character, treating traffic incidents or crimes of sensational nature at great length. At the same time they devote much space to serious information and political debate, and (especially on Fridays) to the discussion of cultural issues.

The two Hebrew Jerusalem Friday papers which I use, are *Kol Ha'ir* ('All the town') and *Yerushalaim* ('Jerusalem') The most radical of the entire Hebrew press, *Kol Ha'ir* is also the most trendy on issues such as modern music and dance, sex, etc. More conservative than *Kol Ha'ir*, *Yerushalem* is still, on many issues, bolder than the national Hebrew press.

In addition to the above I also quote in this book from the following newspapers, all of which closed several years ago.

When it appeared *Hadashot* ('News') used to be the best Hebrew paper, better (especially in the 1980s) than *Yediot Ahronot*. In the long run, however, it showed itself to be too radical for the average Israeli Jewish taste. It concentrated on the very poor and miserable, which in my view angered the working class. When it existed I used it very much. *Ha'olam Ha'ze* ('This World') was a weekly publication. In this book, I quote from a later version of this weekly, not the earlier one which was edited by Uri Avneri and in my view was unworthy of credence until about 1984. The new version, under a completely different ownership and editorship was a serious weekly which had to stop publication, probably because of the competition of the equally serious Friday issues of the dailies. *Shishi* ('Friday') was a continuation of *Ha'olam Ha'ze* under another name, which had to stop publication for the same reasons. *Al Hamishmar* ('On the Watch') was a daily, lately very boring and dogmatic, owned by Mapam, a left Zionist party, and financed by a kibbutz movement Ha'kibbutz Ha'Artzi ('The country Kibbutz'), affiliated with it. It had a very low circulation and, in my view, was of inferior quality. Eventually, the kibbutz movement got tired of financing a paper not read even by its own younger members.

Part I

CENSORSHIP

1

The Struggle Against Military Censorship and the Quality of the Army
2 December 1992

Introduction

This chapter illustrates not only how and to what extent the Hebrew press serves as a source of information, but also shows that the relative freedom it enjoys in the 1990s represents a great improvement on a former situation. Let me add that this improvement coincides, and not by chance, with the decline of the Israeli Labor Party, and more generally with the decline of the Zionist 'left'. Contrary to the opinion of most 'experts', the Zionist 'left' is more hostile to individual human rights and freedom of expression than the main parties (for example, Likud) of the Zionist right. (The quasi-bolshevik nature of the old-style Zionist 'left' and its enmity to freedom for anyone, including Jews, escaped the attention of most left-wing Western writers on Israel in the 1950s and 1960s.) Another important reason for the increase in freedom of the press in the last twenty years, as illustrated in this chapter, were the unsuccessful (or only half-successful) Israeli wars. Another important phenomenon illustrated in this chapter is the great interest taken by readers of the Hebrew press in the Army and everything connected with it, and the way in which this interest can be used to increase the freedom of the Hebrew press.

A similar phenomenon of an increase of freedom of expression following an unsuccessful war occurred in the US, where the actual freedom of the press (although still, in my view, lesser in extent than in the current Hebrew press) increased greatly after the Vietnamese War. Something similar can be observed in other countries.

Among the anomalies of Israeli society none in my view is more glaring than the existence of a fairly free expression in the general and free press in particular, under a censorship which may well be one of the most stringent in the world. This paradox was well described by Yitzhak Gal-Nur (*Maariv*, 25 November 1992):

13

'Legally, [Israeli] military censorship is all-powerful. In practice only a small proportion of press contents are censored in Israel.' Let me first describe the awesome legal powers of censorship: awesome enough to forbid the description of these powers until recent days. I will next proceed to describe the present struggle against accumulation of so much power in the censor's hand, and the deeper reasons for the willing compliance of Israeli Jewish society with those realities and the rarity of protests against them in the past.

Some information is needed to clear the ground. Military censorship is only one of a number of separately operating censorships, some of them abolished only in recent years and others still operative. I will not list all of them, contenting myself with two examples. There used to be a censorship committee concerned with the theatre; no production could be staged without its clearance. Before 1967 its vigilance was targeted primarily at what was thought too sexually explicit or contained sexually explicit language in both contemporary and classical plays. After 1967, when Hebrew theatre became a channel of political protest, the targets of the censors shifted to what they would assess (sometimes correctly) as anti-patriotic, anti-army or pro-Arab, especially when a contemporary play would raise the subject of anti-Palestinian atrocities. Several such plays were banned; in several others, whole portions were excised. Since theatre is popular among Israeli middle and upper classes, this particular censorship engendered outcries of protest. The protests forced the censors to be increasingly careful about their bans. After a struggle, this censorship was abolished a few years ago, with the consent of all secular parties over the opposition of the religious ones.

Another censorship committee oversees the mail, and is empowered to open private letters and to confiscate (but not destroy) them. In the 1950s it acted with few restraints, but in recent years it has busied itself primarily with confiscating those letters of new emigrants from the former USSR to their relatives which could deter the latter from immigrating to Israel.

Of all forms of censorships, however, military censorship has from Israel's inception been by all means the most important, most all-inclusive and most galling. It has been especially so since, as Gal-Nur rightly pointed out, 'in Israel, the underlying principle is that all public information is secret, except if it has been authorized for publication', and since 'the government can be easily tempted to use its powers, for the sake of deterrence or in order to pursue some evil schemes', or simply 'to conceal the extent of its own stupidity or misperformance'. One of the effects is that military censorship is actually furthering the Army's misperformance. Since 1974 when the struggle against military censorship began in earnest, this has been the main and most persuasive argument of its critics and campaigners for its abolition. For the public at large, this argument has certainly carried more conviction than any arguments about the undesirability of keeping people in the dark about the extent of the army's atrocities. When Israel Landers (*Davar* Friday Supplement, 27 November 1992) wants to hit military censorship at its softest spot, he recalls how during the week preceding 6 October 1973, censorship banned all the news derived from usual press sources about the massing of Egyptian and Syrian troops on the cease-fire lines. The Israeli Army then assessed these troop concentrations as devoid of all significance, and therefore didn't want to upset the public unduly. In effect, the ban itself was instrumental in shepherding Israel to its subsequent defeats.

Landers admits, however, that the press itself was then willing to toe the censorship's line, out of respect for the Army whose prestige stood in 1967–73 at its peak. Formal censorial bans were at that time often not needed because 'friendly advice' could suffice. The now raging campaign against military censorship originated from the Army's clumsy efforts to conceal negligence during the 1992 Ts'elim exercise in which five soldiers were killed. A major factor leading to public outrage over that affair were lengthy press interviews with the families of the killed and wounded soldiers. Their common theme was the interviewees' desire to know the causes of the accident. But, as Landers observes, this was not always so in the past. He recalls the explosion of an army truck in Eilat on 24 January 1970. Against all regulations, the truck was loaded with charged mines, killing as many as 24 soldiers, wounding even more and destroying parts of the city. 'No Hebrew paper printed a single story about the dead soldiers' parents', recalls Landers. In the following days some stories did appear about the soldiers' burials, but were relegated to short notes on the inside pages of the papers, very much in contrast to what routinely happens now, when military burials invariably receive maximum publicity. A 'friendly request' of the censor to the newspapers' editors then sufficed to silence the press without any formal ban. Landers quotes from the then published *Davar* editorial that 'when Israel's very survival is in jeopardy, the occasional occurrence of such accidents cannot be avoided.' *Maariv*, then the largest circulation paper, went even further: 'Disasters such as in Eilat are bound to occur in a war.' This particular accident could not be hushed up totally because it occurred in the midst of a city. In general, however, the coverage of accidents involving soldier's deaths as a result of the Army's negligence was banned until the late 1970s. Pictures of wounded Israeli soldiers in pain, or grumbling because of any discomfort, such as were common in the American press coverage of the Vietnam War, are still banned in Israel, but pictures of wounded soldiers smiling in a comfortable hospital beds are encouraged. The Lebanon War brought a change in this respect. Grumblings and protests of soldiers were allowed to be quoted in the media, and even shown on TV. Once the warfare against the Lebanese guerillas turned sour, even anti-war satire was allowed.

Relaxation of military censorship, along with other social changes, must be attributed to the Israeli near-defeat in the October 1973 War. It was this near-defeat which marked the beginning of the yearning of Israelis for more freedom. The transformation of Israeli society in this respect is still under way, yet far from being completed. But until that point in time, unquestioning compliance was by and large voluntary, compensated, as is common also elsewhere, by military triumphs and easy conquests.

Legal documents defining the powers of the military censorship committee, including the texts of agreements reached by the so-called 'Editors' Committee' with the committee, were published for the first time ever by *Haaretz* on last 26 November. They are based on the British 'Defence Regulations' of 1945, originally devised to suppress Jewish underground organizations. Advocate Dov Yoseph, subsequently the Israeli Justice Minister from Labor, defined them in 1946 as 'worse than Nazi laws. True, the Nazis committed worse atrocities, but they at least did not legislate them.' These laws were adopted by the State of Israel. Their stipulations regarding censorship are still binding (except for strictly nominal amendments such as the replacement of 'His Majesty' by 'Defence Minister', or the like). They empower the censor to ban any publication considered as 'possibly jeopardizing the defence of Israel, or public peace and order' without providing any reasons for the ban. This applies to any printed matter, from books to crosswords, including reprints of what has been already published. All periodical publications, except for those which appear in single issues, need to be licensed. The censor can also close newspapers, and confiscate printing machines, faxes and duplicating machines, as was done in the Gaza Strip at the onset of the Intifada. An amendment adopted in 1988 commands that 'anything authored by anyone which may possibly affect the state's security in any way' be submitted to preventive censorship. And there are additional stipulations, still in force, which bestow on the censor further powers that know virtually no limits.

It begs the question how could the Hebrew press function at all under such laws, even with all the self-restraint it exercised before 1973, and certainly after 1973 when it was already capable of winning some freedoms for itself with increasing success? There can be several answers to this. In the first place, the 'Defence Regulations' were adopted, first by the provisional 'National Council' in 1948, and subsequently by the first Knesset in 1949, on the understanding, shared by Ben-Gurion who then was both

Prime Minister and Defence Minister, that they were to be applied mainly against the Arabs, whereas the Jews were not to be hindered by censorship from political debate and criticism of the goverment, no matter how truculent. This distinctively Israeli mixture of democracy and racism was at first informal, because the Labor Party was loath to acknowledge openly its racism. Eventually censorship was nevertheless institutionalized, not by law, but in an agreement, first signed in 1951 and amended in 1966, between the military censorship and the Editors' Committee, which represented the bulk of the Hebrew press, though no Arab newspaper was included. The text of the agreement was kept secret until published recently by *Haaretz*: '1. The sole purpose of the censorship committee is to prevent publications of security-related information apt to help the enemy or prejudice the defence of Israel. 2. Censorship will not be applied to political arguments, opinions, comments, evaluations or any other contents, except when they contain, or can involuntarily disclose some security-related information. 3. Censorship is to rely on cooperation of the army authorities with the [Israeli] press aiming at meeting the purpose defined in section 1.'

This statement of principle is followed by detailed specifications in regard to forms of the mentioned cooperation, to be discussed below. But it needs to be first admitted that the promise of Section 2 has been fully kept. From the beginning the Hebrew press could freely criticize and abuse the government, as well as other politicians. And it used its freedom fully, in the 1950s even more than in the 1990s. (In the Arabic press the situation was different, in that its freedom of expression has been limited. But this matter will not be discussed here.) The meaning of the phrase 'security-related information' was stretched to cover topics whose bearing upon security was most tenuous, but comparing the Israeli Prime Minister (or any other politician) even to Hitler has always been allowed in the Hebrew press.

The remainder of the agreement sets terms of the cooperation between the two parties to it, with the aim of ensuring its smooth functioning. Its primary tool was to be the Editors' Committee, comprised of the editors of the then existent Hebrew daily newspapers and the director of the Broadcasting Authority. In sheer numbers there were more daily newspapers in the 1950s than now, because every party owned one, in addition to non-party newspapers operating on commercial principles. As I recall in the mid-1950s there appeared as many as twelve daily Hebrew newspapers, representing the entire spectrum of Zionist political parties.

Commenting on the agreement, Dori Klasenbald ('Voluntary agreement to be censored corrupts', *Hadashot*, 19 November) stated that it was slanted in favor of censorship. 'The worst aspect of the agreement under discussion is that it imposes on both the newspapers and the censoring bodies an obligation to submit a disputed issue to a "censorship committee" comprised of an army representative, a newspapers' representative, and a representative of the public. Much as it may sound incredible, no rulings of this committee are binding, unless they are approved by the Chief of Staff. On this point, the agreement is very specific. In effect, therefore, it delegates the overriding authority to the Chief of Staff, which in itself should be a sufficient cause for annulling it ... The committee referred to has all the flaws any censorial authority is bound to have. It has no clear procedural rules for conducting deliberations and reaching decisions. Its decisions cannot be invoked as binding precedents. Its deliberations are secret. If it hears an appeal, the very lapse of time between submitting that appeal and obtaining a ruling is bound to reduce the value of an information whose ban is appealed. Finally, the composition of the committee is not such as to guarantee qualified and informed decisions needed in cases of conflict between the opposite interests of the contending sides.'

But the factual subordination of this committee to the Army was not everything. As Klasenbald explains, 'The agreement rested on the notion that the security of the state was the overriding value, compared to which freedom of expression in general and of the press in particular was something marginal, a kind of favour the censor would agree to render to the press and its readers.' He concludes that 'the public should not delegate to any "censorship committee" the powers to determine how far freedom of the press and the public's right to be informed can go. Delegation of such powers to anyone is contrary to the freedom of expression as a whole.' And his final conclusion is that 'any voluntary agreement with censorship corrupts, because it hurts the freedom of expression.' Moshe Negbi (*Hadashot*, 19 November) concurs: 'The newspapers which signed the agreement hoped to operate under comfortable conditions, at the cost of imposing hardships on other papers, left vulnerable to sanctions permissible under the draconic Mandatory regulations, which even entitle the censor to close newspapers, as he actually did with the *Hadashot* eight years ago.' They won their relative freedom at the cost of renouncing their right to appeal to the Supreme Court against the censor.

Statements like these by Gal-Nur, Negbi or Klasenbald represent in Israel a novelty. No opinions of this kind have ever been voiced by the so-called Zionist left. Zionist parties could, for example, differ from each other on whether the Army or the settlement should have higher priority, but they were unanimous in prioritizing Zionism over human rights, even those designed to accrue to the Jews alone. The Zionist left has never been an exception in this respect. The drive toward freedom of expression as well as toward other elementary freedoms, originates in Israel with the centre of the political spectrum, or with some marginal groups, or else with some individuals on the non-Zionist left. Their influence is in my view primarily catalytic: effective not by itself but by virtue of succeeding in attracting youth and the media to their ideas. This explains why military censorship was accepted voluntarily when the Zionist left wielded much power in Israel. It had to be so as long as censorship was perceived as advancing Zionism's cause.

Why has this changed? What social factors promoted that change? There were many reasons. One was the influence of Western ways of life on the Israelis, especially upon younger age cohorts no longer prepared to tolerate the stifling atmosphere of the Zionist left as supinely as their predecessors did. But the crucial factor of change were in my view profound transformations in the profile of press readership which roughly took place between 1974 and 1988, in the aftermath of the first major gains won in struggles for extending the margins of freedom.

The character of the Hebrew press itself changed in this period markedly. A number of local commercially-oriented Friday papers began to appear, quickly becoming very popular. Moreover, the press learned to address itself to the mass of readers who were also regularly watching television. Far from losing the competition with television, the press prospered as never before. It is enough to say that Hebrew newspaper sales on an average Friday reach up to 3.5 million copies within a national population of about 5 million which contains substantial minorities which don't read Hebrew. But the social composition of the readership has also changed markedly since the mid-1950s. Within that population, the less educated, the poorer and consequently the more religious and right-leaning 50 per cent (or even more) tend to shun newspapers, contenting themselves with television. The other half, with opposite social characteristics, tend to buy each Friday two or even three papers, typically one national and one or two local ones, and read them assiduously. The same readership favours more sophisticated and more liberally-minded daily papers. By contrast, the tendency of the religious to refrain from reading any papers (even special weeklies published for their consumption are not overly popular among that public) has been reinforced by denunciations of the entire Hebrew press by their rabbis. Such denunciations became in the last decade increasingly immoderate: to the point of branding that press as a tool of Satan, capable of dooming its pious Jewish reader to untold calamities, not necessarily spiritual but also as physical as death in a traffic accident. By refusing to read the newspapers (as well as all other 'immoral' printed matter), Israeli right-wingers become increasingly illiterate.

The bulk of this 'new press', as it is called, is commercial. Two still extant papers of the Zionist 'left' (at the time of the writing), *Davar* and *Al Hamishmar*, have steadily dropping circulations. Even when owned by the right-wingers, the commercial press, lest it incurs financial losses, needs therefore to cater to the tastes of its readers, becoming in effect more liberal-minded than the Israeli Jews – as best proven by electoral returns – are on the average. When the late Robert Maxwell bought *Maariv* with the intention of supporting the views of Sharon and Shamir, its circulation dropped alarmingly, to the point that after Maxwell's death it faced the prospect of imminent bankruptcy. It was then bought, however, by the right-wing gun merchant Ya'akov Nimrodi of Irangate fame and given as a present to his son Ofer, a man in his thirties. The new management found that the only way to increase the paper's circulation was by revising its earlier practice and publishing critical commentary. The financial situation improved almost instantly as a result of this decision. Not by chance, *Maariv*'s specialty soon became critiques of the Army, the favoured topic of the newspaper-reading 50 per cent Israeli Jewish public at the present moment. Not by chance either, this discussion opens with a quote from *Maariv* in favour of freedom of the press and the right of the public to know. During the last three months *Maariv* has published, for example, a remarkably well-researched study of the Army's criminal negligence at the time of the Sabra and Shatila massacres of 1982, a dispatch on the spreading use of drugs and alcohol in the elite units of the Army, and a story on how a sergeant-major beating the soldiers under his command was subsequently exonerated by the Army authorities.

Roughly similar is the story of the Tel Aviv local Friday paper *Ha'ir*, founded by the same Schocken family which owns *Haaretz*. Its circulation was anyway impressive, but the Schockens found that they raised it even more, when they published full-page ads depicting a stereotypical Haredi Jew or a stereotypical right-winger saying 'I don't read *Ha'ir* because for me it is not religious enough' or 'nationally-minded enough'. Those ads, intended to lure the more open-minded public to buy the paper, met their purpose. On the eve of the last Independence Day the same paper published an article describing the massacres of Palestinians during the War of Independence. I have reliable information that the sales of this particular issue amounted to about 40 per cent in excess of average ones.

No wonder the first legal triumph in the struggle against the awesome powers of military censorship was won in 1988 by *Ha'ir*. *Ha'ir* appealed to the Supreme Court against the censorial ban of an article criticizing the head of Mossad and speculating about the timing of his replacement. In the late 1950s it was forbidden to even utter the word 'Mossad', and all references to any branches of Israeli Intelligence, no matter how oblique, were banned routinely. Being no party to the Editors' Committee, *Ha'ir* was not bound by any commitment not to appeal to the Supreme Court. Responding to *Ha'ir*'s suit, the Supreme Court voided the decision of the censor, and ruled that since freedom of expression was a supreme value, it needed to be protected from potential impairments by all means available, and that it could be allowed to be impaired only when it would be necessary to uphold the value of state's security. In the wake of this ruling, a new clause was added to the 1966 agreement between the Editors' Committee and the military censorship. The clause remained secret until disclosed by Hayim Tzadok ('An improper use of censorship', *Yediot Ahronot*, 17 November) and then by *Haaretz* 26 November. The clause reads: 'From now on, censorship will be bound by the Supreme Court ruling 680/88, which forbids the ban of any contents for publication, except in cases of near-certainty that a given publication can tangibly hurt the security of the state.' As Tzadok points out, 'the quoted "near-certainty" clause clearly means that security of the state can be upheld at the expense of freedom of expression only under extreme conditions of high and ascertainable risk to it. The censor can use his authority only for this purpose, never for any other purposes, extraneous to his functions.'

The circumstances of the last censorship-related scandal can be described briefly. A fatal Army training exercise in Ts'elim resulted in death of five soldiers. The news that the Chief of Staff and his deputy attended that exercise was cleared for publication only after an Inquiry Committee chaired by General (Reserves) Einan, appointed to investigate that disaster, had reached and announced its findings. Only then was the press allowed to inform the public that reports of the presence of the Chief of Staff and his entourage at the scene had been submitted for the censor's approval right after the accident, first by *Haaretz*, and then by other papers, but the censor banned their publication. The news to this effect were finally cleared with a week's delay, simultaneously with the Einan Committee's findings. This infuriated the press, since the clearance was delivered on Friday, one hour before the beginning of the Sabbath, postponing publication until Sunday and enabling the authorities to fine-tune the impact by suitably dosing the news in the government-owned electronic media which broadcast throughout the Sabbath.

As Tzadok and other commentators pointed out, the initial ban had constituted a flagrant violation of the 1988 amendment quoted above to the agreement between the press and the censorship.

Tzadok wrote, 'It is evident that the publication of the news about the presence of the Chief of Staff and his entourage during the Ts'elim accident could not *impair* the security of the state, let alone *impair tangibly*, let alone *impair ascertainably*, let alone with *near-certainty*. It defies all logic to suppose that right after the accident there was "near-certainty that the publication could tangibly hurt the security of the state", whereas a week later all risk to security already disappeared, to the point that the story could be found fit for publication. One may understand the Army's preference for publishing the story about the Chief of Staff's attendance more or less simultaneously with the publication of the Inquiry Committee report. The use of censorship for purpose of ensuring such simultaneity is nevertheless absolutely inacceptable, because it flatly contradicts both the Supreme Court ruling and the agreement with the Editors' Committee. Military censorship exists in order to protect the security of the state, not the convenience of the Chief of Staff. The discussed affair represents an instance of the flagrantly unlawful use of 'censorship'. Tzadok's function as the legal adviser of the Editors' Committee, as one-time Justice Minister in a Labor government and a prominent leader of that party, could only add weight to his opinions, even though for years he has maintained his distance from the Labor leadership, while supporting more liberal policies. No wonder Tzadok's position has been widely supported.

Soon afterwards, *Haaretz* took an unprecedented step and announced its decision to withdraw from participating in the Editors' Committee. Coming together with the mentioned first-ever publication of the previously banned texts of the agreements, *Haaretz*'s decision reopened public discussion of the censorship. As Klasenbald explains, 'In practice, *Haaretz*'s renunciation of the agreement means that the Editors' Committee will no longer make decisions in disputes between the paper and the censor, and that the Chief of Staff will no longer have the supreme authority to approve or disapprove such decisions. It seems likely that *Haaretz* will continue to submit to censorship those items which were agreed upon between the press and the censorship as requiring submission there, but the paper will feel free to bring suits against the censorship to the courts.' The subject-matters requiring such submission were listed and the lists periodically revised by agreements between the editors and the censor. Everything falling under a listed thematic category had to be submitted to preventive censorship. But the government also retains its power to ban the publication of any contents whatsoever. For example, all references to Ethiopia were for a time banned in order to maintain a good relationship with the Ethiopian dictator Mengistu. The suits may range from appeals against any censorship decisions or sanctions to the Supreme Court, to appeals against criminal accusations for ignoring the censorial bans to lower courts. As Klasenbald points out, 'The advantage lies in that the outcome of such legal actions will depend on legal procedure, the quality of evidence rules, timing of sessions, the value of precedents and the openness of the hearings: i.e. on all that was for the most part missing from the deliberations before the Editors' Committee.'

The remainder of this discussion will deal with the latitude the Israeli government still has for deviously concealing information not normally concealed in other democratic countries, on the pretext that it may be security-related, no matter how tenuous in fact. Some concealed information is eventually described by the Hebrew press through recourse to all kinds of circumlocution. In other cases, however, the press is forced to keep silence, at best being allowed to acknowledge its inability to inform the public. By far the best-qualified practitioner of the art of circumlocution has in my view been Amir Oren, who invariably manages to provide in this manner valuable information whenever he cannot talk straight. After the Ts'elim accident, there were many who wondered why the Investigating Military Police hadn't arrived on the scene instantly to investigate. On November 20, Oren wrote in *Davar*: 'The Military Police Commander might well have gone to Ts'elim right upon learning of the calamity, but on the way there he might have had to turn back when an officer senior in rank requested that the Investigating Military Police stay away. If so, we might perhaps learn something of value about the subordination of the Military Police to the Army's hierarchy.' The quoted sentences, convoluted as they are, nevertheless enable Oren's readers to formulate a reasonable conjecture that it was the Chief of Staff who ordered the Commander of the Military Police to desist from investigating the case, because he had his reasons to be afraid of an investigation that would be too professional.

As early as December 1981, Oren was the first to warn the Israeli public that the invasion of Lebanon was in the making, and he even managed to correctly predict its aims and extent: all this with the help of circumlocutions similar to those quoted above. Somewhat later, his art was emulated by Ya'akov Erez, then a military correspondent of *Maariv*, who authored the sequence of 'Legends for natives' describing how tribal chiefs on a Polynesian island, bearing suitably devised names, visited a civil war-ravaged part of another exotic island. It didn't take much sophistication to decipher that Erez's stories referred to the pre-June 1982 visitations of Falangist-held part of Beirut by the chiefs of the Israeli Army and Mossad. Elsewhere, instead of disguised locations, the Talmudic proverb 'For the astute a hint will suffice' would be used

to alert the reader to a recondite message in an innocuous
information.

Let me give an example which shows the extent to which Israeli
censorship is still capable of stifling a public discussion of what is
anyway public knowledge. On the top of a new Ministry of Defence
building, located in the downtown of Tel Aviv, a spire of sorts
stretches upward to about 50 storeys. Of course, the structure can
be seen by everybody and must have been photographed many times
by the most incompetent agents of the most incompetent intelligence
services of the world. In the initial stages of the construction, the
elongation was photographed as a tourist site and commented on
by the Hebrew press, until the cost-benefit questions about this
oddity of colossal dimensions began to be seriously raised. In
response, the Ministry instructed the censors to bluepencil absolutely
everything connected with this building, beginning with its
photographs and including any statement which would as much
as mention its existence. Everyone living in or visiting Tel Aviv may
see the strange spire, but no one can mention it in public. Granted
that, the Hebrew press has found ways to outwit censorship, even
on this point, for the benefit of those who care enough to read
newspapers between the lines. Of course, such attempts to thwart
public knowledge smack of plain crassness. But this crassness must
be taken into consideration in discussions of Israeli military
censorship, as well as of the authorities behind it, namely the
Commander of the Military Intelligence and the Chief of Staff.

All evidence indicates that the Army needs military censorship
in order to further its own interests, in particular in order to
maintain secrecy over its financial operations and over the ever more
lucrative privileges of its cadres. Even the salaries of the professional
Army personnel, down to the rank of private, are a top security secret
in Israel, though they are talked about by virtually everybody
except, as it seems, the top-rank Israeli politicians, who alone
remain ignorant of their magnitudes. Yair Fidel's account (*Hadashot*,
27 November) gives us an idea of how strict is the secrecy
surrounding this matter: 'The previous Finance Minister, Moda'i,
strongly opposed the remunerations received by the professional
Army, considering them far too exorbitant. After he succeeded in
learning their exact scale, he submitted a memo to his Prime
Minister Yitzhak Shamir, presenting the figures involved. According
to people close to Shamir, the Prime Minister was downright
astounded by Moda'i's memo, to the point of requesting his
Defence Minister, Moshe Arens to meet him for clarifications.
Before their meeting could take effect, the government fell. Since
the new Prime Minister, Yitzhak Rabin, also holds the Defence
portfolio, he will at least not need himself as Defence Minister to
brief himself as Prime Minister on the Army budget itemization.'

Fidel raises the subject of secrecy explicitly: 'We need all be aware that all such data have long been top secret, concealed not only from the public which had the right to know them, but from its representatives who had the duty to know them.' They have also been kept secret from the income tax authorities. Hence the suspicion raised by Fidel and other commentators: that the Israeli Army has for years cheated the income tax office by not reporting a whole lot of taxable benefits granted to its cadres. I find it impossible to comment on such suspicions any further because censorship cuts have succeeded in making this affair unclear. I want only to stress that the Israeli Prime Ministers' ignorance of 'top secret matters' which the citizenry commonly knows and talks about, places Israel in the same rank as the defunct East European regimes, and – although most Israeli Jews would furiously resent such comparisons – as the still existing Arab or other undemocratic regimes.

Fidel's reference to the itemization of the Army budget accords with an article by Aluf Ben ('Far away from public eyes', *Haaretz*, 25 August). Ben informs us that 'since Israel exists, all specifications of the Defence budget have always been kept secret. By now its secrecy is even legislated by a Basic Law, namely the State Economic Affairs Law, which stipulates that "details of the Defence ministry's proposed budgets may never be put on the Knesset's table, but are to be deliberated only by a joint committee appointed by the Knesset's Finance and Foreign Affairs and Defence Committees". Gazetted annual budget laws contain only a single line devoted to the Defence ministry, namely the sum total allocated to that ministry that year, without any breakdowns.' As Ben further states, even such data as 'the expenditure of the Ministry of Defence publishing house', which mainly publishes what goes under the name of 'edifying literature' (with political contents depending on whether the Defence Minister is from Labor or Likud), 'remain classified as top secret'. The size of Defence Ministry donations 'to various associations, such as the "Beautiful Land of Israel" organization', are likewise kept top secret. Even 'the weaponry sales of the US to Israel, which are being systematically reported to the Congress and published in its documents and in the professional literature, are here kept secret. The Israelis are forbidden to know what every American citizen can know.'

The Hebrew press has since long done its best to penetrate this wall of totalitarian secrecy. Press attacks on censorship seem to have had some effects, especially when the country is in economic straits. Government ministers in charge of economic affairs expect to be blamed for economic woes, with the effect that censorial shielding of the Army's financial secrets from exposure slackens a little. Owing to the censorial laxity, Fidel could finally inform the Israeli

public that 'without counting the entire American military aid to
Israel, 52 per cent of the Israeli Defence budget goes for salaries
of the professional Army staffers, their perquisites and their pensions.
In absolute figures this amounts to 5.8 billion shekels [\$2.2 billion]'.
But, as Ben rightly observes, this sum does not cover the unknown
sum spent on the salaries, perquisites and pensions of the civilian
officials of the Defence Ministry and other branches of the Security
System, e.g. Intelligence. (The number of employees in the latter
can be assumed to be considerable.)

While providing data on perquisites of the professional Army,
Fidel cautions his readers that other data still cannot be disclosed.
He is at least able to say that 'added to the basic salary is a lot of
variegated perquisites'. For example, all dental care expenses of not
just the professional Army staff but also of their families are covered
by the Army. Since the Army wants its people to practice sports,
it pays for their sport outfits and implements, also when used by
their families. The army participates in their expenses for entry
tickets to sports events, concerts, theatres and 'other cultural
events'. In addition to that, there are paid vacations with families,
subsidies for renting or building apartments or houses, and the so-
called 'white vehicles', that is, cars used not for work but for private
purposes of Army officers and their families, which cause much
resentment among the public when they appear conspicuously in
Israeli towns, especially parked outside luxurious entertainment
venues. Fidel adds that 'according to the Finance Ministry, the
number of employees on the professional Army's payroll has in the
last decade decreased by 10 per cent, but the number of "white
vehicles" has risen by 15 per cent, to the level of 1.1 "white vehicle",
per officer.'

To sum up, because of its use of censorship, in addition to other
factors, the Israeli Army is growing rapidly more corrupt. Since the
public and even the politicians are denied access to knowledge about
the extent of its corruption, its impact must be all the greater. With
the help of generous American aid to Israel, flowing without any
strings attached the quality of the Israeli Army deteriorates even
further. In the first place, that aid only encourages Israel to further
conquests and aggressions. In my view this situation may yet get
much worse. Judging from well-known precedents, states can be
stuffed with military aid from the US to the point of both military
and political indigestion. Ample evidence indicates that US military
aid, contrary to its avowed purposes, only contributes to making
the Israeli Army more corrupt and less efficient. Israel's power to
influence US policies, especially via Congress which holds the
purse-strings, is for Israel more decisive than any vaunted strategic
or diplomatic assets. In domestic social terms, however, it means
that Israel increasingly resembles those Latin American countries

in which the role of the Army is reduced to extorting money from the taxpayers for maintaining its own bureaucracy. Military censorship helps achieve this effect bounteously. Israel, however, has shown itself capable of waging aggressive wars, which may enable its Army to lay its hands on sources of wealth capable of gratifying its growing appetite. This must be seen as a major factor in Middle Eastern politics. Although the stupidity of the Israeli Army brass is by now proverbial, they are still capable of grasping (especially when briefed by academics on their payroll) that Israeli economy cannot be endlessly drained just to gratify their increasing appetite, and that even the US Congress, so generous in supplying armaments, cannot be hoped to disburse forever free monies for luxuries. This is why they would do anything to redeem their dwindling prestige and at the same time lay their hands on other nations' wealth by wars of conquest. This much they are capable of understanding, in the same way as military oligarchies in the past have understood it.

Part II

FOREIGN RELATIONS

2

Israel's Strategic Aims and Nuclear Weapons
27 April 1992

Introduction

This chapter illustrates, quoting the most important Israeli generals and intelligence experts commenting, in the pages of the Hebrew press, what I consider to be the real aims of the Israeli policies: establishing a hegemony over the entire Middle East, 'stabilizing' the regimes which do not disturb too much the Israeli progress toward that aim and a possible use of nuclear weapons for this purpose. General Amnon Shahak-Lipkin, mentioned in this chapter, is now, under the name of General Amnon Shahak, the Chief of Staff of the Israeli Army. General (Reserves) Shlomo Gazit was one of the Israeli negotiators in the talks with the PLO (or rather with the PLO's secret police commanders) which led to the Oslo I Accord.

On April 17 1992, the Passover Eve, two Israeli Army generals who can be regarded as the next in rank after the Chief of Staff gave exhaustive interviews to the Hebrew press. The Deputy Chief of Staff, General Amnon Shahak-Lipkin [now Chief of Staff] was interviewed in *Maariv* by Ya'akov Erez and Immanuel Rozen; the Commander of Military Intelligence, General Uri Saguy was interviewed in *Yediot' Ahronot* by Ron Ben-Yishay. On the same day Oded Brosh, a distinguished expert in nuclear politics who can be presumed to speak in a semi-official capacity, published an article in *Haaretz* which for the first time in the Hebrew press openly discusses the options for the actual use of Israeli nuclear weapons during a war. The contents of these items should be juxtaposed with some recent press articles to generalize our knowledge of Israeli strategic aims and of the nuclear factor in Israeli strategic planning.

Before doing so, however, it may be worthwhile to remind non-Israeli readers that since Israel's strategies are regional in their orientation, their concern with the Palestinians is secondary. In fact, the oppression of Palestinians does not interest the Israeli strategists in the least. It follows that what goes under the name of 'the solution of the Palestinian problem', whatever the nature of that 'solution' is, cannot bring about peace, because Israeli strategies are aimed at establishing a hegemony over the entire Middle East, conceived of as extending from India to Mauritania. Of course, the first victim of Israeli expansionism in search of such a hegemony is the Palestinian nation. But, it should be added, establishing a hegemony over the entire Middle East is more important in Israeli strategic thinking than the extension and the perpetuation of Jewish jurisdiction over the entire land of Israel, however extravagantly its borders may be defined.

Before really proceeding to the subject-matter of this report, let me retell a story, described by one of the better-informed Israeli strategic commentators, Yoav Karni ('Old fashioned Israeli methods', *Haaretz*, 25 March). The story needs to be placed in the context of the American factor in the Israeli grand strategy. Karni is critical of the idea of a world-wide strategic cooperation between the US and Israel as proposed in public by the Israeli Ambassador in Washington, Zalman Shoval but not mentioned in the US press. According to Karni, 'The White House was asked to ignore the misdeeds of the [Israeli] government and their consequences, and to overcome its understandable resentment [of Israeli conduct] in recognition that Israel can be for the US an irreplaceable strategic asset.' Why? Because 'the new Muslim republics in Central Asia, emerging from the ruins of the USSR, "will certainly become Muslim fundamentalist and anti-Western states and thereby terrorize the Middle East more than the USSR ever terrorized it."' Shoval 'expressed his astonishment that the US does not understand' how imminent this danger is, and the fact that only Israel is capable of countering it. While poking fun at Shoval, Karni shrewdly (so as to confound the censors) revealed for the first time an authentic story of Israel's diplomatic pursuit of its strategic aims: 'Even India, which nine years ago expelled a garrulous Israeli consul who wanted to elicit its participation in a cosmic struggle against all Muslims, recently requested to be placed on the Israeli Foreign Ministry's mailing list.' The episode referred to occurred in 1983. Sharon, then a Defence Minister, felt self-confident after signing, with full American blessing, a 'peace' with the puppet Lebanese government. With all complacency, he proposed to India an alliance for the sake of jointly attacking Pakistan, with the aim of destroying the latter's budding nuclear capability. In this scheme Israel was to supply the aircraft and India provide the bases. Incidentally, only two years earlier, in 1981, Sharon made a speech, later widely publicized, in which he defined the extension of Israel's influence 'from Mauritania to Afghanistan' as an Israeli aim. There is plenty of evidence from openly available

Israeli sources that this is Israel's strategic aim. The only problem is that this conflicts with US policies, whether avowed or actually pursued. Still, Israel has an enormous latitude for action when the Americans know nothing about Israeli aims because they don't want to know. Interestingly, all branches of American Intelligence may be even more wilfully ignorant in this respect than the US media.

Karni by no means exaggerates when he speaks of an Israeli 'cosmic struggle against all Muslims'. The same or similar notions crop up constantly in official explanations of the Israeli Security System's current policies. Thus, the chief political correspondent of *Haaretz*, Uzi Benziman describes on (20 March) how his sources in the Security System reacted to his mild and censorship-conscious reservations about the wisdom of the assassination of the Lebanese Sheikh Mussawi and his family, in view of possible adverse consequences for Israel. The reaction was: 'The killing of Mussawi can be considered a retaliation for murders and deadly assaults against the Israelis committed by Muslim fanatics of any stripe. Some people are always ready to remind us that Israel is engaged in the long-term struggle against all Arab states and against all Islamic fanaticism, which all accept murder as a norm of behaviour. Because of that, blood-price-calculation-based criticism of the [Israeli] government is inherently unjust. The [Israeli] norm is best expressed by the words of [the then Labor Prime Minister] Levy Eshko: "The account book is open, but it is our hand which is filling it." This means that blood accounting is to be made by the State of Israel *vis-à-vis* all its enemies treated as a single whole, rather than on the basis of calculations which particular citizens of Israel want to use against their own government.' (Notice Benziman's peculiar censorship-conscious vocabulary, e.g. his use of such terms as 'some people'.) This view may seem to be mad, but it has been held by the Israeli Security System from time immemorial, since long before Israel's inception. In Hebrew, it has been quoted often enough by prestigious commentators, Benziman included. But to the best of my knowledge, it has never been quoted by any mainstream paper outside Israel. But even in Israel, open challenges to this strategic madness are relatively rare, due not only to censorship but even more so to the customary adulation of Israeli Intelligence. Yet, translated into plain language, this strategy assumes a perpetual warfare to be carried out by Israel against a sizeable proportion of humanity.

Recent announcements by Israeli generals and nuclear experts can be properly understood only when these overall strategic aims are taken into account. Let me open my list of quotes with the Deputy Chief of Staff, General Amnon Shahak-Lipkin, whose rise in the ranks began in 1982–85, when, still a mere Military Intelligence Colonel, he escorted Israeli newsmen on visits to

Falangist leaders, using this occasion for peddling to the media his views on how strong Falangist forces were, and how firmly Israel could rely on them in the pursuit of its own goals in Lebanon. His crucial statement was made in his reply to the questions 'Assuming that the Middle East becomes nuclearized, hasn't the time come to change our attitudes towards nuclear realities? Shouldn't we begin thinking about them in terms of negotiations, of secret diplomacy? Will we be always able to prevent the progress of nuclearization?' His answer: 'It is never possible to talk to Iraq about no matter what; it is never possible to talk to Iran about no matter what. Certainly not about nuclearization. With Syria we cannot really talk either. I also don't agree that preventing or postponing [nuclearization] is not in our power. A postponent by one week may be crucial, while a postponent for ten years would be magnificent. Today, not a single Arab state has a proven nuclear capability. I believe that the State of Israel should from now on use all its power and direct all its efforts to preventing nuclear developments in any Arab state whatsoever.' Question: 'Does this imply the need for violent means as well?' Answer: 'In my opinion, all or most [available] means serving that purpose are legitimate.'

Shahak-Lipkin's reference to Iraq should not be construed, however, as his opposition to the rule of Saddam Hussein. The interviewers reminded him that 'at a meeting held on the last day of the Gulf War, [but not reported then] you opined that it was in the Israeli interest that Saddam Hussein remained in power.' When they probed whether he considered 'this opinion still correct', the General answered, 'As far as I am concerned, it would be preferable if Saddam Hussein had not been born. We tried to prevent his birth but we failed. Now we need to decide what to do. It would have been ideal for everybody if it were possible to change the character of the Iraqi regime, and its insane attitude of hostility toward the entire world. But in Iraq no change will ever be possible. Iraq will always remain the same, bent on defying the entire world. True, it was helped by the entire world to become what it became. But since Iraqi thinking can never change, a possible removal of Saddam Hussein alone can only lead to the emergence of another dictator who will smile nicely to the entire world. And the entire world, anxious to somehow recompense Iraq for hardships it had inflicted on it, will help in its recovery and in restoration of its capabilities. Therefore, if I have to choose between a boycotted Iraq with Saddam and an Iraq without Saddam again supported by the entire world, then I opt for Saddam, because Saddam will never be helped by anyone.'

Before discussing the little that is known about how Israel is actually helping Saddam Hussein to survive in power in accordance with the just declared preferences, let me yet comment on the recurrent phrase 'the entire world'. This phrase reflects another concept underlying Israeli strategic thinking. The concept is that in addition to the Arabs or the Muslims who are open enemies, other Gentiles, regarded as a single entity and united in pursuing aims correctly detectable and decipherable by Israeli Intelligence, are without exception both evil and stupid. This concept, at least, has been frequently challenged in Israel in public, in contrast to perception of the evil nature of the Arabs or the Muslims. A typical example of such a challenge is a critique of Shamir's speech in the Knesset, eulogizing (and misrepresenting) Begin, authored by Amnon Abramovitz (*Maariv*, 10 April). In his speech Shamir said that during World War II 'the Jewish nation was left to be ground between the two belligerent blocs equally hostile toward the Jews and indifferent to their bitter fate.' Abramovitz comments: 'What does it mean that "the Jewish nation was thus left to be ground between the two belligerent blocs?" It can only mean that the two sides in World War II had the same moral qualities, while we, the Jews, were being ground as they fought each other. Is it possible that the news of extermination of 6 million Jews by the Germans hasn't yet reached Shamir's notice? What does it mean that "both [were] equally hostile toward the Jews and indifferent to their bitter fate"? It can only mean that the Nazi Germany was merely indifferent to our bitter fate. Does Shamir mean to say that Churchill and Hitler treated us in the same way? Yet it is not hard to conjecture what Shamir had in mind. In his view, the entire world has always been against the Jews and so it remains. In this respect, Churchill is no different than Hitler, George Bush no different than Saddam Hussein and Mitterand no different than Gaddafi.' Israeli strategical ideas are incomprehensible without the realization that a vision of the world such as Shamir's is shared by the Israeli Security System. The pronouncements of its generals and highly placed 'sources' are the best evidence of that.

In the remainder of his interview, General Shahak-Lipkin reiterates, often verbatim, the conventional views of the Israeli Security System which require here no more than a quite cursory presentation. Israel acts under 'a threat to its survival', Syria is 'a terrorist state' and 'almost all terrorist infiltrations from Lebanon [to Israel] originate from Syria.' (Interestingly, Iran is not mentioned in this context, nor is Libya; there is no comment about these by Saguy either.) Shahak-Lipkin's other arguments of the same type are that Iraq's military power is still great, that the killing of Mussawi was fully justified, (his family is not mentioned), that the Israeli public is guilty of criticizing the Army and that 'we [the Army] have received only 40 per cent of the money we requested' and therefore need a lot more. Although little space is devoted to the situation in the Territories, it is assessed as satisfactory, since a lot of wanted Palestinians have been killed.

General Saguy fully shares the notion of a threat to Israel's very survival: 'Syria has always been and still is a threat to the security and very survival of the State of Israel', the reason being that 'Syria continues to arm itself.' This statement is documented by a long list of Syrian weaponry purchases, without mentioning Israeli ones. Saguy does admit that Syria is afraid of Israel and that its armament is motivated by the wish 'to confront the Israeli strategic [i.e. nuclear] weaponry, which the Arabs believe Israel possesses'. He also admits that Syria is afraid of a massive Israeli invasion of its territory: 'According to the Taif Agreement [between Syria and Lebanon] Syria is allowed to keep the bulk of its armed forces in the [Lebanese] Baalbek area. The Syrians believe that such a deployment can be an answer to an Israeli attempt to outflank Damascus [from the north] in the event of a war.' Let me comment on this. As is known, the area between Damascus and the Golan Heights is heavily fortified, but no fortifications seem to exist north of Damascus or along the Syrian–Lebanese borders. Since outflanking a fortified defence line has been the Israeli Army's favourite method of attacking, Syrian fears appear to me well-grounded.

What Saguy says he is afraid of, is 'a Syrian–Iranian alliance'. The exchange on this subject with his interviewer deserves to be quoted *in extenso*: 'Question: Can an alliance of Syria with Iran serve as a substitute for an alliance between Syria and Iraq in the formation of the eastern front against Israel? Answer: There is a collaboration between Syria and Iran in plenty of things. It is going to be closer. Perhaps even in strategic weaponry, and the non-conventional ventures. Question: Is Iran helping Syria to obtain nuclear weapons? Answer: At this stage not yet. But when Iran itself becomes nuclearized, I cannot see how it can avoid cooperating [in this matter] with Syria. Such a prospect should worry us, even though it is still distant … In ten years' time Iran will certainly become a decisive factor in the entire region, and as such an ever-present threat to its peace. This can hardly be prevented, unless somebody intervenes directly. It is quite probable that outside factors such as the US, alone or together with other states, would intervene to halt the progress of Iranian rearmarment. But a historical paradox is also possible: Iraq may rearm itself, with the effect of checking the growth of Iranian armed power.'

A long-standing Israeli custom commands the generals in active service to stop short of saying too much in interviews, but it lets semi-official experts or retired generals reveal the Israeli strategic intentions to the nation's elite in a more informative manner. The explanation of the crucial and most sensitive Israeli strategic aims, concerning the role of nuclear weapons in overall Israeli strategy was left to Oded Brosh. Brosh begins by saying that some Israelis are now raising the question whether 'Israeli nuclear power' helps or obstructs a transferral of the regional conflict to diplomatic channels. This he deplores, since the very phrasing of this question in such terms 'introduces a bias in favour of the recent opponents of Israel's nuclear option, while casting a negative light on the supporters of this option'. He is particularly virulent against some unnamed advocates of an 'appeasement' in the form of only 'a limited use of Israeli nuclear power, referred to as "the last-minute option"'. Those obscure remarks may refer to the bare beginning of a belated but at least serious discussion of the health hazards contingent on the existence of nuclear installations. Brosh's article was indeed, 'balanced' in *Haaretz* by another article, printed right next to it which for the first time in Israel's history reported how people had organized themselves in protest against health hazards stemming from the existence of a civilian nuclear installation in their neighbourhood. But without any attribution, Brosh also refers to claims, still unattributable, to the effect that 'Dimona might yet become another Chernobyl'. He concedes that 'the responsible authorities indeed need to test again and again' their precautionary measures, forgetting that 'the authorities responsible' for Chernobyl also claimed that they had been recurrently testing their precautions. He leaves unanswered the question of who in Israel can be authorized to test the testing undertaken by unnamed 'authorities'.

Brosh must be presumed to aim his polemic at critics more prominent than those concerning themselves with health hazards, because he mentions some unnamed Israelis who are said by him to argue 'that in view of what the foreign media report from time to time about the growth of Israel's nuclear assets, their further growth should be halted. Sometimes it is even being argued that somebody authorized or unauthorized might activate one or several Israeli nuclear warheads through either error or accident. Moreover, some argue that Israel's unremittent nuclear development only propels Arab countries, Iran and other Muslim states to equip themselves with all sorts of non-conventional, but primarily nuclear, weapons.' None of these apprehensions have ever appeared not only in the censored Hebrew press but, to the best of my knowledge, in the mainstream international press as well. All of them are nevertheless in my view quite justified. Not only is the prospect of Dimona one day becoming another Chernobyl something to be seriously discussed. The prospect of Gush Emunim ('The Block of the Faithful'), or some secular right-wing Israeli fanatics, or some of the delirious Israeli Army generals, seizing control of Israeli nuclear weapons and using them in accordance with their 'knowledge' of politics or by the authority of 'divine command' cannot be precluded either. In my view the likelihood of the occurrence of some such calamity is growing. We should not forget that while Israeli Jewish society undergoes a steady political polarization, the Israeli Security System increasingly relies on the recruitment of cohorts from the ranks of the extreme right.

Brosh hurries to admit to his readers that 'not everybody who hates Dimona – whether in Israeli or abroad – hates Israel. On the contrary, a great many foreigners who perceive the Dimona reactor as an evil have an affection for Israel.' Yet the Israelis who 'hate Dimona' are apparently not quite the same. Brosh is worried by their critique, especially since they are said by him to propose 'that the Dimona reactor be closed' in order to be thereafter 'accessible to international controls capable of proving to our neighbours that we no longer produce any fissionable substances'. Such a proof could be offered 'to our neighbours' either in a gesture of good will or within the framework of a regional settlement. But while admitting the desirability of more frequent and thorough checks to preclude Chernobyl-like accidents, Brosh disqualifies 'all other apprehensions of the enemies of Dimona as flunking the test of technical and political realities in our region'. We need to keep in mind that Israeli censorship has thus far prevented the publication of what 'the enemies of Dimona' have to say. We know about their existence and their arguments only what their open enemy, Brosh, wanted and was permitted by that censorship to tell us.

Let me ignore Brosh's brief, superficial and in my view inaccurate presentation of the mentioned 'technical realities'. Let me just mention that he highly commends 'what goes under the name of the neutron bomb, developed by the Americans in the 1970s'. Let me concentrate on what, apparently reiterating the lessons learned from his mentors, he has to say about 'the political realities in our region', in so far as they have a bearing upon Israeli nuclear power. Regarding the uses of Israeli nuclear weapons during a war, Brosh sees two major options. The first, 'the last-minute option' is defined as 'a scenario which in fact presumes that Israel will refrain from making any nuclear threats unless it is defeated by conventional weapons, or can realistically expect such a defeat as imminent, or is threatened by use of non-conventional weapons'. In this way 'the Arab leaders can be denied a victory' by the threat of 'the destruction of Arab civilization'. In my view, this can be interpreted as meaning that Israel has contingency plans for cases of extreme emergency which envisage a devastation by nuclear weapons of a considerable number of Arab urban centres and such crucial installations as the Aswan Dam (whose destruction was envisaged in Israel before 1973). This awful possibility needs to be faced, however horrifying may be the thought about its direct effects on the Arab world and indirect effects upon the entire world in terms of massive human casualties and the long-term effects of radioactivity. The likely existence of such plans needs to be considered jointly with a passage about 'somebody authorized or unauthorized [who] might activate one or several Israeli nuclear warheads through error or accident'. A juxtaposition of the two passages adds to both clarity and horror. By 1992, Israel already abounds in Jewish religious zealots whose influence within the Security System is growing steadily. Gush Emunim or the followers of any extremist Hassidic rabbi are quite capable in my view of activating such scenarios even in peacetime for the sake of thus advancing their Messianic prophecies which by definition imply that God will protect the Jews from any injury and inflict devastation on Gentiles alone.

But Brosh does not favour 'the last-minute option'. Being by no means a religious fanatic he does clearly realize that this option implies not just 'the destruction of the Arab civilization', but also 'our own national suicide'. He also has strategic objections against this option which can be conjectured to draw on the experience of the October 1973 War. He anticipates that the Arab leaders might attack Israel, not for the sake of defeating it but for other reasons. In case the attack turns militarily successful, 'the last-minute option' might prompt the Israeli leaders, even the relatively sane among them, to a nuclear response. When dealing with the long-concealed events of October 1973 War, I documented that the Israeli Army High Command of that time, possibly including Moshe Dayan, favoured Israeli nuclear response against Syria, but were halted in doing so by Golda Meir, backed by Kissinger. Much as I abhor what Brosh says I have to admit that he is not the most extremist among Israeli experts anticipating the use of nuclear weapons.

Brosh's own proposals, which can be assumed express the views of the Israeli Security System, rest on the assumption that 'it is preferable to competently elaborate a system of options which would include the instrumentalities of handling the problems arising from a potential massive missile or armoured attack against us, if it one day materializes, and which would prepare means to deter such an attack, or to foil it, if the deterrence fails'. He adds that pertinent Israeli 'decisions should better not be dictated by outside factors', a transparent allusion to the US. This option should not be resorted to in his opinion, 'as long as the threat to us comes from no more than a single, even if major, Arab state such as Syria' and if it involves only the use of conventional weapons. He immediately stipulates, however, that 'even in such a case, it would be preferable to leave the enemy befogged about our intentions'. Let me clarify, however, that in Israeli terminology, the launching of missiles on to Israeli territory is regarded as 'non-

conventional', regardless of whether they are equipped with
explosives or poison gas.

Still arguing against his unidentified opponents, Brosh contends
that 'there is absolutely no connection between unremitting Israeli
nuclear development and Arab, Iranian or Pakistani pursuits', in
spite of the fact that Israeli nuclear weapons are, or at least may
be, aimed at those countries. But Brosh goes even deeper in his
arguments: 'Generally, in long-term security planning one cannot
ignore the political factors. Israel must take into account, for
example, that the Saudi royal family is not going to reign forever
or that the Egyptian regime may change.' Precisely because of
such political contingencies Israel must remain free to use or
threaten to use its nuclear weapons. Brosh argues that 'we need
not be ashamed that the nuclear option is a major instrumentality
of our defence as a deterrent against those who may attack us. The
three big democracies have relied on the same deterrent for decades.'
The very comparison of Israel's strategic aims with those of the US,
Britain and France is an irrefutable proof of Israel's ambition to
achieve the status of a superpower. But Israel can become a
superpower only if it succeeds in establishing a hegemony over the
entire Middle East. Meanwhile, there is one crucial difference
between Israel and 'the three big democracies'. The French, for
example, pay themselves for developing their own nuclear power.
The development of Israeli nuclear power is, by contrast, being
financed by the US. Money for this purpose can be obtained only
if Congress toes the line of the organized segment of the American
Jewish community and of its various allies. And in the process, the
American public must be effectively deceived about Israel's real
strategic aims.

The Israeli grand strategy has diverse strands. The task of
blending them together into a single overarching concept was
undertaken by General (Reserves) Shlomo Gazit in an article
remarkable for its lucidity and forthrightness (*Yediot Ahronot*, 27
April). Gazit is a former Military Intelligence commander who often
explains in the media the strategic aims of the Israeli Security
System, or else provides apologias for what the public tends to regard
as its blunders or failures. His article has two avowed aims. The
first, common also to several other prestigious Israeli press
commentators writing at about the same time, is to convince the
public that what 'we used to hear for many years, almost since the
birth of the State, about Israel as a strategic asset for the US and
of the free world', remains no less valid after the demise of the USSR
and the termination of the Cold War than it had been before. Let
me ignore a greater part of his historical presentation of how and
why Israel could become so wonderful a strategic asset in the past,
except for a single point which contains something new. The point

is this: 'Israel proposed to the American armed forces that in the event of a war [with the USSR] it might provide the Americans with a variety of services, namely harbour, resupply, storage, medical treatment and hospitalization services.'

However, Gazit admits that the value of Israel's actually rendered services of the Cold War period 'did dwindle, perhaps even completely, as [the US] no longer needs to be prepared for war with the Soviet bloc'. This became apparent 'over a year ago, when the largest military force since World War II assembled during the Gulf War in our own region, in the very heart of the Middle East. Israel was ignored when this war was fought. Moreover, hope was expressed and concrete steps taken for the single aim of precluding Israel's involvement in that war.' Gazit even admits why it was so: 'due to what from the Israeli point of view is a very sad but salient fact, namely that (with the possible exception of Egypt which had signed a peace treaty with us), no other Arab state can be a party to any military or security-aimed alliance, if Israel is also a party to it.' This was why, explains Gazit, 'the Israeli Army was not actively involved in the war against Iraq'. This was why the armed forces of the anti-Iraqi coalition were not stationed on Israeli territory, as a result of 'the Arab veto'. Expecting his readers to consequently ask, 'What has still remained of Israel's traditional role as a strategic asset, then?', Gazit proceeds to lay bare the more decisive and lasting aspects of that role.

This is the second purpose of Gazit's article, even more important than the first. He believes, correctly in my view, that Israel still remains a strategic asset as it was in the past. His lucid explanation deserves to be quoted extensively: 'Israel's main task has not changed at all, and it remains of crucial importance. The geographical location of Israel at the centre of the Arab-Muslim Middle East predestines Israel to be a devoted guardian of stability in all the countries surrounding it. Its [role] is to protect the existing regimes: to prevent or halt the processes of radicalization and to block the expansion of fundamentalist religious zealotry. Israel has its "red lines", which have a powerful deterrent effect by virtue of causing uncertainty beyond its borders, precisely because they are not clearly marked nor explicitly defined. The purpose of these red lines is to determine which strategic developments or other changes occurring beyond Israel's borders can be defined as threats which Israel itself will regard as intolerable to the point of being compelled to use all its military power for the sake of their prevention or eradication.' In other words, the red lines are Israeli dictatorial ultimata imposed by it on all the other Middle Eastern states.

Gazit distinguishes 'three kinds of developments' among the processes of radicalization 'which qualify as intolerable' [to Israel]. The first category is constituted by acts of anti-Israeli terrorism originating from the territory of another state. Gazit is forthright enough to say that Israel retaliates against a given state not only in its own defence, but more in the best interest of an Arab government concerned: 'An Arab government allowing a terrorist organization to run free, creates a monster which sooner or later will turn against it. If it does not take steps to halt any development hostile to itself and to re-establish its total control, it will eventually cease to rule its own country.'

The second category of the red line is applied in case of 'any entry of a foreign Arab military force on to the territory of a state which borders on Israel, i.e. practically Jordan, Syria and Lebanon.' (Although Egypt borders on Israel, it is not mentioned.) As in the previous case, Gazit is anxious to show that Israel has in such cases a benevolent concern for the stability of a given Arab regime: 'An entry of a foreign Arab military force poses also a threat to the stability of the regime of the country thus affected, and sometimes also to the latter's sovereignty. There can be no doubt, therefore, that the Israeli red line which deters and prevents entries of foreign Arab military forces to countries neighbouring with Israel is also a stabilizing factor which really protects the existing states and regimes in the entire Middle East.'

The third category of the 'red line' is in Gazit's view, and in mine as well, the most important. It is intended to preclude the developments which he defines as 'threats of a revolt, whether military or popular, which may end up by bringing fanatical and extremist elements to power in states concerned. The existence of such threats has no connection with the Arab–Israeli conflict. They exist because the regimes [of the region] find it difficult to offer solutions to their socio-economic ills. But any development of the described kind is apt to subvert the existing relations between Israel and this or that from among its neighbours. The prime examples of such a red line are concerns for the preservation of Israel's peace treaty with Egypt and of the *de facto* peaceful cooperation between Israel and Jordan. In both cases it is Israel's red lines which communicate to its neighbours that Israel will not tolerate anything that might encourage the extremist forces to go all the way, following in the footsteps of either the Iranians to the east or the Algerians to the west.' Gazit backs this statement by mentioning the Israeli intervention in defence of the Jordanian regime during the 'Black September' uprising of 1970. He discussed more extensively the developments in Lebanon in the wake of the outbreak of the Civil War in 1975: 'When the Syrians were invited by some Maronites to intervene to stop the fighting and trounce the Muslims, they were at first deterred [by Israel] from advancing. When in the end the Syrian forces did advance, they clearly avoided anything which Israel could interpret as aberrant and thereby violating its red line.' It is well known (at least in Israel), that Syrian advancement had culminated in the 1976 siege of Tel El-Zaatar and the massacre of the Palestinians there. The massacre was perpetrated by Falangists supported by the Syrian army, with Israel fully approving. Senior Israeli Army officers were then spotted as observers in the Falangist camp, located in the vicinity of where the Syrian troops were stationed.

According to Gazit, however, this form of 'Israeli influence' may well extend beyond the Arab countries neighbouring with Israel: 'Indirectly, it also radiates on to all the other states of our region. In almost all of them, some kind of radicalization is going on, except that the radical forces are deterred from pushing all the way through out of fear that their maximalism might prompt Israel to respond. Although no one would say so openly, I am positive that the regime of President Mubarak benefits from such an Israeli deterrence. If power [in Egypt] is ever seized by Islamic extremists, they will at once have to decide whether to recognize the peace treaty with Israel as binding or not. It will be a most difficult decision for them. If they do recognize the treaty, they will compromise their own ideology. And if they don't recognize it, they will at once have a war for which they cannot possibly be ready.'

In Gazit's view, by virtue of protecting all or most Middle Eastern regimes, Israel performs a vital service for 'the industrially advanced states, all of which are keenly concerned with guaranteeing the stability in the Middle East'. He speculates that without Israel, the regimes of the region would have collapsed long ago. He concludes, 'In the aftermath of the disappearance of the USSR as a political power with interests of its own in the region a number of Middle Eastern states lost a patron guaranteeing their political, military and economic viability. A vacuum was thus created, adding to the region's instability. Under such conditions the Israeli role as a strategic asset guaranteeing a modicum of stability in the entire Middle East did not dwindle or disappear but was elevated to the first order of magnitude. Without Israel, the West would have to perform this role by itself, when none of the existing superpowers really could perform it, because of various domestic and international constraints. For Israel, by contrast, the need to intervene is a matter of survival.'

Let me recall in this context several facts of crucial importance. First, that speaking in the context of possible uses of Israeli nuclear power, Brosh revealed that Israel has contingency plans to be applied if 'the Egyptian regime may change' or because 'the Saudi royal family will not reign forever'. By comparing Gazit with Brosh, we can grasp better the nature of Israeli strategic aims. Israel is preparing for a war, nuclear if need be, for the sake of averting domestic change not to its liking, if it occurs in some or any Middle

Eastern states. At some time after the fall of the Shah it was disclosed that in the last days of his regime the Israeli Army planned to dispatch its elite units to Tehran in order to relieve the hard-pressed Iranian generals, except that Begin, in a display of relative moderation refused to okay the venture.

However, as Gazit rightly points out, the USSR collapsed. As long as it existed, it was a strategic factor of prime importance, because threat of Soviet intervention was to some extent deterring Israel from a direct and undisguised pursuit of hegemony over the entire Middle East. Now, as Gazir rightly observes, 'a vacuum was created' which neither the US nor any other 'industrially advanced state' can fill up, at least in Gazit's sense of the term. No faraway power will in the foreseeable future be able to invade a Middle Eastern state, while using or threatening to use its nuclear arms in the process, only because it would dislike a domestic radicalization occurring within the internationally recognized borders of that state. Let us recall that even when Iraq persisted in its annexation of Kuwait, Bush could obtain only a slim majority in the US Congress in favour of opening the Gulf War. Can Congress be envisioned to approve an invasion of a Middle Eastern state in a mere response to a popular revolution there? The answer cannot but be either categorically negative, or at least anticipative of nearly unsurmountable obstacles that the US or any other Western power would in such a case have to cope with. There can be no doubt that in Israel, where even the Knesset doesn't need to be consulted before an armed aggression, no analogous obstacles exist. The Israeli government has the legal right to initiate a war, and it can be certain of an initial approval for it by a huge majority of the Jewish public, regardless of circumstances under which that war breaks out. In the past, whenever the Knesset was notified of an aggressive war already in progress, it would approve it enthusiastically, by a huge majority.

Knesset ratifications of the already ongoing wars actually occurred in 1967 and in 1982. But the best example of it, allowing us to probe deeper into the pattern of the Knesset's behaviour, is its ratification of the Suez War in 1956. After Ben-Gurion told the Knesset, on the third day of the war, that the war's purpose was 'to re-establish the kingdom of David and Solomon' by annexing Sinai, our ancestral property 'which is not a part of Egypt', as well as to liberate the Egyptians and the whole world from the tyranny of Nasser, the entire Knesset, with the exception of the four Communist MKs, got up and stood to attention to sing the Israeli national anthem. Only threats from Khrushchev and from Eisenhower eventually convinced Ben-Gurion to reverse himself on this score. Yet Ben-Gurion was a realist and he ruled over the Army with an iron fist.

Under the new conditions of 'a vacuum [which] was created' by the demise of the USSR, and by the increasing vulnerability of the US, Israel clearly prepares itself to seek overtly a hegemony over the entire Middle East which it has always sought covertly, without hesitating to use for the purpose all means available, including nuclear ones. Contrary to what Gazit, Shuval or other Israeli spokesmen say, however, this venture is not being undertaken for the sake of benefiting the West. The West is comprised primarily of Gentiles, and Israel is a Jewish state whose sole purpose is to benefit Jews alone. Israel's search for hegemony stems from its own time-honoured ambitions which now dictate its strategic aims.

3

Syrian Cities and Relations with Saddam Hussein

24 September 1991

Numerous translations of mine from the Hebrew press envision, from time to time, a 'pre-emptive' Israeli war as likely and as directed against Syria, which has been long regarded by Israel as its enemy number one. Particularly relevant in this context is the 18 February 1991 speech by Yitzhak Rabin (as the head of opposition) to the Labor Knesset faction. Rabin's speech contained three crucial points. The first point was that Israel was doomed to live forever in war, or under the threat of war with the entire Arab world, but at this point of time especially with Syria. The second was that in all its wars Israel 'must assume an essentially aggressive role, so as to be in the position to dictate the terms of a conclusion'. Prerequisite to that is 'a further increase of the offensive power of Israeli Air and Armour forces needed to achieve a quick victory'. The third was Rabin's criticism of Arens (then the Defence Minister) for letting Iraqi missiles hit Israel: 'What had we told them [the Arabs]? If you send missiles on Tel Aviv, Damascus will be turned into a ruin. If you send missiles also on Haifa, not only Damascus but also Aleppo will cease to exist. They will be destroyed root and branch. Without dealing only with missile launchers, we will devastate Damascus.' Various Israeli commentators, e.g. Uzi Benziman and Reuven Padatzur of *Haaretz* and Ya'akov Sharett of *Davar*, understood these words as intended to mean that Israel had already threatened Syria (and other Arab countries as well) with obliteration of its cities by nuclear weapons.

Here I will describe what probably was the first instance when the highest Israeli authorities actually contemplated the razing of four Syrian cities: Damascus, Aleppo, Homs and Latakia. The story which occurred during the October 1973 War is documented by Yigal Sarna (*Yediot Ahronot*, 17 September 1991). Sarna's facts are based on extensive documentation supplied by Aryeh Brown, the then military secretary of the Defence Minister, Moshe Dayan. Sarna's article contains an interview with Brown who defines himself as 'loyal to Dayan, and trusting his judgement fully, both during that war and on other occasions'. Significantly, Brown also says that he owed his quick rise in rank to Dayan.

Sarna's article appeared on the Eve of Yom Kippur when analyses of the 1973 Yom Kippur War are customarily published by the Hebrew press. I find it significant that no other Israeli war, such as the War of Independence and the Six Day War, duly commemorated as they are, receive even a fraction of printed space which the history of the 1973 War continues to receive. Sarna himself fought in that war as a tank commander on the Syrian front. As for Sarna's personal attitude, he says that together with 'a whole generation of Israelis, then traumatized to the core', he has since that war 'acquired a split personality with half of it remaining in the past and the second half facing the future'. This can mean that the attitudes of the entire generation then changed. As Sarna says, that generation 'now passes on the emotions then learned to their sons'. All Israeli politics from 1973 can best be understood as a reaction to the Yom Kippur War. That reaction, however, may assume antithetical directions.

The personality of Moshe Dayan needs to be taken into account here. I have always been very critical of Dayan, but I think that whatever can be said of his politics, there can be little doubt that, while the Israeli grand strategy precedes his time, he was also a master tactician, who invented the Israeli Army's doctrine of deterrence, along with other tactical innovations which still largely determine the Israeli Army's strategies and tactics, but above everything else in its attitudes towards the Arabs. Just before October 1973 Dayan was at the peak of his popularity, not only in Israel but also among the diaspora Jews. His popularity rested in my view mainly on his radiant confidence that Israel could retain the Territories conquered in that war indefinitely. He argued that the the Arab states either would not dare attack Israel, or, if they did, their resounding defeat after a short war was assured.

Already on the second day of the Yom Kippur War (7 October), however, Dayan together with all other Israeli leaders realized that the war was going badly, with all their hopes for a rapid victory dashed. As Brown recounts, they nevertheless kept pretending to the Israelis as well as to the whole world (including their friend Henry Kissinger) that everything was going on according to the Israeli Army's plans. (A major carrier of this deception was Hayim Herzog, then the chief TV commentator and now President of the state.) The deception only aggravated the situation.

As Brown recounts it, on 7 October, at 11:45 a.m., 'Moshe Dayan and his chief military adviser General Rehavam Ze'evi (now the leader of the transfer-advocating Moledet ('Fatherland') party) already recognized the full dimensions of the [Israeli] defeat.' They came to this recognition in spite of being misinformed by some generals, especially the commander of the Southern Command responsible for the Suez front, Gonen (alias Gorodish) who 'kept reporting favourable developments only'. Shortly afterwards Dayan reported his conclusions to several Israeli ministers and then to Prime Minister Golda Meir. The next day (8 October), counter-attacks by fresh Israeli forces, were, according to Brown, 'predicated on the Air Force's false reports of smashing successes'. No wonder the counter-attacks ended up in another defeat, more decisive than the defeats of the previous day. Although at the session of the Israeli government held on the evening of that day Dayan did not reveal the extent of the defeat, he was well aware of it. On a piece of paper guarded by Brown he sketched guidelines to be followed during the next several days. After summarizing the adversities on the Egyptian front he wrote there: 'Everything possible should be done to terminate fighting on the Northern [Syrian] front at once, so that we have only one [the Egyptian] front to cope with.' He decided to discuss this with the Chief of Staff, David Elazar. Next morning he met senior officers to whom he presented another argument for terminating the war against Syria 'at once': 'I expect traumatic reactions when the Israelis discover the truth.' As subsequent developments showed, in this respect Dayan was a good prophet. Possibly, the crucial consideration underlying his subsequent decisions was to prevent Israelis from learning the truth.

'At the meeting [with senior officers]', continues Sarna, 'instructions were drafted which even Brown considered devoid of all precedent.' In addition to orders to Israeli troops fighting the Syrians on the ground to destroy the Syrian Army without regard for their own casualties, they also included 'the orders to find out by any means, including the most bizarre ones, what could be done' in order to defeat the Syrians rapidly. Brown explains to Sarna that 'it was Dayan who first advanced the idea that Syria must be crushed to pieces. When he talked about "the bizarre means", he meant to stress that anything was conceivable ... In the diaries of Brown from that time, the word "Damascus" from that moment onward begins to appear very frequently. Dayan, the Chief of Staff, the commander of the Air Force, all talked about Damascus. "We must smash Syria within the next 24 hours", said the Chief of Staff to the accompanying officers. "We have 400 tanks now fighting like hell. Therefore the Syrian cities of Damascus, Aleppo, Homs and Latakia should be obliterated. I must do something dramatic enough to make Syria cry 'Whoah!', to make them beg us 'Please stop firing!' For that purpose I need something that will deprive them of all electricity, destroy all their power stations, and scorch their earth"'.

But in order to use such 'bizarre means', Israeli generals needed an authorization by civilian authorities. The next day Dayan, accompanied by Yigal Alon [a renowned Palmach commander in 1948 and former Foreign Minister] 'who backed him', held an early morning meeting with Golda Meir. Sarna does not know what transpired there, except for the outcome. No permission to use 'bizarre means' was granted. Instead, 'the Air Force was instructed by the Chief of Staff "to smash Syria"' by conventional means. The government which met later that day was informed that during the air raid on Damascus taking place simultaneously, 'all targets had already been hit'. Only after the ministers dispersed, a report arrived 'that only some targets had been hit, among them the Soviet cultural center'. Damascus was not obliterated by conventional means. The Air Force attributed its failure 'to heavy cloud'.

At this point Sarna's narrative breaks for about seven to eight days. This may be due either to Brown's reluctance to talk or to a censorship ban. Judging by references to events on the Syrian front, the narrative resumes from 15–16 October. By then, Israeli commanders, instead of working alone as they did at the beginning of the war, were working in close coordination with Henry Kissinger. The planning aimed no longer at obliterating Damascus (other Syrian cities were no longer even mentioned), but at besieging or conquering it. Only some of the generals demanded sterner measures. The idea animating everybody was to conclude the war by a great victory in the style of the Six Day War, but on a larger scale.

One October night Dayan wrote an instruction: 'I plan complete destruction of the Syrian army. If Damascus can be conquered, its conquest should be considered ... Our entry into Damascus could balance our retreat from the [Suez] Canal.' Next morning 'the Chief of Staff asked for a missile of 40-km range to be launched on to Damascus. Dayan rejected that request.' We can make the conjecture that the missile which the Chief of Staff requested was not meant to have a conventional warhead. Then Dayan went to the command of General Rafael Eitan on the Syrian front to tell him: 'Our aim is to reach Damascus. The conduct of the war depends on our ability to reach Damascus ... We should proceed toward it, attacking on a narrow front, and [then] make an assault on the city, so that they will be forced to beg us to refrain from conquering it.' Eitan is recorded by Brown as promising Dayan that Damascus would soon be conquered and as issuing the requisite orders at once, while Dayan watched to see what would follow: 'After two hours the spearhead of the advancing Armour brigade commanded by General Lerner, reported having been hit by a Syrian anti-tank force. The Syrians awaited the Israelis in ambush and inflicted heavy casualties. Yet Dayan continued to think about the conquest of Damascus.' After several hours, when Lerner's brigade retreated and began reassembling, 'Dayan radioed Lerner: "I want to tell you that if you reach the gates of Damascus with speed you will vindicate our loss of the [Suez] Canal." At the same time, however, he received a report from the Chief of Staff: "I cannot reach Damascus." Dayan answered: "I now want to reach the vicinity of Damascus, rather than the city itself. It will suffice if they say to the Russians: "Help us to get rid of the Jews"".'

Yet the same day Dayan promised Golda Meir to either conquer Damascus or at least reach its outskirts, and he repeated this at a government meeting. Then he went to the generals commanding the Syrian front, telling them: 'Our troops need to advance no more than 5 or 7 km. From there we can reach Damascus which lies at the distance of only 25 km. further. This can be accomplished easily enough.' What he apparently expected was that after an initial offensive the Syrian Army would break apart and run away, in the same way as the Egyptian Army had done in 1967. In fact, his (and his generals') reasoning relied entirely on folk psychology: on their own preconceptions about 'Arab mentality'. Theirs was a 'strategy based on the presumed psychology of the Arabs'. This strategy prevailed at the same meeting, when the commander of the Air Force, Benny Peled, proposed that Damascus be bombed from the air rather than conquered. Dayan responded: 'The Syrians know that aircraft sows destruction but cannot conquer. But if we shell them with artillery, they will feel that we are about to conquer the city soon.'

But another factor also played its role. Brown records that 'the State Secretary [Kissinger] instantly receives the reports of all the movements of the Israeli troops. He is deliberately staying the political process in order to enable Israel to negotiate later from a more advantageous position. Kissinger is certain that Damascus will be conquered, to the point of having quipped to Dinitz [Israeli Ambassador in the US]: "As soon as you reach the suburbs of Damascus, all you will need for the rest is the public transport"'. He said it 'ten days before the end of the war'. It was due to his interaction with Kissinger that Dayan insisted on 'the conquest of Damascus within a few days'.

The role of Begin, then head of the Israeli opposition, was downright comical. Prompted by 'the phone calls I keep getting from Sharon at the [Egyptian] front', Begin told Dayan that the conquest of Damascus was imperative 'for the sake of liberating the Syrian Jews'. (He apparently meant those who would survive the bombing of Damascus.) Dayan dismissed him courteously. Dayan was still so sure that Damascus could at the very least be besieged by the Israeli forces that 'he began to worry about what might happen to those forces in the vicinity of Damascus during the entire rainy season', i.e. the winter.

Sarna, who served all that time at the front, records that the aim of conquering Damascus was passed on to the troops. 'In fact, the [Israeli] forces in the Golan Heights were already exhausted and unable to break through the [Syrian] defence lines separating them from Damascus. Still, the goal of conquering Damascus raised the morale of the troops, their faith in the continuous attack and their ability to be always able to advance toward designated targets'. Yet he reflects: 'I now think that distances on the Chief of Staff's maps must have seemed short compared to the slowness of our advances and to the scale of our casualties in human lives and also in armour which we suffered for each of 100 meters we have traversed ... As a tankist advancing on "a narrow front" towards Damascus, I recall how distant we were from the city, how dispirited while watching their defence lines, how worn out by their continuous mortar shelling of our night encampments. The attempt to conquer Damascus was unreal but at the same time it was essential because it restored our morale after our war-machine broke down'. This is indeed a telling testimony of ignorance of the Israeli warlords about the conditions their own soldiers were fighting under. To all appearances, that ignorance has deepened since.

Sarna's story is ominous because the fundamental aims of the Israeli army top commanders can be presumed to remain the same and the folk psychology guiding their decisions can be presumed not to have changed either. The ideas of fighting Syria with nuclear weapons are unlikely to have been discarded. The recourse to nuclear weapons on Israel's part, whether for the sake of obliterating the four mentioned Syrian cities or of Damascus alone seems to have been prevented in 1973 by the opposition of Golda Meir and Henry Kissinger, both of whom preferred Israel to conquer Damascus by conventional means.

Past contacts between Israel and Saddam Hussein
10 November 1990

In the middle of the present Gulf crisis it is worth recalling that until a few months ago Saddam Hussein persistently offered to make peace with Israel on the latter's terms. One of his attempts took place about a year ago. The then Defence Minister, Yitzhak Rabin, was during one of his visits to the US then approached with an offer that he meet Saddam Hussein. Information to this effect appeared in two articles by the senior strategy and military correspondent of *Haaretz*, Ze'ev Shiff, who in matters of historical fact can be considered quite reliable (*Haaretz*, 5 and 6 November 1990). Interestingly, Rabin refused to either confirm or deny the revelations, after *Haaretz* accorded them publicity by printing them on its front page.

The middleman chosen by Saddam Hussein was 'an American businessman of Arab descent ... Bob Abud. At present he is the president of the First City Bank of Texas. In the past he presided over the oil company owned by the multi-millionaire Armand Hammer ... He is 62, well-known for his good relations with some heads of Arab states, for whom he arranges personal loans on easy terms. He also maintains good relations with the Arab-American community. After twelve years of heading Hammer's oil company 'Occidental Petroleum', he became president of a Chicago bank', where 'he developed an interest in advancing the cause of peace between Israel and the Arab states' (Shiff, 6 November). It is not irrelevant to note that Armand Hammer, who is Jewish, has for many years been a fervent Israel supporter, a generous contributor to United Jewish Appeal [of the US] and a major investor in Israel, in addition to being used by Israeli diplomacy as a middleman in political ventures, for example arranging the immigration of Soviet Jews to Israel through his contacts with top Soviet leaders.

As Shiff reports it (5 November) the offer was made by Saddam Hussein, who proposed through Abud 'to meet with Yitzhak Rabin, then [Israeli] Defence minister. The dates of two meetings, to be held in Europe were already fixed, although the Iraqis requested to reschedule them. A secret meeting between Rabin and the middleman was held in Philadelphia.' According to Shiff, Abud, 'was held by the Israelis in respect, as somebody with useful connections. Considering this, Rabin expressed his desire to meet him in order to hear directly about the Iraqi proposal.' Prior to meeting Rabin, Mr Abud met several times 'an Israeli businessman living most of his time abroad, Azriel Einav', known for having good connections within the Israeli Defence Ministry and other components of the Israeli Security System. When those meetings proved successful and the consent of Rabin to establish contacts with Saddam Hussein was obtained, an influential aide and personal friend of Rabin, Eytan Haber 'was appointed as a go-between in charge of arranging the meetings' of Rabin with Saddam Hussein. When confronted by Shiff with the evidence, Haber responded that '"something like that" had indeed occured', but refused to provide any further information.

The Philadelphia meeting of Abud with Rabin was held when the latter attended the opening of an Israeli Bonds convention in that city. Haber and the military secretary of Rabin, Kuti Mor were present during a part of the meeting with Abud. To prevent the press from noticing the meetings, Mr Abud 'entered the hotel through the kitchen door and proceeded to Rabin's suite by a service elevator'. On the agenda was, first, 'the proposal [of Saddam

Hussein] to meet in order to talk about reconciling the interests of the two states', and, the second, means of averting an Israeli attack on Iraq which was rumoured to be under preparation: 'Rabin accepted the proposal to meet Saddam Hussein at a location to be determined, but rejected the proposal to include a PLO representative during part of these talks.' After this agreement, Mr Abud suggested in the name of Saddam Hussein, that 'Rabin may be invited to a meeting in Baghdad', instead of a meeting in Europe. There is no information about how Rabin responded to this interesting suggestion, except that he 'opined that all leads toward peace with all the Arab states deserve to be examined'.

Contacts between Israel and Iraq and the timing of various meetings were negotiated and renegotiated by Israel and Iraq through the above mentioned go-between during several subsequent months, 'but when the tension between [Israel] and Iraq began to mount after Saddam Hussein's speech at the last February's conference of the Council for Economic Cooperation between Egypt, Iraq, Jordan and Yemen, the idea of meeting was shelved', apparently by Israel. Shiff (5 November) writes in conclusion: 'Supposedly, the American businessman was reporting all the details of the negotiations to the White House.'

4

Israel versus Iran
24 February 1993

Since the spring of 1992 public opinion in Israel is being prepared for the prospect of a war with Iran, to be fought to bring about Iran's total military and political defeat. In one version, Israel would attack Iran alone, in another it would 'persuade' the West to do the job. The indoctrination campaign to this effect is gaining in intensity. It is accompanied by what could be called semi-official horror scenarios purporting to detail what Iran could do to Israel, the West and the entire world when it acquires nuclear weapons as it is expected to a few years hence. A manipulation of public opinion to this effect may well be considered too phantasmagoric to merit any detailed description. Still, the readers should take notice, especially since to all appearances the Israeli Security System does envisage the prospect seriously. In February 1993 minutely-detailed anticipations of Iran becoming a major target of Israeli policies became intense. I am going to confine myself to a sample of recent publications (in view of the monotony of their contents it will suffice), emphasizing how they envisage the possibility of 'persuading' the West that Iran must be defeated. All Hebrew papers have shared in advocacy of this madness, with exception of *Haaretz* which has not dared to challenge it either. The Zionist 'left' papers, *Davar* and *Al Hamishmar* have particularly distinguished themselves in bellicosity on the subject of Iran; more so than the right-wing *Maariv*. Below, I will concentrate on the recent writings of *Al Hamishmar* and *Maariv* about Iran, only occasionally mentioning what I found in other papers.

A major article by the political correspondent of *Al Hamishmar*, Yo'av Kaspi bears the title that summarizes its contents: 'Iran needs to be treated just as Iraq had been' (19 February 1993). The article contains an interview with Daniel Leshem, introduced as 'a retired senior officer in the [Israeli] Military Intelligence, now member of the Centre for Strategic Research at the Tel Aviv University'. Leshem is known to be involved in forming Israeli strategies. His account of how Iran is going to nuclearize is too dubious to merit coverage here as are his lamentations that 'the world' has been ignoring the warnings of the Israeli experts who

54

alone know all the truth about what the Muslim states are like. However, his proposals for the reversal of the progress of Iranian nuclearization are by all means worth of being reported. Leshem begins by opining that the Allied air raids had very little success in destroying Iraq's military and especially nuclear capabilities, but, owing to Allied victory on the ground, UN observers could succeed in finishing the job. Harping on this 'analogy', Leshem concludes: 'Israel alone can do very little to halt the Iranians. We could raid Iran from the air, but we cannot realistically expect that our aerial operations could destroy all their capabilities. At best, some Iranian nuclear installations could in this way be destroyed. But we couldn't reach their major centres of nuclear development, since that development has proceeded along three different lines in a fairly decentralized manner, with installations and factories scattered widely across the country. It is even reasonable to suppose that we will never know the locations of all their installations, just as we didn't know in Iraq's case.'

Hence Leshem believes that Israel should make Iran fear Israeli nuclear weapons, but without hoping that it might deter it from developing their own; he proposes 'to create the situation which would appear similar to that with Iraq before the Gulf crisis'. He believes this could 'stop the Ayatollahs, if this is what the world really wants'. How to do it? 'Iran claims sovereignty over three strategically located islands in the Gulf. Domination over those islands is capable of assuring domination not only over all the already active oilfields of the area, but also over all the natural gas sources not yet exploited. We should hope that, emulating Iraq, Iran would contest the Gulf Emirates and Saudi Arabia over these islands and, repeating Saddam Hussein's mistake in Kuwait, start a war. This may lead to an imposition of controls over Iranian nuclear developments the way it did in Iraq. This prospect is in my view quite likely, because patience plays no part in the Iranian mentality. But if they nevertheless refrain from starting a war, we should take advantage of their involvement in Islamic terrorism which already hurts the entire world. Israel has incontestable intelligence that the Iranians are terrorists. We should take advantage of this by persistently explaining to the world at large that by virtue of its involvement in terrorism, no other state is as dangerous to the entire world as Iran. I cannot comprehend why Libya has been hit by sanctions, to the point that sales of military equipment are barred to it because of its minor involvement in terrorism; while Iran, with its record of guiding terrorism against the entire world remains entirely free of even stricter sanctions.' In true-blue Israeli style, Leshem attributes this lamentable state of affairs to Israel's neglect of its propaganda (called '*Hasbara*', that is, 'Explanation').

He nevertheless hopes that Israel will soon be able 'to explain to the world at large' how urgent is the need to provoke Iran to a war.

Provoking Iran into responding with war or measures just stopping short of war, is also elaborated by many other commentators. Let me just quote a story published by Telem Admon in *Maariv* (12 February) who reports that 'a senior Israeli', that is, a senior Mossad agent, 'about two weeks ago had a long conversation with the son of the late Shah, Prince Riza Sha'a Pahlevi' in order to appraise the man's possible usefulness for Israeli '*Hasbara*'. In the 'senior's' opinion, 'Clinton's America is too absorbed in its domestic affairs', and as a result 'the prince's chances of reigning in Iran are deplorably slim. The prince's face showed signs of distress after he heard a frank assessment to this effect from the mouth of an Israeli.' Yet the 'senior's' appraisal of the prince was distinctly negative, in spite of 'the princely routine of handing to all visitors copies of articles by Ehud Ya'ari' (an Israeli television commentator suspected of being a front for Israeli Intelligence). Why? In the first place because 'the prince shows how nervous he is. His knees jerked during the first half-hour of the conversation.' Worse still, his chums 'were dressed like hippies' while 'he kept frequenting Manhattan's haunts in their company and addressing them as if they were his equals'. The 'senior' deplores it greatly that the prince has emancipated himself from the beneficial influence of his mother, 'who had done a simply wonderful job travelling from capital to capital in order to impress everybody concerned with her hope to enthrone her son in Iran while she is still alive'. Her valiant efforts look to me as connected, to some extent at least, to the no-less-valiant efforts of the Israeli '*Hasbara*' before it had written off her son.

But what might happen if both Israel and Iran have nuclear weapons? This question is being addressed by the Hebrew press at length, often in a manner intended to titillate the reader with anticipated horrors. Let me give a small sample. In *Al Hamishmar* (19 February), Kaspi interviewed the notorious 'hawk', Professor Shlomo Aharonson, who begins his perorations by excoriating the Israeli left as a major obstacle to Israel's ability to resist Iranian evildoing. Without bothering about the left's current lack of political clout, says Aharonson: 'The left is full of prejudices and fears. It refuses to be rational on the nuclear issue. The left doesn't like nuclear weapons, full stop. The opposition of the Israeli left to nuclear weapons is reminiscent of the opposition to the invention of the wheel.' Profound insights, aren't they? After spelling them out, Aharonson proceeds to his 'scenarios'. Here is just one of them: 'If we established tomorrow a Palestinian state, we will really grant a sovereignty to an entity second to none in hostility toward us. This entity can be expected to reach a nuclear alliance with Iran at once. Suppose the Palestinians open hostilities against us and the Iranians deter us from retaliating against the Palestinians by threatening to retaliate in turn against us by nuclear means. What could we do then?' There is a lot more in the same vein before Aharonson concludes: 'We should see to it that no Palestinian state ever comes into being, even if Iranians threaten us with nuclear weapons. And we should also see to it that Iran lives in permanent fear of Israeli nuclear weapons being used against it.'

Let me reiterate that the Israelis are also bombarded ceaselessly with official messages to the same effect. For example, General Ze'ev Livneh, the commander of recently established Rear General Command of the Israeli Army said (in *Haaretz*, 15 February) that 'it is not only Iran which already endangers every site in Israel', because, even if to a lesser extent, 'Syria, Libya and Algeria do too'. In order to protect Israel from this danger, General Livneh calls upon 'the European Community to enforce jointly with Israel an embargo on any weaponry supplies to both Iran and those Arab states. The EC should also learn that military interventions can have salutary effects, as proven recently in Iraq's case.'

Timid reminders by the Hebrew press that Israel continues to have the monopoly of nuclear weapons in the Middle East, were definitely unwelcome to Israeli authorities. In *Hadashot* of 29 January and 5 February, Ran Edelist, careful to rely only on quotes from the US press, raised the problem of nuclear waste disposal from the rather obsolete Dimona reactor and of other possible risks of that reactor to Israeli lives and limbs. He was 'answered' by numerous interviews with named and unnamed experts, all of whom fiercely denied that any such risks existed. The experts didn't neglect to reassure their readers that the Israeli reactor was the best and the safest in the entire world. But speaking in the name of 'the Intelligence Community' Immanuel Rosen (*Maariv*, 12 February) went even further. He disclosed that the said 'community' felt offended 'by the self-confident publications of an Israeli researcher dealing with nuclear subjects. This researcher has recently been found by the Intelligence Community to pose "a security risk", to the point of observing that in some states such a researcher "would have been made to disappear".' Ran Edelist reacted in a brief note (in *Hadashot*, 14 February), confining himself to quoting these revealing ideas of 'the Intelligence Community', and drawing attention to threats voiced there. But apart from Edelist, the press of 'the only democracy in the Middle East' either didn't dare comment, or was not allowed to.

The press is allowed, and even encouraged, to discuss one issue related to Israeli nuclear policies: to say how clever Peres was in pretending to agree to negotiate nuclear disarmament and then raising unacceptable conditions for entering any such negotiations.

An example of this is Akiva Eldar's coverage in *Haaretz* (19 February), of Rabin's excoriation of Egypt on television a few days earlier. Rabin scolded Egypt for suggesting that a Middle East regional nuclear disarmament agreement would be desirable. Eldar comments that 'The Prime Minister is known to loathe anything that relates to Egypt. Aiming at Boutros Ghali, he said [in a public speech]: "What can you expect of him? Isn't he an Egyptian?" Rabin is particularly averse to Egyptian insistence that the Middle East should be completely denuclearized. Peres, by contrast, favours using Egypt as an intermediary in various diplomatic pursuits, while recognizing that Cairo's reminders on the subject of Dimona obstruct his real mission, which is to mediate between Egypt and the grand man in Jerusalem.' Therefore, after 'Egypt recently invited Israel to a symposium that "would deal with both conventional and non-conventional armed confrontations", a high-level discussion was held in the Foreign Ministry on how to pretend to accept the invitation and then "to decline it elegantly". The solution was to communicate to Egypt the Israeli agreement in principle to attend the symposium on three conditions: that it be chaired by the US and Russia; that its agenda be unanimously determined by the chairmen and all the participants; and, most interestingly, that nothing be discussed unless the presence of all other Arab states, not just of Syria and Lebanon, but also – hard to believe – of Libya and Iraq, be assured in advance. In this way, any conceivable discussion of nuclear affairs was effectively precluded.' I find it superfluous to comment on Eldar's story.

But I do want to make some comments on the incitement of Israelis against Iran. I am well aware that a lot of expert opinions and predictions quoted here will sound to non-Israeli readers like fantasy running amok. Yet I perceive those opinions and predictions, no matter how mendacious and deceitful they obviously are, as politically quite meaningful. Let me explain my reasons. In the first place, I have not quoted the opinions of raving extremists. I was careful to select only the writings of respected and influential Israeli experts or commentators on strategic affairs, who can be presumed to be well acquainted with the thinking of the Israeli Security System. Since militarily Israel is the strongest state in the Middle East and has the monopoly on nuclear weapons in the region, strategical doctrines of its Security System deserve to be disseminated world-wide, especially when they are forcefully pressed upon the Israeli public. Whether one likes it or not, Israel is a great power, not only in military but also in political terms, by virtue of its increasing influence upon US policies. The opinions of the Israeli Security System may mean something different from what they say. But this doesn't detract from their importance.

But there is more to it. Fantasy and madness in the doctrines of the Israeli Security System are nothing new. At least since the early 1950s those qualities could already be noticed. Let us just recall that in 1956 Ben-Gurion wanted to annex Sinai to Israel on the ground that 'it was not Egypt'. The same doctrine was professed in 1967–73 with elaborations, such as the proposal of several generals to conquer Alexandria in order to hold the city hostage until Egypt would sign a peace treaty on Israeli terms. The 1982 invasion of Lebanon relied on fantastic assumptions, and so did the 1983 'peace treaty' signed with a 'lawful Lebanese government' put in power by Sharon. All Israeli policies in the Territories are not just totally immoral, but also rely on assumptions steadily held and advocated without regard for their fanciful contents. It will suffice to recall how Rabin together with the entire Israeli Security System perceived the outbreak of the Intifada first as an Iranian manipulation and then as a fabrication of western television and press. They concluded that if the Arabs are denied opportunities to fake riots in order to be photographed, the unrest in the Territories could be suppressed with ease.

Relevant to this is the fact that Israeli policies bear the easily recognizable imprint of Orientalist 'expertise' abounding in militarist and racist ideological prejudices. This 'expertise' is readily available in English, since its harbingers were the Jewish Orientalists living in English-speaking countries, like Bernard Lewis or the late Elie Kedourie who had visited Israel regularly for hobnobbing on the best of terms with the Israeli Security System. It was Kedourie who performed a particularly seminal role in fathering the assumptions on which Israeli policies rest and who consequently had in Israel a lot of influence. In Kedourie's view, the peoples of the Middle East, with the 'self-evident' exception of Israel, would be best off if ruled by foreign imperial powers with a natural capacity to rule for a long time yet. Kedourie believed that the entire Middle East could be ruled by foreign powers with perfect ease, because their domination would hardly be opposed except by grouplets of intellectuals bent on rabble-rousing. Kedourie lived in Britain, and his primary concern was British politics. In his opinion the British refused to continue to rule the Middle East, with calamitous effects, only because of intellectual corruption of their own experts, especially those from the Foreign and Commonwealth Office at Chatham House, who were misguided enough to dismiss the superior expertise of minority nationals, particularly Jewish, from the Arab world, who alone had known 'the Arab nature' at first hand. For example, in his first book, Kedourie says that as early as 1932 (!) the British government was misguided enough to grant Iraq independence (it was faked, but never mind) against the advice of Jewish community in Baghdad. On many occasions during his recurrent visits to Israel, from the 1960s until his death, Kedourie would assure his Israeli audiences (one of which I was a member) that Iraq could 'really' be still ruled by the British with ease, under whatever disguises it would be convenient to adopt, provided the grouplets of rabble-rousers would be dealt with by a modicum of salutary toughness. That, the opportunities for education would be restricted so as not to produce a superfluous number of intellectuals, prone to learn the western notions of national independence. True, Kedourie also opposed the idea of exclusive Jewish right to the Land of Israel as incompatible with his imperialistic outlook, but he favoured the retention of Israeli permanent rule over the Palestinians. The rather incongruous blend of Kedourie's ideas with the Land of Israel messianism is already an innovation of Israeli Security System vintage.

The implications of the Kedourie doctrine for Israeli policy-makers are obvious. First, Israel always seeks to persuade the West about what its 'true' interests and 'moral duties' in the Middle East are. It also tells the West that by intervening in the Middle East they would serve the authentic interests of Middle Eastern nations. But if the western powers refuse to listen, it is up to Israel to assume 'the white man's burden'.

Another implication of Kedourie's doctrine, acted upon by Israel since the early 1950s already, is that in the Middle East no other strong state is to be tolerated. Its power must be destroyed or at least diminished through a war. Iranian theocracy may have its utility for the Israeli Hasbara, but Nasser's Egypt was attacked while being emphatically secular. In both cases the real reason for the Israeli threat to start a war was the strength of the state concerned. Quite apart from the risks such a state may pose to Israeli hegemonic ambitions, Orientalist 'expertise' requires that natives of the region always remain weak, to be ruled always by their traditional notables but not by persons with intellectual capacity, whether religious or secular. Before World War I, such principles were taken for granted in the West, professed openly and applied globally, from China to Mexico. Israeli Orientalism, on which Israeli policies are based, is no more than their belated replica. It continues to uphold dogmas which, say in 1903, were taken for granted as 'scientific' truths. The subsequent 'troubles' of the West are perceived by the Israeli 'experts' as a well-deserved punishment for listening to intellectuals who had been casting doubt on such self-evident truths. Without such rotten intellectuals, everything would have remained stable.

Let us return to the special case of Iran, though. Anyone not converted to the Orientalistic creed will recognize that Iran is a country very difficult to conquer, because of its size, topography and especially because of fervent nationalism combined with the religious zeal of its populace. I happen to loathe the current Iranian regime, but it doesn't hinder me from immediately noticing how different it is from Saddam Hussein's. Popular support for Iran's rulers is much greater than for Iraq's. After Saddam Hussein had invaded Iran, his troops were resisted valiantly under extremely difficult conditions. All analogies between a possible attack on Iran and the Gulf War are therefore irresponsibly fanciful. Yet Sharon and the Israeli Army commanders did in 1979 propose to send a detachment of Israeli paratroopers to Tehran to quash the revolution and restore the monarchy. They really thought, until stopped by Begin, that a few Israeli paratroopers could determine the history of a country as immense and populous as Iran! According to a consensus of official Israeli experts on Iranian affairs, the fall of the Shah was due solely to his 'softness' in refraining to order his army to slaughter thousands of demonstrators wholesale. Later, the Israeli experts on Iranian affairs were no less unanimous in predicting a speedy defeat of Iran by Saddam Hussein. No evidence indicates that they have changed their assumptions or discarded their underlying racism. Their ranks may include some relatively less-opinionated individuals, who have survived the negative selection process which usually occurs within groups sharing such ideologically-tight imageries. But such individuals can be assumed to prefer to keep their moderation to themselves, while hoping that Israel can reap some fringe benefits from any western provocation against Iran, even if it results in a protracted and inconclusive war.

5

Israeli Foreign Policy after the Oslo Accord

1 November 1993

The right word to describe the thirty-year-old dependence of Israeli policies on the US was coined by *Davar*'s political commentator Daniel Ben-Simon, who speaks of the 'former American tutelage' of Israel (18 October 1993). Ben-Simon's view is correct when he says that 'until quite recently Israeli foreign policy was carried out according to the rules imposed by the State Department and the White House. Nothing was done in defiance of those rules. All former peace initiatives in the Middle East were launched by the Americans.' Yet Ben-Simon also says that 'the Oslo Accord put Israel's patron to shame. While chiefs of the State Department were busily overseeing the progress of Israeli–Palestinian negotiations in Washington, Rabin and Peres closed the deal in distant Oslo. The US was notified of the Accord barely a few days before its finalization, as a gesture to spare them an overt insult, and in order to make it still possible for them to disburse money needed for its implementation.'

His conclusion, with which I again concur, is that 'the main loser from this rapid increase in the Israeli power of diplomatic manoeuvre is the US. The Accord with the PLO which generated sympathy for Israel has also made it more confident of its power than it ever was.' Commenting on this new self-confidence, Ben-Simon elaborates that 'some factions of major importance within Israeli establishment are quite satisfied with this weakening of the American tutelage', but 'Rabin does not belong to them. Regardless of gains in the independence of Israeli policies, he still feels that the American protective umbrella over Israel is the best guarantee of its security.' Right now, however, Israeli foreign policy is noticeably different from what it was before, increasingly aiming at getting rid of 'American tutelage'. This change, placed in a broader historical context, will be described here.

The politically prodigious and financially unprecedented support which Israel was receiving from the US since the early 1960s until this year has actually never determined Israeli policies entirely. To begin with, it superseded the period of frequent conflicts between the US and Israel in the 1950s. These conflicts flared up during the Suez affair of 1956 when Eisenhower forced Israel to withdraw unconditionally not only from Sinai but also from the Gaza Strip. Since the early 1960s, however, Israel has wielded tremendous influence within the US, and it was capable of turning that influence to its advantage. Owing to this, 'American tutelage' has never worked perfectly, as Israel did occasionally pursue policies not in accord with US interests. Even more than that: by exploiting its influence on the Congress and the US media, Israel could occasionally force the US administration to reverse its policies completely. When the Carter administration announced its accord with the USSR as its policy programme for the Middle East, which was not to the taste of the Begin government, the latter dispatched its then Foreign Minister, Dayan to the US. Within three days, Dayan succeeded in making the Carter administration ignominiously reverse itself. Sadat's visit to Jerusalem, the Camp David negotiations, the Israeli–Egyptian peace and the 1982 invasion of Lebanon can all be seen as contingent upon Dayan's humiliation of Carter in this affair.

Israel's economic situation and its standing within the international community can also be reasonably supposed to affect the degree of Israeli dependence on the US. Whenever Israel is in financial straits (whether for economic or other reasons) and whenever its relations with other great powers are strained, its dependence on the US cannot but be on the rise. But whenever the Israeli government and the Israeli wealthy elite are financially well-off (even if the Israeli poor then get poorer) Israel's dependence on the US can be reduced, and Israel can then assume a more independent policy posture.

For example, the invasion of Lebanon resulted in an Israeli conquest of a relatively large territory and in Israel's deep involvement in Lebanese domestic affairs. The invasion was made possible by a long period of steady and enormous increases in the size of the Israeli Defence budgets, beginning in 1967 and continuing until 1984. But the occupation of Lebanon resulted in a bloody guerilla war in which Israel was defeated not only militarily but also economically. Nehemya Strassler, writing in *Haaretz*, (6 August) gave the following vivid picture of the resultant economic situation: 'By the beginning of 1985 the Israeli economy was on the verge of collapse, which could lead to a collapse of Israeli democracy. The only way to avert it was by stopping the hyperinflation. The monthly inflation rate stood then at 15 per cent. The economy was in a shambles, the dollar reserves were already almost spent. The situation was grievous enough to make the Treasury contemplate the imposition of quotas on all imports to stave off the vanishing of all hard currency.' Being in such a shambles, Israel was shunned by all major Third World states. Given such realities, Israel's dependence on the US couldn't but stand at its highest.

In my view, this state of affairs continued until 1992, all the shows of the Shamir government's defiance of the US notwithstanding. The Madrid Conference was convened through American efforts and was run openly by the US. In contrast to that, the signing of the Accord on principles on the White House lawn belonged in a show-business category, constituting a façade behind which true machinations were done by Israel without US knowledge or involvement. In contrast to 1985, the Israeli government now has plenty of money, due to US military aid of unprecedented magnitude granted by the Bush administration during and after the Gulf War, and to guarantees granted by the Clinton administration which are hardly used for their avowed purpose of helping absorb the Jewish immigrants from the former USSR. The fact of their being used for other purposes can best be seen from long lines of those immigrants before the Russian Embassy in Tel Aviv looking forward to their return to Russia.

This is why the present situation is very different. Ben-Simon quotes the [Israeli] Foreign Minister, Shimon Peres, as saying that 'Israeli diplomacy extends all over the world. Israeli representatives are now welcomed in almost every capital and regarded by the international community as its equal members ... Rabin's recent journey to Indonesia can be seen as the culmination of this process of breaking the anti-Israeli taboos. After all, Indonesia is the largest Muslim state in the world, and yet Rabin's visit there was public. After the duly publicized deep Israeli penetration into China and India, Indonesia symbolizes the most radical change in Israel's international status.'

Israel also expects to profit from trade with countries such as China, even if such trade links displease the US. Of course, Israel is vitally interested in maintaining its influence upon the Clinton administration so as to prevent any reduction in the present levels of American aid and any serious US protest against its independent policy ventures. Israeli independence can work as long as Clinton remains ready to finance (or press other countries to finance) that 'independence'. Unless Israel soon acquires its own sources of income, its emancipation from American tutelage will remain contingent on the weakness and crassness of Clinton's foreign policies and on the recent remarkable gains in influence of organized US Jews upon his administration. The situation in this respect was well sumarized by *Haaretz* correspondent Orri Nir who reported (6 July) that 'Clinton feels committed to the Jewish vote and even more to Jewish campaign donations', and that his administration 'has a firm "Jewish connection"'.

Whatever financial benefits Israel expects to derive from its foreign policy ventures, their chief aim undoubtedly remains the neutralization of the power of Iran. To all appearances, Israel would like to overthrow the present Iranian regime and replace it with another one, upon which Israel could maintain an influence comparable to that it had upon the regime of the late Shah. It is again Ben-Simon who described it aptly: 'There is a latent factor behind Rabin's visits to two major countries on his route, that is, China and Indonesia. It is the Israeli fear of Iran. Once the Israeli top establishment came to the conclusion that Iran is the most dangerous enemy not just of Israel but of the entire Middle East, it has spared no efforts to disseminate this conviction abroad. Before departing to China the Prime Minister said that the real purpose of his visit was to explain to his hosts how terrible was the danger posed by Iran to the entire Middle East. "I intend to clarify to them how dangerous Islamic fundamentalism is, not just to Israel and all its neighbours, but also to the world at large", said Rabin in his interview with *Davar*, only one day before he embarked for China.

'China is one of the main suppliers of weaponry to Iran, so the Prime Minister had a good reason to concentrate on this topic during his recent tour. For the same reason Israel has opened the channels for the talks with North Korea, without bothering about the angry response of the US administration to them. The purpose was to do everything possible to halt the non-conventional [that is, nuclear] arming of Iran. For this purpose, Israel is now willing to talk to any state, so as to leave Iran to its own devices, or at least to decrease its receiving any non-conventional armament supplies from anywhere in the world.' It can be taken for granted that in regard to Iran, Israel wants more than 'leaving it to its own devices'. Nevertheless, it is perfectly credible that stirring up any conceivable country against Iran remains the guiding principle of the new and independent Israeli policies.

The case of North Korea may not be the most important, but it is typical. It was described by Nahum Barnea in *Yediot Ahronot* on 20 August, that is before the signing of the Accord with the PLO. Barnea informs us that in its 'talks with North Korea conducted by the Deputy Director of the Foreign Ministry, Eitan Bentzur, Israel asked for stopping the sales of the North Korean Scuds to Iran and Syria. Like so many backward regimes, the North Koreans firmly stick to the myth of the Protocols of the Elders of Zion. From this myth they draw a conclusion that via Israel they can easily win some access to America, and that this access may perhaps rescue their regime in an hour of dire emergency.' Complicated as the deal was, it was almost finalized. There was a third party to it, namely 'a Canadian bank, friendly to Israel, very interested in the project.

The bank proposed to consider an investment of $500 million on the sole condition that the North Koreans sever all relations with Iran.' The expression 'friendly to Israel' may be safely presumed to mean that it was controlled by Mossad. The readers of the Hebrew press realize that at least since the 1960s Israeli foreign affairs are quite often run with the help of financial institutions or individual wealthy businessmen, usually but not necessarily Jewish, who act on orders from Mossad as a quid pro quo for the state of Israel's support for their private business deals. This was the pattern to be observed in the Irangate affair.

But let me return to the story of the deal with North Korea. The secret negotiations were first discovered by the Japanese, who 'became enraged and made a scandal' but had no power to stop them: 'It had already been arranged that Bentzur was soon to meet the daughter of the almighty North Korean leader Kim Il-Sung and close the deal. The daughter is third in the North Korean hierarchy, right after the son.' At the same time 'the Americans claimed that they had opened negotiations with North Korea on the nuclear issue. Consequently, they were upset over Israel's messing up. The Deputy of the National Defence Council Sandy Berger and the Deputy State Secretary Peter Tarnoff put pressure on Christopher to drive Israel away from North Korea. They argued that they themselves could press North Korea to sever its relations with Iran.' Probably because this happened right before the finalization and publication of the Oslo Accord, the Israeli government reluctantly agreed to cancel the deal with North Korea. Barnea draws two conclusions from that affair. The first is that 'unfortunately, Israel does not believe that for the US Iran is as important as it is for Israel.' It can be construed as meaning that if Israel's primary aim is to neutralize the Iranian power, Israel needs to get rid of the American tutelage, at least to some extent. Barnea's second conclusion is that 'the great [Israeli] fear that other states may yet realize that the Protocols of the Elders of Zion are after all a myth – that the Jews do not rule over the US, but the US rules over the Jews – cannot be so easily dissipated. For if this calamity indeed occurs, it is going to be unbearable for us.' Indeed, the Israeli power has two components: one real, based on its own strength and its real influence within the US, and the other imaginary, based on its cultivation of anti-Semitic myths in various countries. Especially under Clinton, these two components are craftily blended.

The most important state whose interests Israel is now advancing against (at least avowed) US interests is Iraq. After many previous hints to this effect in Hebrew press, the well-informed veteran journalist Moshe Zak brought the affair into the open in an article entitled 'Are we ready to make peace with Iraq?' (*Maariv*,

28 October). He thinks Israel is indeed trying to establish friendly relations with Saddam Hussein's regime, his evidence being the words of Israeli Foreign Minister, Shimon Peres, uttered in the course of an interview with the leading Egyptian newspaper *Al Ahram*. Peres said there that 'Israel is ready to make peace with any Middle Eastern state with the exception of Iran.' Zak comments, 'Can this be true? Are we ready to make peace with Saddam Hussein, in defiance of sanctions imposed on him by all the states of the world? Will Israel be involved in an Iraqgate, responding to Iraq's frantic search for a hole in the wall erected by the Free World around Saddam Hussein?' Zak speaks of 'an old Israeli delusion' contributing to its siding with Iraq during the Iran–Iraq War. His crucial argument, however, is that any evidence of good Israeli relations with Iraq will undermine current Israeli efforts to convince states like North Korea, China or 'some European states' to stop arming Iran. He nevertheless concludes his article by formulating an argument in favour of what in my view can only be interpreted as the existence of an Israeli alliance with Iraq: 'Some Arab oil states have already suggested through go-betweens that they may sell oil to Israel even prior to the signing of the Accord with the PLO. After discarding their erstwhile delusions that they will ever be able to prevent oil from reaching Israel, they are already prepared to sell their oil to any purchaser. Therefore, Iraq's possible offer to sell oil to Israel should not be regarded as worth risking a political confrontation with the US. Iraq is not doing us any favour by such an offer, whereas for Israel the main thing is to keep international solidarity with states fighting terrorism.'

Let me comment here that Zak differs from Peres about Israeli relations with Iraq only on purely pragmatic grounds. For Zak, 'a risk of a political confrontation with the US' or the persuasive power of Israeli arguments *vis-à-vis* gangster states like China and North Korea outweigh what in his view are problematic benefits, derivable from purchasing or reselling Iraqi oil. But Peres may know better that under the Clinton administration the US is not going to enter 'a political confrontation' with Israel no matter what the latter may do, or that an appeal to China or North Korea on grounds of 'international solidarity' is bound to be useless. Since Zak has never joined any anti-Iranian propaganda campaign and since he writes under censorship constraints, my impression is that he is genuine in warning the Israelis against an alliance with Iraq, but cannot fully disclose his real arguments against it.

Israeli relations with Kenya and Eritrea seem to belong to the same category as its relations with Iraq. Hami Shalev and Yerah Tal report in *Haaretz* on 18 October, that the main aim of Rabin's visit to Kenya was 'to coordinate ways to prevent the intrusion of fundamentalist Islamic forces into the Horn of Africa. Highly

placed Israeli sources intimate that during his meeting with President
Arap Moi of Kenya, Rabin told Moi that Sudan is increasingly
engaged in subversive activities against Kenya. The two agreed to
coordinate measures against their common enemy, especially in the
realm of intelligence.' Shalev and Tal also say that 'Israel is
conveying similar warnings to Eritrean authorities' with which
Israel maintains good relations. And they add that Kenya was
requested by Israel to convey the same kind of warnings to Tanzania
and Uganda: two countries with which Israel does not have
good contacts.

As is well known, economic exchanges between Israel and China
have been flourishing. But Israeli relations with China have also
their strategic and intelligence aspects to which the Hebrew press
has paid a deal of attention. Those aspects were best summed up
by Moshe Zak in *Ha'olam Ha'ze* (20 October). Zak views 'the
mystery of Israel's power over the Chinese leadership' in the same
terms as Barnea interprets the North Koreans: 'The leaders of China
firmly believe that the US and Israel coordinate their policies and
that Israel has a great influence in Washington. This is why the
Chinese Prime Minister, Li Peng, asked Rabin during their
conversation to act as a go-between to soothe the tension between
Beijing and Washington which appeared after the Chinese
underground nuclear test. Through Rabin, the Chinese Prime
Minister conveyed a message to the US, offering to open
negotiations to discuss this issue.' Zak observes that although many
presidents and prime ministers visited Beijing between the time of
the nuclear test and Rabin's visit, 'none of them was entrusted with
such a message.' He also says that 'when the entire Chinese
leadership spoke with Rabin about the scope of Chinese relations
with Israel, they did not neglect to emphasize frequently that those
relations are with the Jewish people anywhere, whose power and
influence surpasses beyond any comparison that of the four-and-
a-half million Jews residing in Israel.'

Zak says that 'in spite of the regrettably hostile publications in
the American media about the nature of Israeli relations with
China, the US administration is not objecting to Chinese–Israeli
contacts as such.' Zak may be presumed to have had primarily in
his mind a *New York Times* editorial, summarized in *Haaretz* on
17 October, which objected to Israel's sales to China of weapons
and sophisticated technology which may be of an American
provenance. In fact, the US administration may be safely assumed
to be satisfied with such sales, which can hardly be effected by itself
due to the opposition of the human rights lobby. Unlike in the US,
in Israel there is no such lobby of any importance, who would have
objected to arms sales to China (or any other state) on the ground
of the latter's record of oppression and denial of human rights. After

all, the massacre of the demonstrators in Beijing's Square of Heavenly Peace was perpetrated by tanks equipped with Israeli cannon and spare parts. According to Zak, the Chinese government 'is clever enough' to understand that 'the hostile publications in the American media about Israeli weaponry sales to China do not reflect in the least any tension between Israel and the US over this matter.' On the other hand, 'China has promised, and has kept its promise, not to use sophisticated technology purchased from Israel when exporting its own arms to countries hostile to Israel.'

Zak recounts in detail the long story of Chinese relations with the PLO, including their personal relations with Arafat, who visited Beijing as early as 1964, even before the PLO's foundation. I concur with Zak's opinion that the Chinese did genuinely sympathize with the PLO in the 1960s and 1970s, though they were piqued by the latter's systematic rejection of their advice on how to fight a guerilla war. But the quality of Chinese relations with the PLO changed drastically 'some time before 1988, the year in which tanks with Israeli-manufactured cannon appeared at a Beijing military parade, prompting the international press to publish stories about huge arms deals between Israel and China.' From that point in time, the good relations which China had maintained with the PLO began to be used by the Chinese primarily as a convenient camouflage of their ties with Israel. I detect the same pattern of camouflage practised by other countries, some of them Arab, like Morocco or Oman.

Israeli contacts with Indonesia follow the same pattern as with China, except that they have been less important and could be easier kept under wraps which would suit the fact that Indonesia is predominantly a Muslim country. Motti Bassuk, writing in *Davar* (17 October), says that 'in recent years the US imposed trade and other restrictions on Indonesia in response to flagrant violations of fundamental human rights by Indonesian authorities. For Indonesia this was a reason to improve its relations with Israel. In Jakarta, as in so many other Third World capitals, one can encounter a staunch belief that Israel's influence on the US borders on the magic. By the way, in so far as human rights or rather their absence are concerned, Indonesia is hardly any different from Morocco.' (The last sentence is a typical ploy the Hebrew press uses to circumvent censorship. Mossad had excellent relations with the latter country since 1960s.) Let me omit Bassuk's long story of Indonesia's earlier hostility to Israel and begin with the reversal of that attitude, which has been commonly dated to when stories of Indonesian atrocities began to appear in the international media after the invasion of East Timor. Bassuk says that 'in the late 1970s, close relations were established between Mossad and its counterpart in Indonesia. According to foreign sources, in 1979

Israel sold 28 Skyhawk fighter planes and 11 war helicopters from its Air Force surplus to Indonesia.' Let me comment that 'Israeli Air Force surplus' derives from American supplies and that Israel cannot sell anything from it without American approval. According to Hami Shalev (*Haaretz*, 17 October), the Indonesian President, Suharto, 'once tried to keep good relations with Iran in order to control the impact of Iranian fundamentalism upon his country's domestic affairs'. Eventually, however, he was persuaded (Shalev does not say by whom) 'that it would more advisable to establish open relations with Israel in order to coordinate with it the measures designed to contain the fundamentalist threat'. The whole story of Indonesia trumpeting its support for the PLO on every official occasion, especially in the UN, and its simultaneous cooperation with Mossad replicates the Chinese pattern so closely that there is no need to recount it separately.

Let me conclude by providing a list of countries with which Israel now has important Intelligence and/or other unsavoury contacts. The list has been compiled solely on the basis of overt or covert information to be found in the Hebrew press and may be incomplete:

- Asia: Turkey, China, Taiwan, Thailand, Singapore, Indonesia, Kazakhstan, Azerbaijan, Oman. Relations with India have been sporadic and transient and with Sri Lanka have been severed.
- Africa: Egypt, Eritrea, Kenya, Malawi, Zaire, Nigeria, Ivory Coast, Morocco. Relations with South Africa, formerly so close, recently became rather cool and loose.
- Latin America: Guatemala, Honduras, Panama, Colombia, Ecuador, Paraguay, Chile. Some intelligence contacts are also pursued with Mexico, but it is difficult to know what is their exact scope.

6

Coalition Building Against Iran
21 February 1994

Israel's Middle Eastern policies, centered on its enmity to Iran need
to be discussed in a global context. For example, Israeli relations
with a country located as far away from Iran as Estonia have a
lot to do with the Israeli hostility toward Iran. On 5 January
1994, *Maariv* published an article by Shlomo Avineri, Professor
of Sociology at the Hebrew University who, as the newspaper noted
'is a former Director General of the Foreign Ministry', and whose
involvements in shaping Israeli foreign policies are certainly not
yet terminated. In Avineri's view, the recent Israeli arms sales to
Estonia, 'were not an initiative of those in charge of Israeli foreign
and security affairs. The main reason the Israeli government
approved this transaction was the intention to extricate Israeli
military industries (or some individuals within them) from their
present crisis. This was enough to grant Israeli credits to Estonia,
which had no substantial foreign currency reserves at its disposal.'
Avineri's argument against that deal was that it 'might impair Israeli
relations with Russia'. In his view Russia and Israel have 'important
strategical interests in common, such as the struggle against
Islamic fundamentalism'. The Estonian deal 'gave rise to very hard
feelings in Moscow, thus undermining the potential for developing
those all-important relations'. Although information on such
subjects is hardly ever published, Israel does seem to help advance
Russian interests in various Muslim states of the former USSR.

But this is just a case in point, illustrating a broader phenomenon.
Before discussing Israeli policies toward several Middle Eastern
states, let me yet say something about their general background
which normally escapes the attention of observers who merely
monitor the UN Resolutions or diplomacy in general. Since 1991,
Israeli relations with most Middle Eastern regimes have ranged from
good to excellent. For instance, Gabby Bron writes in *Yediot
Ahronot* (25 January), that 'Israel buys 90 per cent of its oil from
Arab countries' (the remaining 10 per cent comes from Norway),
and feels secure enough about these supplies to cancel its oil
purchase contracts with Mexico. Of the 90 per cent oil bought in

the Middle East, 40 per cent comes from Egypt, and no less than 50 per cent 'from Arab states of the Gulf'.

On 8 February, Hayim Handwoker noted in *Haaretz* that Benny Ga'on, the Director General of Koor, one of the largest Israeli corporations, told the *Wall Street Journal* that 'the trade between Israel and the Arab states amounts to $500 million annually.' As *Haaretz* admits, with the exception of Egypt the Arab states concerned are those which are still formally boycotting Israel. On the basis of well-informed sources, I can only see the quoted figure as a gross underestimate, because in 1993 this trade amounted already to about $1.4 billion. Also on 8 February, Zohar Blumencrantz informed *Haaretz* that 'the Israeli Export Institute has very close relations with its partners in Lebanon, Algeria and Tunisia' and that Israeli trade with such traditional Arab outlets for Israeli exports as Morocco had recently increased. Israelis with double citizenship who recently visited Syria on their foreign passports report that a lot of clothes and textiles on sale in Syrian shops or bazaars were recognizable as Israeli-made. Moreover, the fictitious tags to be seen until few years ago, for example, 'Made in the Occupied Territories' or 'Made in Gibraltar' now have disappeared from sight. Syrian customers appeared well aware where the clothes had come from. Palestinians who returned from Iraq report similar sightings in the shops of Baghdad, although without being able to say whether the Iraqi customers, too scared to talk freely, were as aware of the origin of the merchandise as the Syrian ones.

Another example of close Israeli relations with an Arab Gulf regime was provided by Amir Oren (*Davar*, 7 January). Undoubtedly echoing views of some high-ranking officers in the Security System, Oren opines that in addition to using its Air Force as an anti-Iranian nuclear deterrent, Israel should 'plunge its strategic [that is, nuclear] deterrence power into the depths of the sea, where it can be best protected and from where it can threaten potential attackers. Since deterrence rests on the image of power, Israel needs to stress the existence of its submarine weapons.' Oren finds cooperation with the US for this purpose essential, because only the US can sell suitable submarines cheaply to Israel. Oren also has an opinion about where Israeli nuclear submarines should be stationed in order to have a maximum deterrent power against Iran: Oman, with which Israel should fast form an alliance. As seen on a map, Oman is close to what Oren terms 'Iran's hinterland'. Although the US consent to this scheme is problematic, the plan is by no means absurd. Covert Israeli relations with Oman go back at least to 1968, when Israel started drilling for oil in what it then regarded as 'its' part of the Gulf of Suez. The drilling platform on the sea surface used for the purpose was imported from Oman. It was escorted half-way by the Shah's Navy, and the other half by the Israeli one. After the Shah's downfall the Israeli relations with Oman to all appearances improved even further.

Recently, much publicity has been given to the Israeli enticement of Turkey as a prospective ally against Iran. This has obvious implications for Israeli attitudes toward the Kurds and Israeli relations with Turkey's neighbours, Syria and Iraq. A considerable amount of space was devoted by the Hebrew press to the Turkish visit of the President Ezer Weizman of Israel, who was accompanied there by a number of businessmen. I am going to rely primarily on two articles by Aluf Ben (*Haaretz*, 11 and 31 January) and one by Yoav Karni (*Shishi*, 4 February) which emphasizes the Kurdish issue; but I will draw some information from other articles as well. Both Ben and Karni recall that the close relations of Israel with Turkey go as far back as 1958, when Ben-Gurion formed 'the periphery alliance' with Turkey, Iran was still ruled by the Shah, and Ethiopia was still ruled by Haile Selassie. According to Karni, one purpose of that alliance was 'to throttle the very notion of Arab nationalism'. Eventually, the alliance collapsed as a result of the revolutions in Ethiopia and Iran. But as Karni writes, the relations between Israeli and Turkish armies and intelligence services have remained fairly close since, in spite of diplomatic ups and downs.

As Ben informs us on 11 January, the relations between the Israeli and Turkish armies and intelligence services have recently become even closer after 'the 1993 visit of the Commander of the [Israeli] Air Force, General Herzl Budinger, to Turkey' and of several Turkish ministers, including the Prime Minister, to Jerusalem. But apart from marginal matters, like some Israeli weaponry sales to Turkey and some enlargement of the volume of mutual trade, the visits were not crowned by agreement on basic issues, despite American encouragement. Ben reports that 'the Americans are encouraging their allies in the Middle East to cooperate, and officials in the State Department stress to their Israeli opposite numbers the central place of Turkey in US strategic plans, whether in the Middle East, in the Balkan peninsula or toward the states of the former USSR. The American officials recommended to Israel to look upon Turkey through American spectacles.' No doubt as a result of an encouragement by the US, even prior to Weizman's visit Turkey 'proposed to Israel a formal alliance which Israel, Saudi Arabia, Egypt and Turkey would join on equal terms as the four allies of the US in the region'. Although no Israeli commentator said so explicitly, the proposal didn't seem to arouse any enchantment, whether official or non-official and Israel clearly rejected it. It is particularly noteworthy that the Israeli Foreign Minister, Shimon Peres who is so busy advocating 'a regional alliance system' said not a word in commendation of the Turkish alliance. The 'encouragements' of the 'officials in the State Department' have turned out to be of no avail. The talks merely articulated the fundamental disagreements between Turkey and Israel, even though Weizman's visit was officially characterized as 'extraordinarily successful' (31 January).

As reported by Ben on 31 January, the main bones of contention were over nuclear politics, the attitude towards Iran and the policy toward Syria, with their implications for the Kurdish question and the so-called 'struggle against terror and the drug trade'. Ben's comment on the central issues at stake seems to be well-taken: 'Just as Israel hesitates whether to attack Syria, which is Turkey's enemy number one, Turkey hesitates whether to declare publicly its enmity towards Iran, which is Israel's enemy number one'. It turns out that Israel queried Turkey 'whether the latter is as concerned by Iran's nuclearization efforts as is Israel. But President Suleiman Demirel and the Prime Minister answered [Israel] by hinting that Israel is no less involved than Iran. They said that "we oppose proliferation of nuclear weapons in all Middle Eastern states." Demirel further said that "he did not know" whether Iran indeed wanted to produce nuclear weapons, adding a transparent allusion to the effect that "Iran does not talk about it." The Israelis reacted by pressing him: "And do you believe the Iranians?" To that his answer was the same in a different phrasing: "They are denying it."'

The discussion of the nature of Iranian regime also ended in talk at cross purposes. Israel pressed Turkey to denounce the 'Iranian fundamentalist regime', arguing that 'as a secular state Turkey has a duty to do so.' The Turks responded that 'in our view the character of a regime is a purely internal affair of every state.' Ben is quite displeased by the Turkish positions on both issues. In his article of 11 January he quotes Israeli 'experts' who, even prior to the high-level negotiations, communicated to their Turkish counterparts their dissatisfaction that 'the Iranian Vice President, Hassan Habibi, had visited Ankara in December 1993', and that even earlier 'the Iranian Foreign Minister had also visited Turkey'. The 'experts' admonished the Turkish government for ignoring 'the deadly insult to Turkey' on the part of both visitors 'who refused to lay a wreath on Ataturk's tomb'. Catching the Israeli 'experts' off-guard, the Turkish response was that 'although Turkey does speak up against Iranian and Syrian support of Kurdish terrorism, it is vitally interested in cooperating with the two states to solve the Kurdish question.' In line with that, Turkey announced that its overriding interest lay in Iran's fulfilment of promises made by Hassan Habibi during his visit, to the effect that 'Iran and Turkey shall strike powerfully at terrorism and cooperate in finding new ways of guarding their common frontier against it.' Compared to that, symbolic gestures were defined as secondary.

It seems that Turkish and Israeli negotiators spent much of their time discussing Syria, the Kurdish implications of the problem included. In his 11 January article Ben reports that 'Turkey asked Israel to demand that as a precondition for signing a peace treaty Syria stops supporting Kurdish terrorism and close all Kurdish offices and bases, in Syria and in Lebanon alike', and that the US was approached by Turkey with the same demand. In his 31 January article Ben reports that 'during Weizman's visit all pro-government Turkish journalists completely ignored the Palestinians and Israeli intentions in regard to the Territories. Instead of asking any questions about Palestine-related issues, they kept asking Weizman whether Israel would welcome an independent Kurdish state and what is Israel's attitude towards the Kurdish terror.' Ben doesn't bother to say how Weizman answered these questions but he mentions that 'on such occasions Weizman talked about Assad's importance for the peace process.' Such evasion was not likely to please his questioners. Ben also mentions some alternative official Turkish proposals, one to the effect of issuing a joint condemnation of terror 'in which Turkey would condemn Hizbollah and Israel the PKP, the strongest Kurdish terror organization'; and the second to the effect of 'Israeli promises to help Turkey in its struggle against terror, at least by explicitly condemning the PKP', preferably by 'signing a pledge in which the two countries would fight terror and the drug trade together. The Israelis answered that these proposals needed to be carefully examined. In the meantime, therefore, such [Turkish] ideas hang in the air. The only thing Israel agreed to was to set up a joint committee for the purpose of strategic consultations and an exchange of political assessments of the "regional threats".' Apart from that, the only thing Turkey could obtain was Weizman's declaration, described by Ben as 'not committing Israel to anything concrete'. Weizman said that 'every organization which carries out terrorist actions is a terrorist organization', without naming any such 'organization'. After the visit ended, the disapointed Turkish press deplored 'Israel's unwise refusal to sign formal treaties against terror', and claimed that, unlike Israel, 'Turkey believes in open diplomacy.'

Ben and Karni make it clear that Israeli rejection of Turkish proposals did not stem from any sympathy for the Kurds. If anything, Israel is now quite hostile toward them. But, as Ben puts it in his 31 January article, 'Israel refuses to make any public statements which might be interpreted adversely by Syria while hoping that alliance with Turkey "will make a fellow in Damascus sweat a little".' Karni recounts a long history of Israeli relations with the Iraqi Kurds. The story goes back to the 1950s, but the relations were abruptly severed in 1975 to please the Shah after his deal with Saddam Hussein. The details of that deal are too well known to be retold here. Karni, however, says nothing about a later phase of Israeli relations with Iraqi Kurds which occurred after the end of the Gulf War. During the entire Gulf Crisis and War, Israel, seconded by its foreign friends, was supporting the Iraqi Kurds and their national and individual rights. But in March 1991, the then Israeli Chief of Staff, General Dan Shomron, formed a 'broad Knesset coalition', comprising politicians from all the parties in support of Saddam Hussein. Let me quote the argument of MK Avraham Burg, a Labor 'dove' in favor of joining that coalition: 'Unless Saddam Hussein is supported, a vast Shi'ite empire extending from Iran up to the Occupied Territories will become a real prospect.' Some supporters of such a pro-Iraqi coalition, such as Moshe Zak (*Jerusalem Post*, 4 April 1991) explained that it implied leaving the Iraqi Kurds to their own devices, because 'Syria and Iran are lodged behind the Kurdish revolt and hoping to create a territorial link between them.' In vaguer language, other commentators hinted that Israel and Saudi Arabia were jointly exerting their influence in Washington to convince the US to go along with the scheme. Avner Tavori (*Davar*, 4 April 1991) wrote that 'any attempt to introduce democracy to Iraq may only result in its partition into a Kurdish state in the north, a Sunni state in the center around Baghdad and a pro-Iranian Shi'ite state in the south, which would be located too close to Saudi Arabia to please it.' There are reasons to presume that Israeli policies are still based on such assumptions, even if they are also informed by contempt for all the 'Orientals' and fear of democracy in any Arab country.

Karni writes that since the early 1960s Israel has been consistently helping Turkey by whitewashing, especially in the US, its soiled record of human rights violations. Whitewashing extended as far back as the Turkish genocide of Armenians during World War I: 'Israeli diplomats in Washington were mobilized to use their influence in the Congress to try to squash a law establishing the [Armenian] memorial day in 1989.' But Karni also provides examples of Israeli attempts to prevent or at least to postpone holding symposia discussing the Armenian or Kurdish question from either the human rights or the historic point of view. He does not object to such practices in principle, because 'we should not be sanctimonious when Israel is pursuing its legitimate interests in this affair', or elsewhere in the Third World. Yet he says that 'no survival imperative can command Israel to lie non-stop for the sake of profits obtainable in relations with a foreign state for our weapons industry. The Israeli government and even more so a President of Israel whose authority is limited to purely ceremonial matters, can afford to occasionally say something in public in praise of democratic foreign policy that would place moral considerations above profitability.' This can only be interpreted as meaning that Karni wants Israel to be even more sanctimonious than it is.

Roughly the same is the attitude of Motti Zaken (*Davar*, 31 January), introduced as 'the chairman of the Israeli Association of Friendship with Kurdistan', a curious organization almost hardly ever heard of in Israel but quite active among the Kurds in Europe. Zaken objects to Israeli pro-Turkish and anti-Kurdish gestures, but especially if they are publicized. After repeating Ben's story about the cooperation of Turkey and Iran against the Kurds, he says: 'It is impossible not to compare Israeli and Iranian conduct in matters which for the Muslims' own good should be better kept secret from them. Yet Israel stridently talks about a policy which some may find objectionable, already at its designing stage.' After such a preamble, the reader is caught off-guard by the writer's demand for a 'public and parliamentary debate' about Israeli policies towards the Kurds. Zaken speaks about 'love' which supposedly existed between the Kurds and the Kurdish Jews in order to advocate a return to pro-Kurdish policies Israel once pursued. But in spite of his recommendation of a debate, he utters no single word about how would he envisage those 'pro-Kurdish policies'. Unlike Karni, he does not even call upon the President to 'say something in public'.

Minimalistic as the proposals of Karni and Zaken are, there is no hope that they will be put into effect. Even Aluf Ben's lucid views on the problems dividing Israel from Turkey do not square with what the majority of Israeli commentators have written on the subject. To give a notion of a typical account of Israeli–Turkish relations, let me briefly quote Yoram Levy from *Davar* of 31 January. The relations between Israel and Turkey are for Levy based on 'love' and 'true friendship' and secondarily on their common attitude toward 'Kurdish terrorism', which in his view Syria supports for the same reasons it supports Hizbollah. He doesn't even hint that this 'love' and 'true friendship' may be somewhat ragged.

The evidence presented here can only corroborate the conclusions about the more independent nature of Israeli foreign policies reached earlier. At the time of the 'periphery alliance' Israel was quite satisfied with its status of an equal partner with three other US allies, among which Turkey was the most important. The Camp David Accords and the peace with Egypt conformed explicitly to the principle of equality between the two states and tacitly to the fact of their common dependence on the US. Now, however, Israel insists that its special status, superior to all other Middle Eastern states, be explicitly acknowledged. The case of the failed Israeli negotiations with Turkey proves that Israel was guided in them by hegemonic ambitions. Regardless of whether the Clinton administration bows to such Israeli pretensions, they cannot be brought about except by force. And hence the hazards they invite.

7

Israeli Foreign Policies, August 1994

8 August 1994

The scope of Israeli foreign policies can be said to be truly world-wide. This is especially the case when, in the wake of recent terrorist assaults against Israeli and Jewish targets in Buenos Aires and London, the Israeli government professed the eradication of all such terror in the entire world as its aim. At the same time, however, due to Israeli automatic attribution of responsibility for all those assaults to Iran, Israeli foreign policies are also firmly anchored in the region of the Middle East. It can even be conjectured that the primary purpose of the Washington treaty with Jordan recently signed by Rabin and King Hussein was not so much to make peace as to seek to use Jordanian territory for action against Iran. And the same purpose was by no means absent from the 'peace process' pursued earlier with Arafat. Here I will deal with the Israeli anti-Iranian propaganda campaign which is being intensified: its policy context clearly being the Middle East in the widest possible meaning of that term, that is, extending from Afghanistan to Morocco, the Muslim republics of the former USSR included.

Let me proceed to discuss the strategic significance of the Israeli Accord with Jordan. It is both defensive and offensive. Jordan commits itself not to allow any third state's army to enter its territory. (But there is no mention of a possible entry of the Israeli Army into Jordan.) Most Israeli commentators understood this stipulation as precluding the threat of the so-called 'Eastern Front', that is, of allied Arab armies attacking Israel from the east. Even though Israel's border with Jordan is more difficult to defend than its Egyptian border, the whole notion has in my view long belonged to the realm of fiction. With the Jordanian border secure and a firm peace with Egypt, only the borders with Syria and Lebanon remain hostile. They are relatively short, allowing for heavy concentrations of troops and fire, the preferred Israeli method of warfare. The prospect of so shortening the potential front line has been discussed for a long time in professional military magazines of the Israeli Army. But Israeli strategists are also keenly aware of the two-fold importance of the Irbid area of Jordan, located just south of the Golan Heights and Syria. By penetrating this area, the Syrian

Army could outflank the Israeli troops deployed in the Golan Heights. By penetrating the same area, however, the Israeli Army could outflank the bulk of the Syrian Army, entrenched in its fortifications opposite the Golan Heights, and speedily advance toward Damascus. Now, the Israeli military alliance with Jordan (which is what the agreement with that country amounts to), precludes the former prospect while enhancing the likelihood of the latter. All too clearly, it poses a major threat to Syria.

Still, the most likely target of a possible Israeli armed attack is at the present moment Iran. Oren (*Davar*, 7 January 1994) views the agreement with Jordan primarily in that context: 'The agreement is intended to establish a military alliance between Israel and Jordan and thus extend the boundary of Israel's military presence to the eastern tip of the Jordanian desert. Israel's undisguised military presence there, right on the border of Iraq, means that the route of its war planes to Iran will be hundreds of kilometres shorter.' Had they had to take off from Israeli territory, only the most advanced Israeli planes, practically only the F-15s, could reach Iran without refuelling in the air. A glance of the map of the Middle East will suffice to show that the Iraqi–Jordanian border area is already quite close to Iran: close enough to let Israel use its plentiful older model planes (or missiles) for bombing raids on Iran after overflying the Iraqi territory. Oren does expect Jordan 'to grant the Israeli Air Force the right to overfly its territory, at least in emergency situations.' Sure enough, the use of Jordanian territory for a possible assault of Iran implies the existence of a tacit Iraqi complicity with Israel. Oren must imply no less than that when he says that once Israeli alliance with Jordan is fully operational, 'Rafsanjani will be compelled to approach Israel with greater restraint than to date.' In more general terms Oren opines that 'just as Israel had opened the flow of American dollars to Sadat and enabled the Egyptian Air Force to receive advanced planes from the US within no more than year and a half after Sadat's visit to Jerusalem, so the Rabin government which enabled Jordan to receive not a few US dollars, will feel entitled to use its agreement with Jordan not just for the sake of the military status quo, but in order to improve Israel's military strength considerably, to the point of letting the Israeli Air Force and eventually Intelligence reach the western boundary of Iraq.' In my view, this crucial change in strategic configurations in the Middle East either has already occurred or is likely to occur in the coming months.

I feel tempted at this point to digress in order to recount some new revelations about the past relations of the Zionist movement and the State of Israel with the Hashemite regime in Jordan. A veteran of Haganah's Intelligence Service, Yo'av Gelber, recently published a book bearing the title *The Roots of the Lily*, (the lily being the emblem of Israeli Military Intelligence), which heavily relies on documents declassified only in recent years. According to Gelber, King Hussein's grandfather, Abdullah, was recruited as a spy for the Zionist movement in the early 1920s, soon after being appointed 'Emir of Trans-Jordan' by the British. He was instructed to spy on all sorts of Arab leaders, but his main task was to spy on his British masters. Heaps of documents depict Zionist intra-agency squabbles over whether Abdullah's demands for payment for each rendered service should be fully respected or subject to some bargaining, the late Moshe Sharett being a consistent advocate of the latter. All payments to Abdullah were in cash directly delivered to him. Other intra-agency disputes were over Abdullah's occasional demands to be paid not in banknotes, but in gold coins. In addition to this, one of Abdullah's wives was put on the Zionist payroll to spy on her husband. Gelber boasts that the British discovered the whole scheme only after more than twenty years, in 1946. Their reaction was not only to offer Abdullah more money than the Zionist movement could possibly pay, but also to give more military aid for Abdullah's army. Most importantly, however, they dangled before him a vision of becoming king of 'the greater Syria' – Syria, Lebanon and Palestine together. This displeased Ben-Gurion greatly, and relations between the Zionist movement and subsequently the State of Israel with Jordan dwindled to a coordination of policy directed, as Oren defines it, 'against their common enemy, Palestinian nationalism'.

A fuller cooperation between Israel and Jordan was revived by King Hussein in 1958, right after the revolution in Iraq in which his close relatives from the Iraqi royal family perished. As Oren puts it, Hussein 'sent his Armenian Intelligence advisor to Israel' with dispatch. On the Jordanian side cooperation with Israel was carried through solely by the kingdom's Armenian or Circassian functionaries. Azarya Alon (*Davar*, 28 July) informs us that one unit guarding King Hussein is comprised solely of Circassians and considers this fact advantageous to Israel.

The Israeli alliance with King Hussein endured until 1965. Oren points out that, as subsequently revealed by declassified American documents, George Bush, acting in capacity of CIA Director had in that year offered King Hussein personal payment. Bush's scheme was considered in Israel hostile and it was recalled when he became President. But Hussein again became subservient to Israel before the 'Black September' of 1970. After that date he became a virtual Israeli spy, as his grandfather had been. As is well known, it was he who in September 1973 forewarned Golda Meir about the incipient attack of Egypt and Syria on Israel, although he was not believed. Good relations have been maintained since, regardless of which party ruled Israel. As was reported by the Hebrew press on the occasion of the present Washington Accord, Shamir had met King Hussein in London even during the Gulf Crisis, in November 1990, in order to assure him that unless Iraqi land forces are let into Jordan, Israel was not going to invade it, even in the case of it launching hostilities against Iraq. The present Israeli–Jordanian alliance is therefore the crowning point of decades of thinly disguised cooperation.

Let me now quote at some length an instructive portrayal of Israeli relations with Morocco by Daniel Ben-Simon writing in *Davar* (7 June). After gloating about how excellent the relations between the two countries have been, Ben-Simon admits that 'the web of relations between the two states rests on the shoulders of a single individual: King Hassan II. Morocco's kindness toward Israel and all the Jews depends solely on his feelings ... Only a few thousand Jews have remained in Morocco: most of them in Casablanca where they are among the wealthiest people. Hassan II has highly appreciated the Jewish contribution to the development of his country. When the French left in 1954, the Jews tended to replace them in their occupations in industry and commerce.' Ben-Simon fails to understand that if the Jews 'replaced' the French in Morocco with the effect of becoming very wealthy in the process, then the same grudges which ordinary Moroccans had had against the French and their role in Morocco are now likely to be revived against the Jews.

Ben-Simon continues: 'Hassan II has a weakness for Israel. To many of his visitors he expressed his admiration for Israel's ability to turn wilderness into a fertile land. He does not hide his belief that Jews are cleverer than other nations, and that economic, social and cultural revolutions and progress were a product of Jewish genius. In the early 1970s, when the hostility between Israel and the Arab states reached its peak, he indulged in fanciful reveries about what could be achieved by blending Jewish genius with Arab capital. "If there is peace, the Middle East may in this way become the strongest power on earth", he used to say.' This sounds not unlike the Protocols of the Elders of Zion.

But such visions for the future depend on a purely personal factor: 'Hassan II is an absolute monarch, one of the few such still left in the world. All state affairs depends on his decisions and orders. In theory, Morocco has a constitution and democratic institutions. But their impact is very limited. In practice, everything is subordinated to his will. In the West, Hassan II succeeded in manufacturing for himself an image of an enlightened, open-minded, liberal, educated king who relies on democratic institutions. Consequently, the western countries would turn a blind eye to oddities of that democracy, and content themselves with the existence of many parties and periodic elections in Morocco.

Hassan II fights like a lion to maintain this image. It was not too easy, after books appeared depicting his regime as one of the most obscurantist in the world. A French journalist Gilles Perrault wrote a book documenting the outrages committed by the King's regime, in the first place the atrocities in treating the regime's opponents. The King not only banned the book, but also sought to prevail upon President Mitterrand to do the same in France. Regardless of whatever Mitterand might have wanted, the French law precluded the possibility of his satisfying the King.

'On several occasions, the King would berate his Western critics, "Do you want Morocco to become an Islamic state like Iran? Just say so", he would reply to queries about his misdeeds. Western countries do realize that they can ill afford another state resembling Algeria or Iran. This is why western governments prefer to turn a blind eye on whatever the King might do and speculate about what may happen after Hassan II. If he just retires he will be succeeded by the Crown Prince Sidi Mohammed. The Crown Prince is a very different character than his father, gentle, refined, with a penchant for romanticism. Some in the West would prefer the King to appoint his younger son, Moulay Rashid, as his successor. Like his father, Moulay Rashid is tough, determined to hold on to power at any price. He wants to be Crown Prince in order to assure that the country toes the pro-Western line. If Morocco remains a monarchy, its further rapprochement with Israel can be expected. If monarchy is abolished there, everything becomes possible. Then, the very survival of the tiny Jewish community in Morocco may also be in doubt. For in Morocco, everything depends on the will of our friend, the King.' I guess that 'some in the West' is Ben-Simon's codename for Israeli Intelligence whose links with Hassan II have been notorious. But his whole treatment of Israeli relations with the Moroccan regime shows how much Israel and the organized Jewish communities in the Diaspora have always tended to support despotic regimes, especially in the Muslim world.

Let me return to Iran, on which Israeli foreign policies currently focus. Prior to the last wave of terrorist attacks on Jewish targets in Buenos Aires and London the situation in this respect was summed up by Aluf Ben (*Haaretz*, 12 July), whose article deserves to be quoted at some length: 'During the last two years the Iranian threat has been the central element in Israel's foreign and security policy. After the Gulf War ruined Iran's rival Iraq, Iran emerged more powerful than ever. Israel feared that Iran could aspire to regional hegemony and ruin the peace process by virtue of having nuclear weapons and long-range missiles, of building a modern air force and navy, of exporting terrorism and revolution and of subverting Arab secular regimes.' Let me observe that when (as plenty of other evidence shows) Israel 'after the Gulf War' decided that Iran was its enemy number one, the latter was still exhausted after the lengthy war with Iraq and hadn't yet begun its nuclearization. Really, Israeli enmity toward Iran stemmed from the fact that it 'could aspire to [the] regional hegemony' to which Israel aspires. 'Last year Rabin said that Iran was the main threat to Israel's security. The Chief of Staff Ehud Barak described the monster of Tehran as the most terrible danger to peace in the whole world. Why? Because Iran undermines political stability in the Middle East, because it opposes the flow of oil to the developed world and because it wants to upset the cultural equilibrium between the West and Islam. "The Iranian regime poses a danger to the very foundations of world order", said Barak.' I believe the quote from Barak is authentic, but I don't know where he said it. Certainly, it has never been published before. Although I don't disregard the dangers such utterances may entail, the spectacle of an Israeli general concerned about the potential upsetting of 'the cultural equilibrium between the West and Islam' strikes me as having its comic side as well.

Commenting on a terrorist attack on Jewish targets, on 29 July, Uzi Mahanaimi wrote in *Shishi*: 'The Iranians are now busy hiring foreign experts to make the little gifts they obtained fully operational. Is this perhaps why Israel vacillates about knocking the downtown of Tehran with all its might? Is somebody in Israel afraid that the madmen in Tehran may already possess the bomb? Is this the reason they cannot be touched? I hope things are not that bad. I find it absolutely clear that as long as the heads of the Iranians do not get whacked, and as long as Israel keeps playing its games with Hizbollah in Lebanon, our embassies cannot but continue to be blown up.' Mahanaimi has no doubt that the Iranians 'are responsible for the bombing of our embassy and Jewish Centre in Buenos Aires'. He claims that 'the proofs of this abound', but he mentions only one, namely that 'through their Argentinian embassy the Iranians denied any connection with the outrage.' Why should the denial be a proof? Mahanaimi's argument runs as follows: 'I know them bloody well. This is why I can say with confidence that had Israel reacted properly to the bombing of its embassy in Argentina two years ago, the Iranians would have thought twice before sending their saboteurs once again. After the first bombing in Argentina, it was the Commander of Israeli Military Intelligence who accused the Iranians of complicity. Not a journalist voicing his opinion, but the very Commander of Israeli Military Intelligence said that. Why did Israel do nothing then? After all, if Katyushas are fired upon the Galilee, Israel escalates almost to the point of a war. So why didn't we react likewise when our entire embassy was blown sky high? The Iranians have plenty of sensitive targets across their country. Hitting them could make the Ayatollahs think twice before they play with fire next time.' And so on and so forth.

Ron Ben-Yishay (*Yediot Ahronot*, 29 July) says that 'Intelligence sources estimate that one and the same hand in Tehran was behind the terrorist assault in Buenos Aires, the Hizbollah attacks in Lebanon and the two terrorist assaults in London': the operational medium being the 'Iranian Intelligence officers masquerading as diplomats and working in all Iranian embassies the world over'. Ben-Yishay claims that 'until two weeks ago' Israel did nothing against Iran 'except abuse it verbally', but now 'many Israeli politicians, including the Prime Minister, believe that Israel should hit the Iranians right where it hurts.' Ben-Yishay does not seem to mean by that an armed attack on Iranian territory, but only a world-wide elimination of whomever Israel may label as an 'Iranian' terrorist. This transpires from his saying that Israel 'should treat all Iranian terrorists as it treated the PLO's international terror after the 1970 Black September'. He refers to Israeli Intelligence then killing Palestinians and other Arabs (including some innocent people like a Moroccan waiter mistakenly identified as a PLO agent in Lilienhammer, Norway), but stopping short of doing anything more violent. Ben-Yishay says that 'the dragon is already too powerful for Israel to slay it alone'. He hopes the western states will help Israel in its struggle against the Iranian dragon.

However, voices advocating some caution and moderation have resounded as well. Let me quote two. A Labor Party stalwart Shalom Yerushalmi writing in *Maariv* (3 August), admits that 'in Lebanon Israel did commit against Hizbollah, the operational arm of Khomeinism some "eliminations" Iranian style, e.g the Sheikh Mussawi affair [murdered together with his family] or kidnappings, e.g. of Sheikhs Obeid and Dirani. It is not clear what Israel gained thereby, but there also have been massive bombardments of civilian populations. I think we should stop playing such dangerous games.' Yerushalmi advises Rabin to follow in the footsteps of Shamir's judicious conduct during the Gulf War. Shamir then merely threatened that Israel would retaliate but didn't follow his threats through. But restraint toward Iran would, argues Yerushalmi, be even more advisable now than in the past toward Iraq. Iran is stronger than Iraq, larger in size and population. The war against Iraq was really 'only a war against an insane dictator and a handful of his henchmen', whereas Iranians are in their majority 'united in their support for the mad ideology hammered into their heads by the Ayatollahs'. Yerushalmi advises Rabin to ask the West to impose 'some potent economic sanctions against Iran', paired with a propaganda campaign to the effect that Iranian nuclearization threatens everybody.

Even more interesting are the views of some components of Israeli and apparently also US intelligence as relayed by Tzvi Bar'el in *Haaretz* (24 July). Contrary to the quoted commentators who believe (presumably after being briefed by the Israeli Prime Minister's Office) that Iran was solely responsible for the Buenos Aires and London terrorist assaults, Bar'el quotes 'a senior Israeli Intelligence source' as telling him that 'the working presumption [of Israeli Intelligence] is that the assault was committed by local terrorists hired for pay, the money being traceable to Hizbollah. The same source claims that the Iranian connection amounts only to political and economic patronage Iran bestows on Hizbollah: "I presume that under different political circumstances Israel could blame Syria or Libya in the same way as it now accuses Iran. In the same way it was once customary to blame the former USSR for standing behind terrorist acts which gained international publicity".' Bar'el contrasts this point of view with Rabin's and Netanyahu's views. Rabin 'rushed to announce that Iran was responsible. After a while, without retracting the first version, he pinned the responsiblity on Hizbollah.' Incidentally, this seems to be Rabin's *façon de parler.* When the Intifada had just broken out he rushed to blame Iran and Libya for their 'exclusive responsibility' for it. This stupid falsehood was then, for some time, elevated to the rank of Israeli propaganda line. Rabin's mendacity borders on the pathological, even more so than Sharon's or Shamir's. The western media only show how biased they are when they fail to document Rabin's systematic lying. Netanyahu surpasses even Rabin in mendacity. According to Bar'el, Netanyahu opined that 'Iran, Hizbollah and Syria were equally responsible.' A record in lying, however, has been attained in this affair by the Israeli Chief of Staff, Ehud Barak. He is reported by On Levy (*Davar*, 3 August) to have said that 'the intelligence community of the entire world knows for sure that Iran stands behind the terror.' Dissenting from Rabin, Netanyahu and Barak alike, Bar'el reports that 'Israeli Intelligence has so far failed to find evidence linking the Buenos Aires terror with any of the three factors', that is, with 'Iran, Hizbollah and Syria'.

But Bar'el makes also some fairly keen observations about the nature of state terror, which deserve to be quoted at length: 'Iran is a terror state in the same way as Iraq, Libya or Syria. But the list of terror states can be extended. Not so long ago Argentina, Chile and South Africa qualified as well by virtue of committing routinely political murders or terrorist assaults against dissenters living outside their borders.' Let me comment that Israel, and especially the Labor Party was chummy with the three regimes named here as terrorists. Rabin particularly cultivated close relations with the South African apartheid regime. Helped by his present

Defence Deputy Minister Motta Gur, he advanced the ties with Argentinian and Chilean juntas. 'Still', continues Bar'el, 'some states can be said to be more terroristic than others. At the present moment, by far the most terrorist state in the Middle East, and perhaps in the entire world, is Afghanistan. As estimated by various intelligence experts, most subversive and terrorist acts against Arab regimes were committed by veterans of the war against communism, or of the tribal war continuing to grip that country till this very day. The Afghan government and other authorities maintain training programmes in terror for the cohorts of volunteers who for this very purpose come to Afghanistan.

'Paradoxically, however, Afghanistan is not defined as a terror state. Instead, it is glorified by the US as a nation of valiant patriots who expelled the Soviet invaders. On the opposite side, the US seeks to overthrow Saddam Hussein not because his henchmen have committed lots of terrorist acts but because he poses a threat to US interests in the Middle East ... Fortunately for Israel, Iran is nowadays an easy target to be branded as a terror state ... Its diplomats have admittedly been found to be involved in some terrorist acts, but acts aimed only at exiled Iranian political dissenters. Iran is a fundamentalist state, but no more so than Saudi Arabia or the Islamic opposition in Algeria. Yet the US has the best of relations with the former and is perfectly prepared to parley with the latter.

'The crucial factor which helps uphold the definition of Iran as a terror state is the non-operational character of such a definition. By itself, the definition cannot authorize Israel to dispatch its Air Force to raid some targets on Iranian territory. Nor can it by itself warrant the imposition of economic sanctions on Iran, aggravating its economic plight. Intelligence experts commonly estimate that acts of retaliation directed against Iranian targets would hardly deter Iran while mounting trouble for Israel. A senior foreign intelligence source told me that in the absence of decisive evidence linking the recent terrorist assaults to Iran, the definition of Iran (or of any other state for that matter) as a terror state discredits a state advancing such a definition because it brings into relief the dismal failure of its intelligence. Talking of "decisive evidence", my interlocutor meant evidence as decisive as that found by the US linking the Libyan government with the terrorist act in Berlin discotheque.' This 'senior foreign intelligence source' sounds as if he were an American.

Bar'el formulates an interpretation of what he heard from this presumed American intelligence source: 'In other words, the more vague a given state's concept of the sources of terrorism, the more its intelligence can be faulted for incompetence. As the same source put it, "occasionally you may have good intelligence as in some cases in Lebanon. But then you are catching individual criminals, not states. When your intelligence is rather poor, you bomb wide areas, but not close to the borders of Syria, in spite of the obvious fact that without the latter Hizbollah couldn't move a finger. You also take care to spare the Lebanese state machinery as far as possible, even though the Hizbollah are represented in the Lebanese parliament".' After his observations of American Intelligence, Bar'el returns to Israeli Intelligence: 'The problem, as indicated to me by my intelligence source, is that when political authorities choose to put blame for terror on a country according to what under given political conditions may be convenient, intelligence work is bound to suffer. It is because those authorities then want to find "proofs" of what they have already assumed, instead of looking for genuine proofs showing who was really responsible for a given terrorist outrage.'

However, in spite of Israeli military censorship (recently more lenient), the Hebrew press has for years been full of pragmatically-minded criticism of Mossad and of stories about scandals and personal squabbles rampant among its high-ranking staff. This criticism became sharper after the last wave of terror revealed Mossad's incompetence. As Bar'el puts it, 'From the viewpoint of the terrorists the first recent assault in Buenos Aires is already the second terrorist success. For anti-terrorist struggle agencies, whether Israeli, Argentinian or otherwise, the successes of Argentinian terrorism must be particularly embarrassing, because investigations of the first assault [the bombing of the Israeli embassy] failed to yield any clue as to the identity of its perpetrators and because neither assault was preceded by specific advance indication that it was going to occur.' Similar views were widely echoed in the Hebrew press.

Ze'ev Shiff (*Haaretz*, 5 August), whose 'connections' are in my evaluation better than Bar'el's goes farther in his criticism of Mossad, without sparing Military Intelligence either. According to him, 'the latter's complete failure to penetrate Hizbollah's ranks was not its finest hour. With the exception of whatever could be learned through kidnappings, e.g. of Dirani, everything indicates that Israel knows very little about Hizbollah.' Shiff deplores the fact that 'in the past it was much easier to penetrate the PLO organizations in Lebanon and thus obtain information, than is now possible to obtain information about Hizbollah, even by way of continual observation from distance.' Still, Shiff views Mossad as more incompetent than Military Intelligence, the proof being that within the two years which have lapsed since the Israeli embassy in Buenos Aires was bombed 'Mossad failed to learn anything about it.' In spite of lack of evidence, Shiff assumes that the embassy was bombed by 'fundamentalists' who committed the recent assault. But he denies that responsibility for these bombings can be pinned on any state and he backs this conclusion by a finding reached by some unnamed intelligence bodies that explosives used in Buenos Aires and London were manufactured from locally available raw materials, 'which means that the explosives were not smuggled in by any embassy'. He concludes that 'Israel is not in a position to claim that the terrorists have been dispatched by a single agency. It does not know who are their leaders.' None the less, Shiff says that 'we need a lot of Israeli operations of the same kind which were used against Palestininian terrorism in the 1970s, only superior in quality.'

In pursuing its anti-Iranian campaign, Israel seems to aim higher than a mere Mossad operation. To all appearances, the conditioning of the Israeli public for the peace process is to be followed by an alliance with Saddam Hussein. A curious piece of evidence that such an alliance is in the cards is the complete silence of the Hebrew press, which for months already hasn't uttered a single word about the never-ending atrocities occurring in Iraq. The prospect of alliance with Iraq is already being mooted by Mossad veterans. Shmuel Toledano, a ex-Mossad senior who once served as the Prime Minister's Advisor on Arab Affairs and is active in politics, writes in *Haaretz* (5 August) that 'if Israel is attacked from the east, the Jordanian army will at first try to contain the attack on it, thus giving Israel time to mobilize its forces to encounter the attackers.' This opportunity has, nevertheless, one hitch: 'Something may yet go amiss in the Hashemite kingdom's interior, giving rise to unwelcome developments.' This is Toledano's elegant way of alluding to the possiblity that the Hashemite dynasty may yet be toppled by a popular revolution. The remedy, as seen by Toledano, of an Israeli peace and alliance with Iraq, is the best way to protect the Hashemites from 'unwelcome developments'. Although Toledano sees them as unwelcome to Israel, they could be no less unwelcome to Saddam Hussein. And the strategic value of Iraq to Israel would be no mean consideration either.

Toledano is well aware that in the way of making such an alliance 'stands the US which thus far hasn't been favourably disposed toward any state seeking to circumvent the sanctions against Iraq, and especially to help Iraq emerge out of its international isolation.' 'But', says Toledano, 'President Clinton who now badly needs to shore up his domestic ratings, will perhaps be able to explain his approval of Israeli–Iraqi alliance as a step towards advancing peace in the Middle East.' Toledano wants 'Israel to obtain from the US the entry ticket letting Iraq rejoin the family of the civilized nations'. Toledano recalls that 'Iraq still has accounts to settle with Syria for joining the [US-led] coalition during the Gulf War.' This is why 'an Iraqi alliance with Israel is going to hurt Syria badly and reduce its bargaining power. At the same time let us not forget that Saddam Hussein owes a moral debt to Arafat for supporting him fervently throughout the Gulf War and paying a high price for that support. Now Arafat wants as many Arab states to make peace with Israel as possible. But he must be particularly interested in making Iraq do so, simply because Iraq has been so friendly to him. Besides, Iraq may then help him negotiate with Israel. And the Palestinians will then see that Arafat is not isolated.' For all such reasons, Toledano defines the alliance with Iraq as lying in 'Israel's existential interest'.

It is fairly safe to predict the formation of such an alliance, overt or covert, in a not very distant future. It can be also fairly safely predicted that the Clinton administration will either overtly support or tacitly condone the whole scheme. What I cannot predict is whether the envisaged Israeli world-wide anti-terrorist drive will incline the Clinton administration to support Israel. Whatever happens, however, I find it likely that the peace process with Jordan is on Israel's part intended as a preliminary step to a violent contest with Iran.

8

Israeli Policies Toward Iran and Syria
1 October 1994

Here I am going to discuss the continuation and the results of the Israeli anti-Iranian campaign described before. I rely primarily on Aluf Ben (*Haaretz*, 28 September), whose article obviously echoes the views of highly-placed sources in the Israeli establishment, and in particular, the Foreign Affairs Ministry, in the way it presents the Israeli anti-Iranian policies up to the date of its publication.

It seems impossible to write about Israeli foreign policy in general, and Shimon Peres in particular, without bearing in mind Orwell's Ministry of Truth from his novel *1984*. Ben reveals the hitherto unknown fact that under Peres the Israeli Foreign Ministry has had a 'Peace in the Middle East Department'. Right after the Buenos Aires terror assault 'Peres appointed the deputy-director, of this department, Yo'av Biran as a coordinator of Israeli measures against Iran', writes Ben, because 'Israel instantly perceived this assault as a convenient opportunity' to form an anti-Iranian coalition. The fact that Israeli Intelligence has failed to establish any link between Iran and that terror assault, was of course no obstacle in this 'convenient opportunity'. But one may ask a deeper question here: why do terrorist assaults have a tendency to occur exactly when their occurrence is for Israel a 'convenient opportunity'? Leaving this issue aside for the time being, let me quote Ben who invokes 'top-ranking [Israeli] politician' (possibly Peres) as one who 'several days earlier briefed the more notable Jerusalem political correspondents' about the results of a world-wide campaign against Iran.

The campaign was to follow Rabin's strategy and Peres' tactics and to be carried out by Biran in 'Peace in the Middle East Department'. Rabin and Peres agree that 'Iran is the greatest risk Israel has ever faced and a major threat to the stability of the entire Middle East.' This is due not only to 'its support for terror and sabotage and its attempt to become nuclearized', but to its 'being an examplar not only for Islamic fundamentalists but for other resistance movements in Arab countries'. Judging from my familiarity with what goes under the name of Israeli strategic thinking, the reference to 'resistance movements' means that many

Middle Easterners (not necessarily Arabs) take pride in the fact that Iran has not succumbed to American diktat for nearly twenty years. This proves to them that resistance to US policy schemes in the Middle East is possible and conflicts with Israeli attempts 'to convince' everyone concerned that resisting the US is an exercise in futility; and that, since Israel has US support, resisting Israel is futile as well. Iran provides the best evidence to the contrary.

Rabin's strategy was 'to push the US and other western powers into a confrontation with Iran' because if 'Israel confronts Iran on its own, it may get involved in a religious war against the entire Muslim world'. To forestall this danger 'Israeli propaganda [*Hasbara*] was ordered to depict the rulers of Iran as "a danger to peace in the entire world and a threat to equilibrium between Western civilization and Islam".' Peres exerted himself towards this aim by 'sending his personal representatives to capitals of states in the world at large, in order to first announce that Israel and Jordan had reached an agreement and right thereafter to demand that the state concerned should stop giving credits to Iran and radically reduce the volume of trade with it, until it ceases supporting terrorism and gives up attempts to nuclearize'. Peres' representatives were also instructed to say that Israel was highly critical of any state willing to reschedule Iranian debts. The chief offender in Israel's eyes was Germany 'which the was first to sign with Iran a debt-rescheduling accord', but Japan, France, Italy, Switzerland and South Korea were by no means blameless in Israeli eyes either.

Let me omit Ben's reports about the course of this campaign, except to report on the behaviour of Iranian diplomats attending international conferences who, to Israeli regret, didn't behave in conformity with expectations. The Israeli diplomats had instructions to accuse Iran of 'undermining the peace process', expecting Iranians 'either to leave the hall during our speeches or else to corroborate our allegations by admitting that they indeed opposed the peace process'. Instead, the Iranian diplomats used to listen to Israeli representatives' accusations and then take the podium to argue that the word 'peace' has plural meanings. If by using that word Israel means to withdraw from all territories conquered since June 1967 including East Jerusalem and South Lebanon, Iran will by no means oppose it. The Israeli diplomats couldn't but refuse to answer the Iranians straight. Instead, they quoted some admittedly provocative interviews Iranian politicians had previously given to the western press. That was answered by an assertion that the interviewers 'didn't understand what they had been told' and by reiterating the request to discuss the peace that could be brought to fruition by a total Israeli withdrawal.

This sequence of failures couldn't but result in a bifurcation of expert opinion. As Ben reports, two policies are now being recommended to Rabin. The first is that 'since we haven't succeeded in isolating the Iranians, we need to begin to talk straight to them ... Other major figures, however, have urged Rabin to go ahead without bothering about American protection and adopt an activist policy against Iran, relying on Israel's own resources alone.' It is impossible yet to make predictions on which way Rabin may ultimately follow.

I believe the most important single factor now prompting Israel to make an effort to reach accommodation with Syria is the much increased military power of the Syrian Army. The most important recent article dealing with the Syrian army was by Ron Ben-Yishay, an author reputed for his good access to the Israeli Army high command. According to Ben-Yishay (*Yediot Ahronot*, 16 September), 'Assad is very close to realizing his old dream of reaching a strategic parity with Israel.' Ben-Yishay explains that 'during the long years when the USSR and its satellites supported Syria, the latter couldn't really advance toward a strategic parity with Israel.' Although Ben-Yishay does not explain why it was so, I would venture a guess that the USSR's Middle East policies had been for a long time secretly coordinated with the US. Things changed under Gorbachev, who, according to Ben-Yishay, 'soon after assuming power told Assad that he expected him to make peace with Israel, even on Israeli terms. To make it clear that he meant business, Gorbachev stopped Soviet arms sales to Syria. For some time he did allow the supplies of limited quantities of spare parts, but eventually even such sales were stopped.' Ben-Yishay's information seems to me to be accurate. Probably because he believed in unlimited Israeli influence within the US, Gorbachev's policies were pro-Israeli: 'For a different reason those policies were pursued after the collapse of the Soviet Union in 1991. The new rulers of Russia refused to sell any weapons to Syria except for hard currency which Syria then hardly possessed.' Ben-Yishay defines the years 1986–91 as the Syrian Army's most unfortunate period. During the Gulf Crisis 'US officers expressed highly critical opinions about the quality of Syrian troops.' This applied not only to the division the Syrians dispatched to Saudi Arabia but also to any other troops the Americans had chance to inspect.

According to Ben-Yishay, the growth of the Syrian Army's power dates from the aftermath of the Gulf Crisis. The first contribution to it was by the US 'which secretely allocated the best among the captured Iraqi tanks and self-propelled guns to Syrian forces as a reward for their participation in the anti-Iraq coalition'. After having declared Syria a 'terror-state' the US couldn't legally disburse any credits to Syria. But it convinced some unnamed European countries to grant Syria 'several hundred million dollars in credit' after the Gulf War was over. 'At the same time Syria received a grant of $1.5 billion directly from the Saudi royal house.' Such grants seem to continue to flow. Aluf Ben (*Haaretz*, 12 August) says that 'Peres complained to his US colleague Warren Christopher about the Saudis.' His complaint must have had little effect, though, since Ben says that 'Saudi Arabia is the only state in the region whose direct ties with Washington are not pre-consulted with Israel. It is the only state which, unlike Egypt, Jordan, Syria and the PLO, does not need to cope with constant US pressures to be more open toward Israel and accept basic Israeli demands.' This statement should not be construed as meaning that the US had refrained from exerting any pressure on Saudi Arabia, but that the exerted pressures concerned matters of secondary importance. Ben-Yishay believes that Saudi financial aid to Syria keeps flowing with the effect that Assad has plenty of hard cash to buy the best weaponry. Undoubtedly the present equipment of the Syrian Army is much better than it was when Syria depended on Soviet supplies. Contrary to conventional wisdom, the collapse of the USSR does not seem to have weakened Syria; and I would venture the same guess about any Arab state. It might well have been a blessing for them all.

Let me omit Ben-Yishay's elaborate presentation of the current size of the Syrian ground forces and their weapons. The point worth mentioning, however, is his view that the Syrians must have what he calls 'non-conventional weapons', namely quite accurate land-to-land missiles which can be equipped with chemical warheads. I concur with this view. Against these missiles Israeli is in Ben-Yishay's view defenceless. They can wreak havoc across the country. According to him, the acquisition of these weapons by Syria and the Saudi funding of these purchases was attributable to their shared fear that 'Israel might attempt to impose on Syria a peace on Israeli terms, exactly as Israel had attempted to do during the Lebanese War.' Such an attempt could follow an offensive of 'the Israeli Army breaking through the Golan Heights cease-fire lines, with the effect of arriving on the outskirts of Damascus after no more than 24 hours'. In Ben-Yishay's view Israel had this option until a few years ago: 'Right now, however, Syrian armour is capable of stopping an Israeli attack simultaneously on two fronts, in the Golan Heights and in Lebanon. However, if the Israeli Air Force attacks Syria now, as it did in October 1973, in order to destroy half of Syrian military and civilian infrastructure, Assad would be able to retaliate, wreaking upon Israel a no lesser amount of devastation', something he could not do in 1973. Ben-Yishay maintains that 'Israel still retains its qualitative advantage in terms of both the quality of its weapons and the training of its military personnel.' Yet he concludes that 'for the first time in Middle Eastern history a situation has appeared, where a state, namely Syria, is capable of defending itself effectively against Israeli attack. For

Assad it could well have been a reason inducing him to open negotiations with Israel, because he had kept saying that he would proceed to truly decisive negotiations with Israel only from a position of strength.'

Ben-Yishay refers to fears of Syrian strength present 'among security professionals in Israel, including the Commander of Northern Command', General Yitzhak Mordechay, known for his hawkish views. Right-wing politicians and Golan Heights settlers believe that it is Assad who wants to attack Israel. Ben-Yishay, however, is adamant that 'many in the high command of the Israeli Army and all of Israeli Intelligence are convinced that Syria is doing exactly what Israel is doing. Like Syria, Israel conducts *bona fide* peace negotiations while arming itself to the teeth in the event that they fail, the status quo gets stalemated and a war breaks out. Although only time can tell which of the two sides is right in its evaluations, all the signs indicate that Assad wants an honourable peace'. This evaluation is backed by Professor Moshe Ma'oz, an orientalist with close access to the Israeli Security System. He says that 'although Syria keeps arming itself with weapons which can be lethal for us, its claim that the purpose of these armaments is defensive is eminently credible. After all, Syria does need to deter Iraq. Its need to deter Israel is much greater. It needs to avoid a repeat of the 1982 invasion of Lebanon and to conduct negotiations from a position of strength. Rightly so, Israel is doing exactly the same while buttressing its military and strategic standing so as to negotiate simultaneously from a position of strength.' (*Yediot Ahronot*, 28 September)

Ma'oz adds that Israeli military strength derives partly from the US supplies of modern weaponry deliberately intended 'to provide Israel with superiority over all neighbouring Arab states together'. According to him, the US has pursued this objective 'since the early 1960s', that is, since the term of office of John F. Kennedy. I think Ma'oz is right. Kennedy reversed the approach toward Israel adopted by Eisenhower. In my view, the Six Day War was a direct consequence of Kennedy-initiated policies. But Ma'oz is aware that American support for Israel is in turn conditional on Israel's willingness to coordinate its policies with the US: 'Once Israel gives away the Golan Heights to Syria, the US, as it already promised, will keep supplying the Israeli Army with the most sophisticated modern weaponry in abundance, so that the Israeli Army may retain its strategic superiority over the entire Middle East even in peacetime.' Although neither Ben-Yishay nor Ma'oz say it explicitly, they can be understood as arguing against the demand of the Israeli right-wing (including Labor Party hawks) to stop negotiating with Syria for as long as Syria keeps purchasing weaponry. Politicians and publicists voicing this demand (among whom the most vociferous is the Likud leader Netanyahu), believe that while Syria must be prevented from purchasing weapons, Israel must keep arming itself.

Amir Oren, writing in *Davar* (30 September), agrees with Ben-Yishay that until 1991 the Americans, regardless of what they would officially declare, didn't want Israel to withdraw from the Golan Heights. The Syrian participation in the 1990–91 anti-Iraqi coalition changed American attitudes. Oren discusses Israeli relations with Syria against the background of steady reduction of the US Defence budgets. Ma'oz, Ben-Yishay and other Israeli commentators assume that the US may generously reward Israel for any accord with Syria with grants to be used for the purchase of quality weapons for the Israeli Army. On the opposite side stands Oren, who believes that while the budgets of the US Marines are being cut, it may be difficult to persuade Congress to grant Israel the huge sums which it has hoped for. According to Oren, US money may be particularly needed if the peace process fails: 'One Israeli Army general recently requested to speak to Rabin and Chief of Staff Barak at least six times. His aim was to alert them to the gap between estimates of the equipment needed for the coming war and the equipment likely to be actually lost in such an event.' Oren blames Rabin for this state of affairs. As both Prime Minister and Defence Minister, Rabin in Oren's eyes is not able to cut civilian budgets enough to allocate more money for the Army. Yet according to official figures over one half of the Israeli Army's budget goes for salaries and pensions. More weapons means more personnel to look after them, even when they are safely stored. In any event, therefore, more weapons means the further militarization of Israeli society. In Barak's view as reported by Oren 'the gap against which the mentioned general warned does exist but Israel will have time to bridge it. Stopping negotiations with Syria would create a strategic alert. Months before Syria opens fire in a form of static shelling, let alone in an attack, the US can be expected to open its weaponry stores to the Israeli Army and let it pick up whatever it wants.'

Oren reports this optimistic expectation, but does not share it. He admits that 'Clinton loves Israel effusively and even more the American voters who support Israel.' But he warns that 'Clinton becomes ever weaker as President, to the point that his wishes are being less and less taken into account.' Also, the power of the organized US Jews is in Oren's view declining. This is why Oren anticipates that 'in 1994–97 no responsible Israeli Prime Minister and Defence Minister can rest at ease that Assad would suffer rebuffs passively; nor expect that the Israeli Army would win a quick, easy and cheap victory; nor hope for a war in which Israel could accomplish more than without fighting it. It would be like in

October 1973 when we lost 2,600 fallen for what we could approximately accomplish without a single Israeli casualty.' Oren uses this argument also against 'the opponents of the withdrawal from the Golan Heights' who really want a war with Syria, so as to let 'the Israeli Army take advantage of its deployment on the Golan Heights and win a quick victory. This assumption, however, ignores such factors as the loss of morale of the civilians in the rear and of the troops on the front as soon as they realize that the war they fight is unnecessary. It also ignores the fact that the Israeli Army cannot fight a protracted war without having its indispensable supplies constantly renewed.'

In summary, the new factor in Israeli–Syrian relations is the military parity set between them. This factor puts Israel much more at a disadvantage than was the case two years ago. Israeli military and intelligence leadership, foolish as ever, was not aware of the build-up of Syrian strategic strength until it was too late. Of course, now it is aware of that, even if only due to American briefings. As a consequence, Israel is now for the first time prepared to negotiate a deal with Syria. I don't know yet what Israel is really ready to offer Syria. In view of the lack of information I am not going either to try to guess what Israel may yet demand from Syria. With two exceptions, though. First, it is certain that Israel will demand that Syria itself disarms the Hizbollah. And second, it is also certain that Israel will demand Syrian backing for, or at least neutrality in, the coming Israeli contest with Iran, no matter what forms this contest may yet assume.

Part III

ISRAELI FOREIGN TRADE

9

Trade Between Israel and the Arab States
26 April 1991

Officially, all Arab states (except Egypt since signing the peace treaty) have been boycotting Israel since 1949. The boycott assumes two forms. On the one hand, all trade, all postal deliveries and all travel exchanges between Israel and any Arab state are supposed to be banned. On the other hand, the Arab states are also supposed to boycott commercial companies from third countries which do any trade with Israel. Even the films shown in Israel in theory cannot be seen in Arab countries. An overseeing 'Boycott Office', located in Damascus, is supposed to impose specific bans and to issue guidelines binding all the Arab states.

In reality some Arab states for all practical intents and purposes stopped boycotting Israel in 1967, right after the Six Day War, and started pursuing diversified trade and other relations with Israel. This has continued since, to the point of becoming an important prop for the Israeli economy. In the beginning, Israeli censorship saw to it that the subject was never explicitly mentioned in the media. Nevertheless, knowledge of the situation became widespread in Israel. As for the Arab countries, articles and press reports obviously inspired by the authorities have kept appearing, asserting the boycott's success. (The Palestinian press in particular has done its best to maintain this illusion.) As time lapsed, however, some oblique (and occasionally even direct) references to the Israeli trade with Arab states were tacitly allowed to appear in the Hebrew press.

The first extensive discussion of the situation, authored by Yosef Ein-Dor appeared, however, only most recently in *Al-Hamishmar* (20 March 1991). To a great extent Ein-Dor relies on lectures delivered by Professor Gad Gilber, described as 'an expert in the Middle Eastern economy', at Tel Aviv University's Dayan Centre of Strategic Studies. The publication of Ein-Dor's article may be connected with Israel's present demand for the formal termination of the boycott and institution of overt trade relations as a precondition for peace with pro-American Arab countries. While drawing on his article, I will also use other available information, including various Hebrew press titbits which have kept appearing over the years. Incidentally, such titbits began to crop up in June 1982, at the time of the invasion of Lebanon. It could hardly be coincidental that the invasion was, *inter alia*, intended to promote Israeli exports to the Arab world. I will also use private sources of information, albeit, like the aforementioned titbits, without specific references.

Let me begin with the second form of boycott, that is, the boycott of companies trading with Israel. With a few exceptions involving Japanese companies, this boycott had already become economically meaningless in the late 1950s. Professor Gilber states that 'in the early 1960s, both the central Boycott Office located in Damascus and its coordinating branch offices admitted [in their yearly reports] that their venture had turned into an unprecedented fiasco ... An increasing number of foreign companies, which had once feared retaliation on the part of the Boycott Office, started ignoring it. Moreover, even the Arab states from then on began to cooperate with that office rather perfunctorily, often turning a blind eye to a given company's connections with Israel.' The boycott's abject failure was further accelerated by the formation of 'branch or dummy companies, registered in the US or other countries' for the sole purpose of doing business with Israel. The fierce opposition of the US to this form of boycott, highlighted by enactment of legislation against it, brought the whole venture to the point of collapse, especially since other countries resisted it as well. Although Ein-Dor does not say it, the corruption of Arab bureaucracies, the demand of the Arab public for the goods the boycotted companies could offer cheaply and profits the Arab merchants could reap from the sales of such goods did the rest. Whatever boycott continued was focused on the most visible and publicity-liable trade sectors: for example, high fashion or renowned movie stars, and the like. Scattered instances of such token boycotts, intended for their propaganda effects only, may continue to this very day. Everything else was moribund already before 1967, although unknown to both the Arab and the Jewish publics. As an economic factor of any significance, the whole subject can now be safely ignored.

This, however, was not the case with the more important form of direct Arab boycott of Israel which at least until June 1967 was observed quite rigorously. Both in Israel and in the Arab countries this form of boycott was often referred to as 'the wall' surrounding Israel from all sides except the sea. Its existence was by all means a major factor in Israeli policies. But, as Professor Gilber correctly observes, 'the first crack in the wall of the Arab boycott appeared as a result of the occupation of the West Bank in 1967 when Israeli-produced goods started flooding the Arab market, contrary to the boycott's foremost purpose.' As a result of this, 'the wall became a sieve.' Almost at once 'the Territories began to function as a transit point in export of Israeli goods to Arab states east of Jordan', but not to Jordan itself. During 1968–72, the Jordanian authorities, in cooperation with the Boycott Office in Damascus and its Amman branch, issued pathetic appeals to the chambers of commerce in the West Bank which then operated under the Israeli rule and were comprised of the Israeli appointees, to halt this trade by insisting on attaching a label 'made in West Bank' or 'made in Gaza Strip' to the goods passing the Jordanian territory in transit further east. (Subsequently, the label had to specify the name of an 'Arab' factory supposedly manufacturing a given product.) Israeli authorities readily consented. The 'factories', usually owned by the rich chambers of commerce members were quickly set up, to do nothing apart from putting new labels on Israeli manufactures. The PLO which at that time was a power in Jordan, acceded (apparently for a share in the profits) to this all-too-transparent scheme without saying a word about it in public, while repeating *ad nauseam* its then prevalent slogan of 'strangling Israel' by the 'united Arab boycott'.

While Jordan allows transit of Israeli exports to other Arab countries, it has instituted tight and quite effectual controls to protect its own markets. Since 1975 the volume of these exports declined, compared to what it was in 1967–75. Consider, for example, the following Hebrew press story. In 1986, after the US State Secretary Shultz made some rhetoric about 'improving the quality of life in the Occupied Territories', some naive American Palestinians responded with a project of opening a cement factory in the West Bank. Israeli authorities consented, but on a strict condition that all cement produced was to go for export to Arab countries via Jordan, with none to be marketed in the Territories themselves so as not to undermine the monopoly of the Israeli-produced cement in the local market. The prospective investors rejected this condition. But they again raised the matter in March 1991, knowing that Israel still stood by its condition. Now, however, the Hebrew press reported how Israeli policy in the Territories changed under Arens. Contrary to Rabin who turned down Palestinian applications to open a new businesses, Arens tends to grant them, on condition that a given business will also relabel Israeli-made goods destined for export through Jordan.

The implication of the story is, that from the Israeli point of view, the described exports have always had a major disadvantage. They depended on Jordanian consent. Being a sovereign state, Jordan is in a position to impose conditions. The fictitious labels are one such condition. The matter is no more than symbolic. Other conditions, such as the closure of the Jordanian market to Israeli exports are economically detrimental.

This is why Israel has been looking for other outlets for its exports, that could be under its exclusive control. Professor Gilber speaks about it not without a certain finesse: 'In 1975, after the direct ties with South Lebanon expanded, another route was opened for transit of Israeli exports to Arab markets, first and foremost in Lebanon itself, but also in Syria. Israeli trucks with fruit and vegetables, processed foodstuffs, household appliances and other Israeli manufactures, would arrive at the [Lebanese border] checkpost in Rosh Hanikra, where the goods would be reloaded on to Arab trucks which would then proceed to Syria and Lebanon. Every Syrian and Lebanese knew that the goods were Israeli, but as long as the "Made in Israel" label was absent, nobody cared', Damascus Boycott Office included. The new transit via Lebanon has differed from the transit via Jordan in two respects. One is of a rather symbolic nature: there has been no need to relabel anything, as the sheer absence of an Israeli label did the trick. But the other difference was material. Since Israel controlled both sides of Rosh Hanikra checkpost, the reloading did not need to be coordinated with authorities of another state, as it did on the Jordan River bridges. The PLO which in 1975–82 in southern Lebanon had even more power than before 1970 in Jordan, again could not be bothered with a subject as trivial as trade.

Economic motivations behind the unpublicized occupation of parts of southern Lebanon from 1975 onward were never mentioned abroad, but known at the time to many in Israel, myself included. (It was, incidentally, Shimon Peres, who first had the gall to disguise the sordid realities of that occupation under the name of 'the good-neighbourly fence'.) Later, pretty much the same economic reasons were a factor in the full-scale 1982 invasion of that country, in the continuing occupation of its large areas in 1982–85, and finally in the occupation of the so-called 'Security Zone' up to the present day.

Professor Gilber says that 'Israeli exporters operated under strong incentives to seek alternative markets ... after losing the Iranian market for Israeli exports when the Shah had been overthrown.' This explains the Israeli expansion into Lebanon to a certain extent. During the heyday of the invasion in June–July 1982, the Labor hawk Haggay Eshed (a friend of Sharon) published articles in *Davar* explaining that the 'commercial hegemony' over the Middle East was to be won 'by the two trading nations, the Jews and the Maronites'. (The latter won this distinction by virtue of their purported descent from the Phoenicians.) Eshed was emphatic in defining the search for such 'hegemony' as an aim of the invasion and conquest of Lebanon. But it soon turned out that Bashir Jumail had other ideas. After having been elected president of Lebanon he met Begin in Nahariya where, without objecting to Israeli military presence in his country he demanded an immediate restoration of Lebanese customs controls on its border with Israel. The demand made Begin angry and he refused to comply with it. I have a hunch which I admittedly cannot substantiate, that the assassination of Jumail which occurred shortly thereafter was not entirely unconnected with this dispute with Begin over customs control.

No conceivable Lebanese government, of whatever political stripe, can possibly put up with Israeli economic penetration of Lebanon, even if out of weakness or other reasons it would tolerate Israeli military presence on its territory. It is because this penetration amounts to something without parallels in modern history. A great deal of Israeli exports are marketed in Lebanon without passing through any customs or border controls. Only the exports which pass Lebanon in transit to Syria are subject to controls on the Syrian border. Another abnormality is in the modes of marketing. In the areas of Lebanon which are, or were, overtly or covertly occupied by Israel, Israeli goods have been sold as such, without fictitious labels or other disguises. In the rest of Lebanon and in other Arab countries they are being sold, as Professor Gilber informs, through 'the medium of dummy corporations established in Cyprus, Greece and Spain for the sole purpose of disguising the fact of their being Israeli manufactures'.

According to Gilber, the volume of direct trade between Israel and Arab countries carried out in this way has lately considerably increased. He does not provide updated statistical figures; he only says that 'in the early 1980s the value of [Israeli] exports to Arab countries, including the Occupied Territories, amounted to about $500,000.' In my opinion, this estimate must be interpreted as referring only to exports passing through the Occupied Territories and then through Jordan. I cannot reveal the source of my own estimate, which is that in 1988–89 Israeli exports to all Arab states, except the Occupied Territories and Egypt (in the latter case the official figures are available) were in the range between $1.5 billion and perhaps as high as $2 billion. Even this estimate does not cover arms and other security-related products about which I have no detailed information, but whose value has been far from negligible. A notice recently published in the Hebrew press in connection with the current scandal involving the defective quality of gas masks the Israeli government distributed to its citizenry during the Gulf War, sheds some light on this sector of Israeli exports. As it turns out, some gas masks found defective had Arabic language labels on them. Why? Because they were sold by Israel to Germany but, shortly after the Gulf crisis began, they were hastily repurchased back. Why should Israel sell gas masks with Arab language labels to Germany which anyhow produces enough gas masks on its own, if not for the sake of thus transiting them to an Arab state? But apart from

gas masks, reliable reports give information about Israeli mortars
and other military equipment destined for Morocco, Oman,
Lebanese militias and, one can presume, other Arab countries
as well.

In order to show the relative value of trade with Arab countries
for Israel, let me use official data for the year 1988 as published in
The Statistical Abstract of Israel, 1989. Except for Egypt, the volume
contains no particularized data about exports to the Arab countries
(even to Lebanon); only the totals which may or may not cover those
exports. The only open information available is from Professor
Gilber who says, without referring to his sources or providing
breakdowns for particular countries, that 'the total value of all
exports to Arab states (including Egypt and North Africa) for 1988
amounted to about $1 billion.' I think that this is a gross
underestimate. According to the Statistical Abstract just referred
to, all Israeli exports taken together in 1988 totalled $9.739 million,
thereof to the European Common Market countries $3.229 million
and to the US $2.987 million. Since Israeli exports to other
countries were small and to Egypt miniscule, a considerable part
of the remainder can only be accounted for by exports to other Arab
states. Gilber does say that the 'hidden' Israeli exports to Arab states
amounted to about 10 per cent of total exports. This would accord
with his $1 billion estimate. But for the reason just stated, I would
think that the actual figure is at least twice as high, or even higher.

More information can be extracted from Gilber about the nature
and dynamics of Israeli exports to Arab countries. He bewails
what for him is a paradox, that the Arab country with which Israel
is at peace, Egypt, has successfully barred nearly all Israeli exports
while selling to Israel oil for hard cash. This he contrasts with
countries of destination which do not have peaceful relations with
Israel, such as 'all the Gulf states'. He discusses the diversification
of Israeli exports to the Arab countries, which include 'fresh and
frozen fruits and vegetables, processed foodstuffs, textiles, office
supplies, domestic solar heaters, furniture, cosmetics, medication,
fertilizers, electronic equipment such as communication units, air
conditioners, spare parts for cars including tyres, agricultural
equipment such as drip-irrigation pipes, pesticides, fertilizers and
all kind of raw materials', apparently including many chemicals.
He correctly observes that some of the listed products, being
originally designed for the climatic and soil conditions of Israel,
are better suited to similar conditions in Arab countries than the
comparable European or American manufactures, in addition to
being cheaper. For instance, Israeli agricultural drip-irrigation
equipment, which is world-renowned, aroused the special interest
of Arabs, to the point that 'in March 1990, when an agricultural
exhibition was held in Tel Aviv ... several buyers from hostile Arab

states were permitted to attend'. The proximity of Israel to Arab
countries also works, as Gilber observes, to Israel's competitive
advantage over European and other exporters, especially 'in the case
of large-sized merchandise' whose transport is expensive.

In conclusion, let me point to various implications of the described
trade practices, and of the relations between Israel and the Arab
states in general, in terms of the actual political situation and the
potentialities inherent in it. A very important question which Gilber
does not ask, is: how do the Arab states pay for their Israeli exports?
It can be stated with confidence that the bulk of civilian exports
as listed, until the Gulf crisis (which disrupted trade routes) were
destined for Lebanon, Syria, Iraq, Sudan, Libya, Oman and other
Gulf states with the exception of Saudi Arabia. Only in the case of
Lebanon a *quid pro quo* is known: illicit drugs, although sold to Israel
in increasing quantities, can hardly amount to more than a fraction
of Israeli exports to that country. All other listed Arab states export
nothing to Israel. Hence an inescapable conclusion, supported by
quite extensive evidence available to me privately, that Israeli
exports are paid for in hard currencies and occasionally in gold. I
have no information about the breakdown of the distribution of
Israeli exports to each named Arab state, but I know that Iraq and
Syria are now on the top of the list, while exports to Libya (Gaddafi's
frequent anti-Israel posturing notwithstanding) are not negligible.
An interesting fact emerges: beyond the screen of incessant
sloganeering about their unshakable commitment to Palestinian
cause and to 'the armed struggle' against Israel the three 'radical'
Arab dictators, Gaddafi, Assad and Saddam Hussein, have for
long years been supplying Israel with much of its foreign currency
reserves. And it can be assumed that, in the absence of publicity,
they will continue to do so in the future as well.

A generalization is called for here. With the exception of some
minor states such as Yemen, Mauritania or even Algeria (whose case
will yet be discussed), the more an Arab state is or pretends to be
hostile towards Israel, the higher are its purchases of Israeli-made
goods and the closer are its covert relations with Israel. The reverse
also holds true. The two most moderate Arab states, Egypt and
Jordan, have been the only ones which actually barred nearly all
Israeli exports. Among the states which buy big quantities of Israeli-
made goods are not only Syria and (until the Gulf crisis) Iraq but
the Gulf states which do not even permit Israel to be shown on the
maps sold on their territory. Although the Israeli exports to Libya
are not as massive as those to Iraq and Syria it is by no means
irrelevant that much of Libyan oil is marketed by the 'Occidental
Petroleum' company owned (until his recent death) by the notorious
Zionist, Armand Hammer, who was influential in convincing the
USSR to let its Jews emigrate to Israel. Morocco encourages Israeli

tourism, with many Israelis taking advantage of it, using their Israeli passports for the purpose. The actual relations of Israel with Tunisia are quite close, and with Oman even more so, since as long ago as 1968. The only extremist Arab country which does not trade with Israel is Algeria, which can be accounted for by distance and by French competition rather than by any ideological commitments.

The same facts call for yet another generalization. All this voluminous trade can take place only because of the absence of democracy and freedom of expression in the Arab world. It is greatly enhanced by the customary bribery and other forms of corruption rampant in Arab bureaucracies. In this respect the Palestinians are by no means an exception. Many of them must by necessity be aware of the situation as described in this report, but denied both the access to information and the right to speak their minds under the prevailing repression they delude themselves about the attitudes of both the Arab states and individual Arab purchasers towards Israeli goods. This holds particularly true about the so-called 'left' factions within the PLO which have always servilely refrained from criticizing the 'radical' Arab regimes for their trading with Israel on terms advantageous to the latter. The same holds no less true about other 'left' Arab intellectuals, especially on the Egyptian left.

Much evidence points to the fact that Israel has consistently opposed any developments towards democracy in all neighbouring countries. I have firmly believed, for more than 25 years, that this opposition stems not only from political but also from economic considerations. The Israeli–Arab trade rests on deceit and corruption on both sides. Yet it could be carried out normally and openly with tremendous advantages for the peoples of both sides. The primary barrier to the normalization of this trade is the refusal of Israel to renounce the Occupied Territories for the sake of peace. But the absence of democracy and freedom of expression in the Arab states and Palestinian society, together with the concomitant delusions bound to ensnare people under such conditions, can be seen as prerequisite to the success of these Israeli policies. But the US lends its helping hand, by opposing the developments toward democracy in the Middle East as well. It can be surmised that economic considerations play a part in current American policies. Yet in my opinion, a peaceful and prosperous Middle East is likely to be a better market for American exports (weaponry excepted) than a war-torn one. Thus it is political considerations, such as the influence of organized US Jewry which helps shape US policies no less than the hope of making profits.

Note: On 26 April, an article by Gad Gilber ('The labels are not being checked') appeared in *Haaretz*. Without adding anything new, the article repeats what Ein-Dor had already reported about Gilber's lecture.

10

Drugs and Vegetables: The Israeli Trade with Arab Countries

26 August 1994

The ever-increasing volume of Israeli trade with Arab countries is certainly one of the important factors of Middle Eastern politics, but reliable information about it is hard to come by. My report of 26 April 1991 recounted the history of the development of this trade. Since then I haven't seen any novel sources of important information, though incidental information from various sources became in 1994 much more abundant. This dearth of information could be explained by Israeli censorship seeing to it that the subject be never explicitly mentioned in the media except when it would suit its purposes. In the Arab countries press reports obviously inspired by authorities have kept appearing, proudly asserting the boycott's success. The Palestinian press in particular has done its best to maintain this illusion. Such prevarications still go on.

Since then Israeli military censorship has been somewhat relaxed, with the result that I can now supply further information. The first part of this report deals with Israeli exports of vegetables, fruit, flowers and marginally of other produce to Arab countries. It relies on two articles by Ronen Bergman (*Ha'ir*, Tel Aviv's Friday paper, 15 and 22 July 1994) which, as the author admits, rely exclusively on the official Israeli sources. The second part of this report, describing the cooperation of Israeli Security Services with drug merchants in return for intelligence the latter supply, is based on information provided by Israeli lawyers defending Lebanese drug merchants kidnapped and brought before Israeli courts. Their story appeared in an article by Etty Hassid (*Yerushalaim*, Jerusalem's Friday paper, 22 July). While censorship didn't prevent the publication of the article in question it did prevent all other Hebrew papers from uttering a single word in response to the deeply disturbing facts revealed by Hassid and never subsequently denied. Incidentally, both parts of this report, but especially the second, will shed some light upon the rather narrow limits of Israeli democracy.

Bergman deals with those exports of Israeli agricultural produce (plus salt and sugar) to Arab countries which, regardless of their

ultimate destination, after leaving Israel pass through Lebanon.
Although some exports passed and still pass through Jordan, they
must by necessity be ignored here. Let me note, however, one crucial
difference between the two routes. The Jordanian border with
Israel is 'normal' in regard to trade. Merchandise is checked.
Without a valid permit nothing is allowed to pass. By contrast, since
the June 1982 Israeli invasion of Lebanon, there have been no
Lebanese border controls on its border with Israel or with the
Security Zone. Israel alone decides who and what can enter Lebanon
through this border. The border posts between the territory
controlled by Israel (the 'Security Zone') and the Lebanese territory
to the north of it do bar the entry of unwelcome individuals and
merchandise from Lebanon to the Zone and then to Israel but are
passable in the reverse direction. The only Lebanese politician
who demanded a reinstatement of customs and custom barriers
between Lebanon and Israel was Lebanon's President-elect Bashir
Jumail at his meeting with Begin in Nahariya. Begin angrily turned
down this demand. One may speculate that Jumail's demand for
reinstatement of the custom controls was the main cause of his
imminent assassination.

Bergman says (15 July) that Lebanon is treated by Israel as an
ordinary export country. By Israeli law, agricultural exports are a
monopoly of the government-owned company Agrexco. The
director of Agrexco's Lebanese department, Yossi Tzafrir, and its
spokesman Hayim Keller were Bergman's sources of information.
But Bergman was also helped by the director of the Lebanese
department in the Agriculture Ministry, Benny Gabbay. Although
Bergman does not say it explicitly, he must have also derived some
information from the Israeli Army, Shabak and Military Intelligence.
Without their permission, he could not have interviewed veterans
of the 'South Lebanese Army' (SLA), or quoted some of Israeli
Intelligence's assessments of its own role in the whole business. In
view of Bergman's dependence on official Israeli sources, I will often
need to add my own comments.

According to Bergman large-scale Israeli trade with Lebanon
began 'twelve years ago', that is, in 1982. He doesn't mention the
'coincidential' circumstance that this was the year of the invasion
of Lebanon, nor that Israeli–Lebanese trade could soar only due
to that invasion. Though this has hardly been realized, the 'Peace
for the Galilee' War was to a large extent a trade war, comparable
with, say, the Opium Wars, or the trade wars of the seventeenth
and eighteenth centuries. Israeli trade with Lebanon, and through
it with Arab countries, has peculiar characteristics. It is monopolistic
– the sales take place only in selected localities, where they are
overseen by the military. Actually, the Israeli use of military coercion
in trading bears resemblance to the earlier forms of western trade

with Asian countries. True, the Israeli trade with Lebanon began according to Bergman before 1982, indeed, in 1979 (though I would say even earlier – in 1974 under the cover of Shimon Peres' 'Good Fence'). However, before invasion, this trade was small-scale and limited to areas controlled by the Falangists. The monopoly of trade with the Falangist zone of Beirut and the Falangist enclave to the north of it was granted to Camille Chamoun and in South Lebanon to Major Sa'ed Haddad; in both cases as a reward for political collaboration. 'But', says Tzafrir, 'only since 1982 has the entire Lebanon stood open to Israeli trade.'

Tzafrir insists that tough measures on the part of the Israeli security forces (their exact nature is not specified) were needed after the invasion to enforce the monopoly of Agrexco and protect 'the interests of Jewish farmers'. Anyhow, owing to action of the security forces, 'the initial disarray', when 'Arab farmers from the Galilee were allowed to enter Lebanon and sell their produce there' was speedily put to an end: 'Agrexco, in its capacity of authorized state monopoly, requested the Army to act with dispatch against the Arab interlopers.' Also, 'permits issued to some Lebanese merchants who would arrive in Haifa Agricultural Exchange with suitcases full of dollars to compete with us there' needed to be cancelled. Tzafrir describes that competition as 'particularly precarious for us, because the Lebanese merchants were as clever as the Jews'. Border controls were reinstated and the Lebanese and unauthorized Israelis were as a rule denied the right to cross it. Agrexco alone could from then on deliver Israeli agricultural produce to locations right behind the Lebanese border. Few duly authorized Lebanese merchants could appear at those locations in order to buy what they were offered, reload the merchandise on to their trucks and transport it to wherever they pleased. But, complains Tzafrir, after the June 1985 Israeli withdrawal from a large chunk of South Lebanon, 'land traffic became problematic.' At first Israel approached the SLA for help. Bergman does not say what this 'help' was: he only complains about the SLA's incompetence and obstacles set up by its commander, General Lahad, to operations of Israeli trade. He gives some examples: 'At all stages of Israeli trade with Lebanon and other Arab countries, senior SLA officers insisted on pocketing a hefty share of the profits. Worse still, General Lahad's private driver was one of the main go-betweens between Israel and the Lebanese merchants, notwithstanding the fact that Israeli Army branded him as a 'butterfly' on account of his cowardice.' Bergman's article of 22 July describes in detail how General Lahad would from time to time (apparently when he felt relatively strong *vis-à-vis* Israel) temporarily ban imports of specific commodities into his 'Zone' in order to thus extort a heftier bribe.

It was thus found advisable to search for a trade route that would not depend on Lahad's good graces. The first solution adopted was to let some major interested Lebanese merchants live in Israel and thus place them beyond Lahad's reach. In his 15 July article Bergman portrays one of the richest among those merchants, Amin El-Haj: 'Although Shi'ite, he was an old political ally of Camille Chamoun. For over 15 years he was handling a large part of Israeli trade with Lebanon, and indirectly with many other Arab countries.' Let me add that Israel wanted to appoint him as a virtual feudal lord of the entire Shi'ite-inhabited area of South Lebanon, except that the local population rebelled, first against him and then against the Israeli troops behind him. It was this rebellion which led to the establishment of Hizbollah in South Lebanon: 'Right now he is living in a luxurious suite in Nahariya [in Israel], connected by a special phone line to the central Lebanese phone-exchange.' The next solution in bypassing Lahad was to construct a harbour in Nakura which, although located in the 'Zone', was made off-limits to the SLA. From Nakura, ships took Israeli produce to Beirut and other Lebanese ports: 'Sometimes those ships would be escorted by an Israeli Navy warship up to some safe distance from Beirut.' Actually, explains Tzafrir, most of those ships, 'which navigate under the flags of various Latin American countries', don't depart from Nakura, except in their records: 'They really depart from Haifa or Ashdod.' Needless to say, the uninterrupted and massive presence of the Israeli Navy in Lebanese territorial waters, although normally justified as an 'anti-terrorist measure', is in the main intended to protect the Israeli trade.

Yet unexpected incidents sometimes occur. Bergman tells how 'in March 1990 the crew of one of Amin El-Haj's ships declared a strike precisely when the ship was anchored in Haifa. The strikers even turned for help to the Israeli Union of Merchant Marine Officers.' They were fortunate to turn to that union, rather than to the larger one of Merchant Marine Crewmen which is Histadrut-affiliated. The independent union agreed to help Amin El-Haj's crew, whereas the Histadrut (trade union) bosses controlling the latter union dutifully consulted the secret police and refused to do anything: 'A quick inspection by the Israeli union revealed something strange. There was no record of the ship's entry into the port of Haifa, and no document naming any past or future ports of the ship's call, or indication of the origin of its cargo. Officially, the ship didn't exist. In the entire management of the port of Haifa there was no one capable of informing the union inspectors to whom the ship belonged, where it sailed from and what was its destination.' The absence of documentation created the appearance of a pirate ship. At this point Bergman breaks his narrative. Of course, Israeli censorship clamped down on any further news. According to my sources, after several days, a gang arrived from no one could tell where, boarded and took over the ship forcibly under the protection of Israeli troops and made it depart from Haifa immediately. Nothing is known for certain about the fate of the striking crew, but they are presumed to be dead.

The nature of Israeli agricultural exports to Lebanon changed in 1985, after the Israeli pull-out from large chunks of Lebanese territory. In 1982–85, as Tzafrir admits, Israel used Lebanon primarily as a dumping ground for its variegated agricultural surpluses, including such cheap vegetables as tomatoes, and secondarily as a destination for South African exports then boycotted by Europe. Tzafrir recounts with pride how, with the help of the Israeli national airline El Al he organized exports of South African avocados to Lebanon. He also talks about sales of Israeli bananas to Lebanon, without mentioning that Lebanon itself was a large-scale banana producing country. Nor does he mention that the Israeli Army helped Agrexco sell its wares and in the process ruin the Lebanese peasants by imposing bothersome prohibitions, like forbidding them to sell their produce before 11 a.m. or seeing to it that Israeli produce is sold before allowing other sales. In my view, the major cause of outbreak of guerilla warfare in the occupied areas of Lebanon were such Israeli commercial practices. But corruption in Syria, then much greater than today, also played a role. Tzafrir recounts how Lebanese merchants trading in 1982–85 with Agrexco would re-export part of their purchases to Syria, in particular to Damascus, 'since Rifat Assad [Hafez Assad's brother, now exiled from Syria] then in charge of the Syrian trade, was amenable to anything when offered a suitable bribe'. I can confirm this information from my own sources, with the addition that the belated discovery of Rifat Assad's involvement in illicit trade with Israel was probably the main reason for his subsequent exile.

Naturally, after the 1985 Israeli withdrawal such forms of 'export' had to cease. Two cheap exports to Lebanon which survived withdrawal are salt, which according to Tzafrir is destined mainly for the Iraqi market and sugar, which according to my sources ends up in the Gulf states. The post-1985 Israeli exports to and via Lebanon can be said to be of a two-fold nature. On the one hand there are some cheap mass-produced items like eggs or poultry which in Israel are heavily subsidized and whose production is reserved for poor Jewish farmers, especially in the Galilee. The second category is made up by the more expensive vegetables, fruits (for example, avocados) and flowers, whose production is reserved for wealthy Jewish farmers. Most of the expensive produce is exported via Lebanon to the Gulf states where there are enough people of means to create a demand for them. Thus, Bergman tells stories about how Israeli mangoes are *de rigueur* in expensive restaurants in one Gulf Emirate, whereas Israeli roses are *de rigueur* for sumptuous weddings in another.

In other words, Israeli exports to the Arab countries have been since 1985 guided by the rules of apartheid. At the same time, the tame acceptance of Israeli apartheid practices by Arab upper classes is symptomatic of the community of interests between those classes and Israel. In Israel, agriculture is mainly run by the state and guided by racist principles which can be enforced readily because no one can farm anything without government permits whose distribution can be totally arbitrary. Let me quote some figures concerning those products which according to Bergman tend to be exported most to and via Lebanon since 1985. My figures are derived from *The Statistical Abstract of Israel, 1991* which provides the data for 1990 and which clearly distinguishes between what is produced on 'Jewish farms' and 'non-Jewish farms'. (The proportions recorded below have hardly changed since.) The data for the agricultural crops are in thousands of dunams of cultivated land:

	Jewish farms	Non-Jewish farms
Peas for canning	22.3	0
Cotton	319.0	0.8
Groundnuts	27.7	1.6
Avocado	98.5	1.0
Bananas	18.3	0
Roses	2.1	0
Poultry (in thousands of livestock)	26,990	250

No data about the production of eggs are provided in the *Abstract*, but in all likeliood they are roughly proportional to those concerning poultry.

These figures should be juxtaposed not only with the proportion of Arabs in Israel (about 17 per cent in 1990) but also with the ratio of Jewish to Arab farmers, excluding seasonal workers, employed in agriculture: 50,600 Jews compared to 20,300 Non-Jews (28.6 per cent).

Etty Hassid's article shows the complementary aspects of Israeli trade relations with Arab countries. She offers her conclusions in the very beginning of her article: 'Even though it may be hard to believe, the State of Israel is actively engaged in the drug trade, especially on its northern Lebanese borders. The participants are on one side the Israeli Army, Shabak, Mossad and the Israeli police and on the other side Lebanese drug merchants, Israeli Bedouins from the Negev and some retired [Israeli] senior officers. The operational principle is: We will close our eyes to all the filth you stoop to, and even give you money, if only you provide us with intelligence of interest to us. In my article I am going to prove it or at least to substantiate it as highly probable on the basis of the trials of large-scale drug merchants. Since I was forced by the censors to skip some facts, let me tell you that the realities are even more ghastly than what you can find here. True, what I do reveal is ghastly enough. It turns out that State of Israel, which professes to wage an uncompromising struggle with the epidemic of drug addiction, is in reality the largest-scale importer of drugs in the Middle East. It is as if we were trying with one hand to apprehend the drug users and peddlers, or at least pretending to do so, while using the other hand to plunge the syringe deep into the drug addict's veins.'

As evidence for this conclusion, Hassid uses the transcripts of secret trials of both Israelis and Lebanese charged with drug offenses. But she also says that 'in recent years a number of publications have appeared abroad disclosing information about involvement in the drug trade by individuals serving in the Israeli Security Services.' She discusses in detail only one such affair which she investigated by approaching the Israeli lawyers of one defendant so involved, Yosef Amit, formerly a major in the Military Intelligence Unit 504. According to a London magazine *Foreign Report* of July 1993, the unit was known as 'mini-Mossad'. As, may happen to people in 'the only democracy of the Middle East', Amit 'disappeared' in 1986 and even his name couldn't be mentioned in the media. Only after the *Foreign Report's* publication in London was it admitted in Israel that he was secretly sentenced to imprisonment for unspecified 'security offences'. However, he was imprisoned under luxurious conditions. Among his privileges, he was allowed to spend long hours in phone conversations with Hebrew press journalists to whom he professed his innocence. When they then queried the Israeli authorities they were told that Amit was insane. Renowned psychologists would confirm this diagnosis to any journalist concerned. For some unexplained reason, however, neither Amit's lawyers nor his family could ever see any document that would certify Amit's supposed insanity. Only after seven years were the journalists in question permitted to say they had had phone conversations with Amit, some (still unnamed) authorities and some (still unnamed) psychologists. Even after July 1993, the only fact disclosed was that his offence had had something to do with Lebanon. Moreover, the *Foreign Report* disclosures could still not be mentioned in Israel, the reason, as conjectured by Hassid, being that it described Military Intelligence Unit 504 as recruiting agents, particularly 'Arab ones', remunerated by hashish acquired in the course of 'special operations in the Bekaa district of Lebanon'. The drug was said to be stored in the unit's warehouse in Tel Aviv and then transferred to Cairo whenever needed. Neither Hassid nor *Foreign Report* provide any information as to whether such transfers were approved by the Egyptian authorities. Judging from clues provided by my sources, I would conjecture that the Egyptians (who profess their resolve to eradicate drug supplies) might well have been accomplices. According to Hassid, Amit's subordinate was caught selling hashish 'which was apparently derived from the Military Intelligence central stockpiles' for his own profit. Since 'suspicion rebounded on Amit' he was also charged.

Hassid reports that 'in the meantime Amit was released from prison, on condition of keeping silence. Really, however, he disappeared raising a lot of question marks about his actual fate.' Hassid has a tentative explanation of those 'question marks'. A journalist with whom often Amit communicated by phone from prison, Avi Valentin, wrote a novel entitled *The Lost Truth*. As a novel, it couldn't be banned. Its plot, summarized by Hassid, runs as follows. The novel's hero, Haggay Gur, 'resembles Yosef Amit' in biography, the character of Army service, his rank and 'even in the number of the children and their gender'. His job in Military Intelligence is to protect Bedouin caravans delivering hashish from Jordan to Egypt 'while extracting a share of the stuff for Military Intelligence'. Subsequently, he is transferred to make similar deals on the Lebanese border. Some of the thus acquired hashish is, according to the novel, 'processed by known criminals cooperating with Military Intelligence', into heroin and other hard drugs, which are used 'to pay Arab agents'. In my view some such practices may be routinely engaged in by Israeli Intelligence.

But Hassid had access to sources better than a novel: 'The idea of using drugs and overseeing and mediating enormous-scale drug deals in order to remunerate Arab collaborators with Israel, is confirmed by the so-called "police models", used in Israel and abroad. Such models are known to some people outside of officialdom involved in investigations of Lebanese drug affairs and trials before Israeli courts resulting from those investigations. The existence of such models was also disclosed in court protocols ultimately cleared for publication.' In Hassid's view the drug affairs which have reached the courts 'were only the tip of an iceberg' of the drug smuggling condoned by Israel. The trials nevertheless led to the disclosure of two 'police models' used 'by the Israeli Police, together with Lebanese Border Unit (LBU) and the special police unit "*Yahalom*" ["Diamond"], which jointly oversee the drug trade at enormous scale'. Those 'models' were explained to Hassid by advocate Meir Ziv who defended Colonel Meir Binyamin, a former LBU commander charged in 1989 with trading in hard drugs.

After a protracted trial in camera, Colonel Binyamin was acquitted by the court which accepted the argument that his undenied involvement in the drug trade was carried out under orders of his superiors and conformed to an 'officially accepted method of trading in drugs': 'Two Lebanese models were devised about ten years ago by a special division of [Israeli] Police called "Maman" [an acronym for "intelligence department"], in cooperation with the Attorney General's Office.' Their designer was Rafi Peled, then Deputy Commander of Maman who later advanced to the post of superintendent of the Israeli Police. (He had to resign from this job after less than one year, having been caught red-handed accepting a bribe from a hotel owner.) The approval of the Attorney General's Office was sought because the Police feared it may be in trouble if its complicity with crime remains uncovered: 'The first model is applied when an Israeli drug merchant asks the Police to either supply him with drugs of Lebanese origin or connect him with a Lebanese drug merchant. If the [Israeli] Police approve the request it becomes criminally liable on two counts: an incitement and involvement in drug trade. The second model is applied when an Israeli drug merchant approaches a Lebanese drug merchant who is an [Israeli] Police informer, and the Police help smuggle the merchandise across the border.' After some deliberations, the Attorney General's Office approved the two models under some conditions, such as e.g. 'if such a drug dealer is stuck in Israel, the Police will help him return the drugs to Lebanon.' It meant, however, that the Police 'condoned the deals in which Lebanese drug dealers were paid in hard currencies while in Israel which they exported to Lebanon'. The Police became concerned whether they themselves thereby didn't become also criminally liable by infringing on foreign currency-related laws. The Israeli Treasury okayed the procedure 'after being told that the deals with drug merchants are intended solely to improve the methods of suppressing the drug trade'.

However, it seems that the 'models' were not followed to the letter. Hassid's sources discovered that in 1988, when the Police's own Drug Division dealing with drug consumption in Israel had investigated the situation on the Lebanese border, it found that 'the [Lebanese] drug traders were not put under adequate surveillance during their stay in Israel.' In one case it was found that '100 kg. of heroin, which is but a small part of the usual traffic', couldn't be accounted for by the surveillance. No wonder Colonel Meir Binyamin could plausibly claim at his trial that 'in reality the Israeli authorities are manipulated by large-scale Lebanese drug traders exploiting their excellent relations with the [Israeli] Police for the sake of smuggling enormous quantities of drugs behind its back'. In substantiating this claim, two witnesses, both sub-contractors of a large-scale Lebanese drug tradesman Ramzi Nahara, 'both with long records of cooperation with Israel', testified that once they 'smuggled 250 kg. of heroin into Israel' in a single swoop. Hassid explains that 'such an amount suffices for up to a million retail doses of the drug'. Ramzi Nahara himself also testified. Hassid writes that he complained against the two models as limiting the extent of his profiteering and so forcing him, against his better judgement 'to make deals behind the back of the [Israeli] Police for the sake of profit maximization'. Hassid describes Nahara's deals in great detail. I have selected to cover here only one of his feats. A single transport, detected in Israel by sheer chance by the traffic police due to a minor traffic infraction, consisted of 3,000 kg. of hashish destined for re-export to Egypt. Let me quote on this occasion an opinion of the advocate Meir Ziv with which I concur entirely: 'The State of Israel is by far the largest importer of drugs into Israel. The importation is sponsored by the Police, under the hardly credible pretext that it will help catch drug offenders.'

Another of Hassid's sources was the well-known Jerusalemite advocate Avraham Bardugo 'who in recent years had represented many Lebanese drug dealers. Bardugo states firmly that in all major drug smuggling cases in which he represented the defendants, the Israeli Security System had in one or another way been itself involved.' To authenticate his claim he told Hassid about his representing Muhammad Biru, a Lebanese Shi'ite drug trader. In response to Hassid's queries '[Israeli] security sources described Biru as the largest-scale Lebanese drug trader.' Hassid opines that 'Biru's affair shows how intimately is the crime in South Lebanon intertwined with Israeli activities in that area'. In August 1989 Biru was kidnapped by the SLA and brought to Israel to stand trial. He was sentenced to 15 years of prison for a large and complex heroin deal made behind the back of the Police. Biru's heroin was smuggled across the border 'in a car of a Shabak agent codenamed "Assad"'. The transport was stumbled upon when it was about to be smuggled into the Gaza Strip. Biru keeps claiming that he had nothing to do with this particular deal. In spite of his imprisonment, 'Biru continues to make business in drugs from within the [Israeli] prison of Shatta.' Hassid reported that 'an Egyptian court sentenced Biru to death in absentia, and the Interpol is looking for him as well. One may ask why Israel wanted to hold Biru in its prison and to pay for years for his upkeep?' The question remains unanswered, except that, as Hassid notes, 'after Israel had kidnapped Sheikh Dirani, Hizbollah kidnapped Biru's son and son-in-law, accusing them of having helped Israel kidnap Dirani.' Biru's other lawyer, the previously mentioned advocate Ziv, told Hassid that Biru had asked him 'to approach for his sake the [Israeli] Health Minister Efraim Sneh. Apparently Biru and Sneh had amicable relations [during the latter's service in the army in the 1980s] when he was the commander of South Lebanon.'

The name of the Israeli advocate who told Hassid about another legal case is withheld. The case was that of a well-known SLA officer Ibrahim El-Sayad, who had been rising in rank until he became 'the commander of the Shi'ite battalion of the SLA, maintaining amicable relations with the SLA commander, General Lahad and various Israeli army officers'. El-Sayad was incapacitated after stepping on a Hizbollah mine. On recovery, he was appointed liaison officer with *Yahalom* and a 'senior partner' of those Israeli forces applying the two Lebanese models 'in South Lebanon, in plain clothes, of course'. At some point (the date banned by censorship) he was brought by force to Israel and sentenced to twelve years of prison: 'The charges against him were many, but only two have been cleared for publication. El-Sayad acted as an *agent provocateur* implicating the eventually convicted Major Hayim Shahar, a senior officer in the Israeli Army's Liaison Unit with South Lebanon and commander of "Fatma Gate", one of the important entry points between Israel and Lebanon. Exploiting this opportunity, Shahar smuggled enormous amounts of drugs to Israel. The second charge against El-Sayad had to do with November 1991 meeting with the highest Druze officer in the Israeli Army at that time, Colonel Mufir Mu'afak, who was later discharged from Army service.' If the Shahar affair remains shrouded in mystery, in regard to the Mu'afak affair Hassid was able to learn a lot, some of that from Mu'afak himself, who after four years of investigation had been tried, acquitted of all charges and discharged from the army.

Let me quote Hassid about Mu'afak at some length: 'The offices of the command of the Liaison Unit with South Lebanon are located in a building in Marjayoun [a town serving as 'capital' of the 'Security Zone'] two floors above Yahalom offices. One day El-Sayad mounted those two floors to meet Colonel Mu'afak. Sitting down on a chair in Mu'afak's office, El-Sayad told him: "We know that you are going to retire from the army soon. This is why we request you to help us transport 100 kg. of heroin into our area." Colonel Mu'afak became enraged and summoned his soldiers, who surrounded El-Sayad. Next he contacted the Yahalom office which sent men to arrest El-Sayad and interrogate him on the spot. El-Sayad admitted that he had made a proposal of this nature to Mu'afak but explained that he did so on orders of his superiors who sought evidence to enable them to put Mu'afak on trial. Yahalom functionaries, in their turn, did admit that they had used El-Sayad as an *agent provocateur* on other occasions, but denied that they had authorized him to act to implicate Mu'afak. The conclusion was that El-Sayad this time wanted to make a real drug deal. El-Sayad retorted: "Your real aim is to appease the Druze community in Israel. For that you are scapegoating me." To the disappointment of Shi'ites who served under El-Sayad's command he was brought to Israel. The ties between Israel and the Shi'ites of the Zone were by then strained: the case in this discussion is believed to have contributed to their complete severance. In Israel El-Sayad was put on trial before District Judge Zu'abi, who specialized in such cases.' (It may not be irrelevant to mention that Judge Zu'abi also served as a member of the Shamgar Inquiry Committee investigating the Goldstein massacre in Hebron.) 'Since no drugs were found on El-Sayad, his trial in camera focused on the meaning of what he said to Mu'afak, especially on the words "our area". If those words referred to Lebanon an Israeli court had no power to deal with the case. After this question was resolved, the court began deliberating whether El-Sayad acted as an *agent provocateur* or as a drug dealer.

'El-Sayad wanted to prove the former by describing the methods he had used while working for Yahalom. But here he encountered a difficulty. The Police Minister issued an order of secrecy in the name of protecting state security, as rigid as had never before been issued in the history of Israeli judiciary. The lawyers for the defence were prohibited by that order from summoning witnesses or referring to issues other than those approved by the Minister in advance. On top of that, the defendant was prohibited from testifying in his own defence on anything he had done in the past. On the other hand, the prosecution encountered no obstacles in summoning Nassif Biru, Muhammad Biru's oldest son to testify against El-Sayad. Under cross-examination by the defence, Nassif Biru admitted that he was still overseeing the world-wide drug dealings of the Biru family, while collaborating with Israeli authorities, in particular with the Yahalom unit. In the latter capacity he helped supply evidence needed to convict Major Hayim Shahar. We cannot reveal anything else about this part of his testimony.'

In another part of Nassif Biru's testimony there was revelation which 'stunned those who fancied themselves as knowledgeable about the Biru family's affairs. After Muhammad Biru was sentenced to 15 years, his family petitioned the Supreme Court for the right to visit him in prison. The State of Israel objected, arguing that visits should not be allowed, because Muhammad Biru continued to direct the drug traffic from within the prison. Incidentally, the state's objection applied in particular to the visits of Muhammad's son Nassif.' Unfortunately, censorship banned the publication of the Supreme Court's deliberations of this case; this is why nothing can be said about the nature of its response to the state's argument: 'Strangely enough, in his testimony in the El-Sayad case, Muhammad Biru, who was also a state witness, testified that his son Nassif was after all allowed to visit him in prison, on condition of being accompanied by security agents in plain clothes. The latter even took him out to luxurious nightclubs and other fleshpots where they entertained themselves together most amicably, except that the security agents kept trying to persuade him to talk.' The censors didn't let it be specified what was he supposed to talk about. Hassid speculates that 'they expected information about some sort of targets in Lebanon'.

Hassid assures her readers that there have been many other incidents which she couldn't disclose. She concludes: 'The apparent conclusion from those affairs is that the entire Israeli Security System – that is, the Police, Shabak, Mossad, Military Intelligence and such units as operate independently – are involved in drug deals. The supposed aims of those deals are to capture drug merchants, to obtain security-related information, money and whatever else that can be conceived. Methods used in such deals create a situation no less sensitive, lethal and explosive than nitroglycerine. Israel's needs, real or imaginary, are compromised through gangsters' account-settling, through vendettas between clans, through the untrammelled pursuit of profits, and so on. In the name of these sacred aims the State of Israel is either closing its eyes to, or even actively cooperating with and encouraging the drug trade on an enormous scale ... Regardless of other factors, performance of this type is bound to corrupt deeply the Security System officers involved. It cannot be assumed that every single Israeli Army or Intelligence officer can resist the temptation of pocketing huge sums of money likely to be offered to him by professional drug dealers. Let me ask: has it been calculated what proportion of drugs available on Israeli market were imported under the patronage of the Police, Army or other Security branches? Some reputable Israeli lawyers are perfectly willing to testify under oath that Israel is the largest-scale importer of heroin into its own territory.

'The Israeli Army spokesman requested by me to comment on some issues tangential to this article, refused adamantly. He only said: "All this is claptrap".' Together with the mentioned ban on further disclosures, this comment is in my view the best confirmation of the accuracy of Hassid's revelations.

The Mu'afak affair had an interesting sequel. After about four years in detention he was recently completely exonerated and freed. He then described in interviews to the Hebrew papers a method of interrogation which had been used against him. He was brought every morning at 8 a.m. to some office in Tel Aviv where an interrogator would ask him whether he wanted to confess. On his refusal, he would be handcuffed and chained to the chair he was sitting on until 4 p.m. During that time the handcuffs would be once removed to let him have lunch and he would be allowed to go the restroom under guard, but only 'infrequently'. This went on for eight months, six days a week. (Torture is in Israel not inflicted on Saturdays except in emergency cases, so that the Jewish torturers would not violate the Sabbath.) I have two comments on the story. First, the form of 'moderate physical pressure' (as torture is officially referred to in Israel) applied against Colonel Mu'afak was indeed moderate if compared to torture routinely applied against non-Jews. For example, others are being chained to a very small chair rather than to an ordinary one, so as to inflict more pain. Secondly, no Jew charged with drug offences, spying or security offenses in the last thirty years has ever complained of being tortured. Like so much else in Israel, the use of torture is subject to rules of apartheid: applicable only to non-Jews, no matter what their Army rank may be.

The facts described in this report warrant some general conclusions. First, Israeli agricultural produce re-exported from Lebanon to other Arab countries must transit through Syria. Considering the bulkiness of the commodities and their uninterrupted flow, their transit cannot take place without the connivance of Syrian authorities, probably in return for payments. There exists some evidence that some cheaper produce, in particular eggs, are in fact destined for the Syrian market. After all, in recent years not a few Israeli Jews with double citizenship have visited Syria. Some of them do speak Arabic, so that they were in the position to engage in friendly conversations with people in the bazaars of Syrian cities. They noticed that Israeli eggs are commonly on display in these bazaars, and that both buyers and sellers were aware of their Israeli origin, even though this fact is never mentioned in the strictly controlled Syrian media. The same happens with textiles. This fact casts some light on an usually ignored aspect of Syrian-Israeli relations: namely that there exists covert cooperation alongside overt hostility. The same is the case in Israeli relations with Arab countries with which Israel is trading. This cooperation is not a side-effect of 'the peace process' with the Palestinians, the best proof being that it existed earlier and independently from it. The trade in question proves, contrary to the conventional wisdoms, that Israeli policies are regional in nature and that Israeli oppression of the Palestinians is only one and not even the most important aspect of those policies.

Israeli involvement in the drug trade warrants even more important conclusions in regard to the nature of political realities in the Middle East. In the first place, we should bear in mind the date when the two Israeli Police 'models' were approved. The conclusion is inescapable that Israeli involvement in drug trafficking in Lebanon was initiated by the 'national unity government' formed after the 1984 elections, that is, by the twin architects of 'the peace process', Shimon Peres who then became Prime Minister and his Defence Minister, Yitzhak Rabin.

Second, there are grounds to suspect that Israeli encouragement of the drug trade and consequently also of drug consumption, cannot be entirely explained by the categories of acquiring intelligence, extending influence and reaping profits. Part of the motivation must have been to weaken the disaffection of Middle Eastern masses with policies of their governments (Israeli and Arab alike) by encouraging drug addiction and thereby political apathy. The suspicion can be buttressed if we consider the effects of Israeli succour for Lebanese drug traffickers upon the Lebanese population (a factor which Hassid probably is not allowed to discuss by censorship), and the well-known facts about the encouragement of Palestinian drug dealers by Israeli occupation authorities. The coddling of Palestinian drug dealers was one of the reasons of the outbreak for the Intifada, but it was resumed in 1991.

Lastly, massive involvement of Israeli Intelligence in drug trafficking must be well known to (and is probably approved by) its American opposite numbers. Ample precedents for that exist. During the Vietnam War the CIA was engaged in encouraging its allies in drug trafficking. Moreover, US indirect support for the Israeli drug trade is much safer than direct involvement in this business. If Israeli involvement in the drug trade were exposed in the US, some powerful organizations such as the American Israeli Political Action Committee (AIPAC) and organized American Jewry in general would scream bloody murder. A lot of American liberals, usually happy to denounce American Intelligence for encouraging drug traffickers, would protest if Israeli Intelligence were denounced for anything. The combined influence of organized American Jews and such pseudo-liberals upon the US media is immeasurable. The invasion of Panama was said to be launched for the sake of suppressing the drug trade: yet well-documented Israeli connections with Noriega passed almost unnoticed in the US. It can therefore be tentatively presumed that in its encouragement of drug traffic and traffickers, as in much else, Israel acts as a proxy executor of the American will. This would at least partly explain why this policy works.

But it works for another reason as well. All reporting on Lebanese affairs since the Israeli withdrawal to the borders of the 'Zone' in June 1985 has been subject to censorship then imposed by Peres. Since then Hebrew press journalists can enter the 'Zone' only in exceptional instances. As Ron Ben-Yishay (*Yediot Ahronot*, 17 August) wrote, the censorship run by the Northern Command of the Israeli Army in charge of Lebanese affairs (in place of Israeli censorship), is strict enough to see to it that 'very little information reaches the [Israeli] public', and that 'senior government officials can never be sure if they indeed have all relevant information.' Ben-Yishay says that 'it is difficult to understand how the Chief-of-Staff lets the Northern Command commander treat Lebanon as his private estate and use his military censorship to deny the Israeli public meaningful information.' Ben-Yishay also noted 'a suspicion angrily voiced by a senior government minister in Jerusalem that "sometimes it is Hizbollah which tells the truth"'.

Finally, the reluctance of most Arab intellectuals to discuss the issue of drug addiction in their society plays into Israeli hands and only helps Israel encourage Arab drug addiction. Generalized and often incorrect claims about Israeli 'subversion of the Arab culture' cannot substitute for the badly needed open and democratic discussion of the issues. Israeli policies depend on cooperation and support not only of the Arab regimes but also of some social classes in Arab society. Far from proving that Israel is 'an alien body in the Middle East' as many Arab intellectuals like to claim, Israeli policies show that Israel is adapting remarkably successfully to what is worst in the Middle East and that it knows how to exploit it to its advantage. Boycotts (whether real or faked) didn't stop Israeli trade in agricultural produce and will not help against Israeli encouragement of the drug traffic. The only way of effectually opposing such policies is the implementation of democracy in general and freedom of expression in particular, because only in this way can real issues be analysed and effective remedies devised.

Part IV

AMERICAN JEWS

11

Israel and the Organized American Jews
20 September 1993

The politically prodigious and financially unprecedented support
which Israel has received from the US since the early 1960s can
be attributed to two reasons. On the one hand, Israeli policies do
serve American interests, not only in the Middle East but all over
the world. Whenever the US finds it inconvenient to get directly
involved in a particularly unsavoury act, for example, in supporting
a regime or an organization whose reputation is particularly heinous,
Israel comes in handy to do the job on the US's behalf. On the other
hand, Israel wields a tremendous influence within the US, in my
view regardless of whether Israeli policies accord with US interests
or not. Although to some extent this can be attributed to the
support Israel receives from many strains of Christian
fundamentalism, there is no doubt in my mind that its primary
reason is the role performed by the organized Jewish community
in the US in backing Israel and its policies. The proportion of
organized Jews within the body of US Jewry can be roughly
estimated as close to 50 per cent. Here I will describe the newly
emerging strained relations between the organized American Jews
and the Rabin regime, and their impact on possible shifts in the
extent of Israeli influence upon US policies.
   Curiously, Canada represents a case where influence of its
organized Jewish community upon that country's policies is even
more palpable than in the US. The effect is that, although Canada's
interests in the Middle Eastern are quite secondary, its dedication
to Israel surpasses even that of the US. In both countries, major
Jewish organizations support Israel as loyally and unconditionally
as the Communist parties for so long used to in regard to the
USSR. Israelis are well-aware that the chauvinism and fanaticism
of organized Jews in those two countries in supporting Israel
exceeds by far the chauvinism of the average Israeli Jew.
   Why should some American Jews be so inclined to pro-Israeli
chauvinism? The first factor is the exclusivism of Jewish
organizations. They do not admit non-Jews in their ranks and
draw social and therefore also political power from that fact. Those
who can be called 'organized Jews' spend most of their leisure time

solely in the company of other Jews, thus upholding Jewish exclusivism and, as a natural consequence, reinforcing their Jewish chauvinism. Amounting to no more than 3 per cent of the US population, it would be impolitic of them to express openly their real attitudes toward non-Jews in the US. An exercise of their influence in support of Israel as the 'Jewish state' compensates them for this constraint upon freedom of their expression.

Let me describe the current relations between Israel and the organized American Jews. Yo'av Karni (*Ha'olam Ha'ze*, 8 September) describes a new and important stage in these relations which began with the rise of the Rabin government to power in Israel, but was prepared by American sympathizers of Labor even earlier. Karni fully concurs with my assessment of chauvinism and, more importantly, of the totalitarian streak manifested by organized American Jews. He quotes the words of Norman Podhoretz, the editor of the journal *Commentary*, to the effect that 'Israel needs criticism as much as the Sahara desert needs sand'. Karni treats this as descriptive of the opinion of organized US Jewry for years. Incidentally, *Commentary* is affiliated with the American Jewish Committee, which in the US has the reputation of being a 'liberal organization'. I find it hard to imagine an American liberal saying that any other state, and particularly the US, 'needs criticism as much as the Sahara desert needs sand'. It is only if they belong to the ranks of organized Jewry and says it about Israel that their liberalism may remain unquestioned. But, as Karni notes, the same Podhoretz, first among the better-known organized Jews, began in April 1993 to oppose viciously the Rabin government, to the point of casting doubt over whether this government 'is loyal to the Jewish people'. It had obviously never crossed Podhoretz's mind that Israeli governments are legally obliged to be loyal to the State of Israel and its laws, as Israeli ministers undertake in an oath they give upon taking office. In my view, there can hardly be a better illustration of the contrast between Israeli law, however grim are the discriminations it prescribes, and the expectations of Jewish chauvinists in the US. But why did Podhoretz change his attitudes about criticizing Israel in the first place? According to Karni, the reason was that 'a criticism such as his, unlike that of the doves made against the Shamir government, could not encourage the anti-Semites.' While, in my view, Jews, like all other human beings, have an obligation to speak their minds with all candour, and without concerning themselves over whether a particular view of theirs may or may not encourage anti-Semitism, I also think that nothing I can imagine does actually encourage the anti-Semites more than the opinions of Norman Podhoretz.

With 'the exception of the "Who is a Jew?" issue', over which the Reform Movement shepherded a rather timid protest campaign against the threat of enacting in Israel a law which would in effect define a large part of their movement as non-Jews, Karni cannot recall any other occasion when organized American Jews would oppose any Israeli policies. He recalls how their support of the extremist positions of Golda Meir, Menachem Begin and Yitzhak Shamir surpassed in zeal all such manifestations in Israel. He finds it even more important to note that respectable American organized Jews show no restraint in abusing not only, say, Jews who support the right of the Palestinians for self-determination and their state, but also faithful Laborites who oppose such self-evident rights. For evidence of this, he relies on the experience of an organization named *Nishma* [in Hebrew 'We shall hear'] set up some years ago by Laborites to make their views legitimate in the eyes of the organized US Jews. Nothing can better illustrate the rabid militarism and total-itarianism of the latter than the methods resorted to by Nishma at Shamir's time in order to publicize its views. For the most part it avoided expressing them directly. Instead, it invited Israeli colonels and generals in the reserves to lecture or write articles for its organ. One of generals in the reserves whom Nishma used extensively for the purpose, was the ex-commander of Israeli Military Intelligence, Shlomo Gazit, who advocated the toughest possible repression of the Palestinians unless they give in to Israeli demands; but who nevertheless did support the autonomy plan. Karni says that this recourse of Nishma to the cult of the military can be explained by 'the founders of Nishma's sophisticated approach to grappling with the instinctive urges of US Jews'. Their last propaganda effort was a pamphlet displaying on its cover a photo of Rabin in the Chief of Staff's uniform against the background of a 1967 battlefield. The caption under the photo claimed that 'no one knows better than Yitzhak Rabin' what Israel needs. It can be safely presumed that in Israel a photo with such a caption could only be an object of ridicule.

Karni, who is an Israeli Jew, scoffs at what he calls the 'Yitzhak-is-always-right pamphlet'. He recalls that Rabin 'is the man who 24 years ago proposed to wipe out all Egyptian cities located close to the [Suez] Canal from the earth's surface; who 19 years ago did everything he might to encourage the growth of Gush Emunim; who twelve years ago foreclosed the chances of his own party's return to power to make sure that Shimon Peres would not be Prime Minister; who eleven years ago supported the devastation of Lebanon, and who five years ago virtually stupefied the friends of Israel in the US by ordering the Israeli army soldiers "to break the bones" [of Palestinian detainees]'. The enthusiasm with which Nishma tries to sell Rabin in the US can only arouse suspicion.' Karni nevertheless notes that Rabin's is the first Israeli government which is not only openly criticized but also abused amongst organized American Jews. An AIPAC leader, 'a dealer in used cars in Florida' by profession, went public by referring to Israeli Deputy Foreign Minister Yossi Beilin as 'scum', even though he was subsequently forced to resign as a result. Karni quotes some Jewish hate letters, all equipped with sender's slips which the Nishma director, Tom Smerling, keeps in his office. One of them, while 'returning the "Yitzhak-is-always-right pamphlet" reads: "Rabin in effect murders the Jews. The time has come to kill him." A retired colonel of the US Army, now a lawyer in a New York Jewish neighbourhood, after placing on his stationery a pathologically abusive set of imprecations about some sponsors of the pamphlet, refers to Yossi Beilin as "that kind of filth", and follows it by asking the Nishma directors: "Can you at all tell the difference between a rifle and a teaspoon?"' And so on and so forth.

Let me here parenthetically add a personal recollection concerning hate letters which some American Jews are capable of writing. In 1974, after I was invited by the Dutch Association in Support of Palestinian Rights for a speaking tour addressing only human rights issues, in Holland, I was attacked by Amnon Rubinstein (now a minister in the Rabin government on behalf of Meretz). He demanded, unsuccessfully, that I should be dismissed from my position at the Hebrew University for expressing my views within the limits of the Israeli law. After Rubinstein's attack on me I received 1081 hate letters within two months. (They continued coming except that I ceased to count them.) Only 36 were in Hebrew and 3 in French: the remaining 1042 were in English. Almost all of their senders provided their US addresses and indentified themselves as Jews. They showed a complete ignorance of the matters at issue, confining themselves to calling me an enemy of Israel or of the Jews, or a 'self-hating Jew'. All of them wrote, however, that they 'were reliably informed' that I was a Holocaust survivor and hence my 'treason' was particularly heinous. Some deplored that I had not been exterminated while others expressed a rather curious view that had I been exterminated, 'a better' or 'more loyal' Jew could have been saved instead of me. Obviously Smerling has much to learn about hate letters which organized US Jews are capable of writing.

Smerling claims that the letters he showed Karni 'are more abusive than those his organization used to receive in the years he was criticizing the Israeli government' under Shamir. Their vehemence took him by surprise since he had taken the trouble to publicize it widely that 'Nishma was already supported by the [Israeli] government. What a delight now! Our relations with the [Israeli] embassy in Washington have dramatically improved. The embassy staff have become wonderful. They had campaigned against us in the Jewish community before, whereas now they are first to appreciate our efforts to help the US understand the recent changes in the Middle East.' Smerling says that he has always supported the right of diaspora Jews to criticize Israel, but Karni qualifies it by observing that his attitude was dictated not by support of the freedom of expression as a principle, but by Jewish national interest: 'When you see your Jewish brother injuring himself', says Smerling, 'you are duty-bound to help him by raising your voice.' Karni says that 'the problem is that different Jews have different opinions about "injury to oneself". Some believed that Yitzhak Shamir was injuring himself, while others claimed that he was doing his best to advance his own and other Jews' cause. And the same goes for Rabin.' For a long time I have believed, and I suspect Karni shares this belief, that the opinions of organized US Jews, whether they support Rabin or Shamir, are bound to remain anti-democratic as long as they are based solely on considerations of Jewish national interest.

As the formation of Nishma proves, the sages of the Israeli Labor Party anticipated long ago the troubles to be caused by the chauvinism of organized American Jews. By July 1993 the Hebrew press was already quite apprehensive about the noxious impact of organized American Jewry upon Israeli policies. Let me mention two writings in this vein. Orri Nir, then *Haaretz* correspondent in Washington, reported (6 July) a frantic appeal of US Jews to 'the Israeli government' to open a campaign intended to 'restore the harmony' between that government and themselves, which was sadly upset of late. Otherwise, comments Nir, 'they would continue to perceive Labor as an interlude between the two Likud governments.' After recounting some scandals within AIPAC, like the forced resignation of its director, Tom Dine (which in Nir's view was particularly detrimental because it was reported at length in the *New York Times*), and deploring 'the plight in which AIPAC finds itself these days', he proceeds to his main point: 'A major part of the organized Jewish community in the US, including some activists who form the real backbone of AIPAC, have not yet accommodated themselves to changes in policies of the new [Israeli] government. After more than a year, many US Jews still disdain the Rabin government as deficient in displaying as much proper Jewish pride as they would expect. In their view this government is weak, and by making unnecesary concessions it betrays the sacrosanct interests of the Jewish people in their own patrimony. Through years of Likud rule the US Jews learned a sequence of Pavlovian reflexes: "Never withdraw, say no to any American pressure on Israel, no to any contacts with any representatives of the Palestinian diaspora, no to contacts with any Palestinian representatives from East Jerusalem, no to any improvement of US relations with any Arab state." Official representatives of the Likud government kept telling Jewish activists in the US day and night that Israel's survival depends on making all these noes effective.' Let me clarify that by saying 'long years of Likud rule', Nir also means the period of the 'National Unity Government' (1984–90), when Labor was an equal partner in the government and fully supported all these 'noes'.

Nir approves the fact that 'the Washington-based leadership of AIPAC accommodates itself to changes on the political agenda of the new Israeli leadership', but, like a real Bolshevik, deplores AIPAC's inability to impose its authority over 'the 55,000 AIPAC activists scattered all over the US whose accommodation to those changes is much slower'. Unless the American Jews so accommodate themselves, they can in his view damage Israel badly, when 'an administration with a "Jewish connection" as firm as Clinton's sits in the White House. Since Clinton feels so committed to the Jewish vote and even more to Jewish campaign donations, Jewish opinion has a great importance. A danger exists that the present US administration may stop heeding the voice of US Jewry as carefully as heretofore.' In order to avert this danger, Nir proposes several measures closely resembling the Nishma methods, like sending 'people with authority in security affairs, plenty of generals', to educate the US Jews, because their prestige in the eyes of US Jews remains intact, while that of the Rabin government sadly does not.

A deeper, but still unsatisfactory insight came from the pen of Meron Benvenisti writing for *Haaretz* (15 July). His opinions deserve to be quoted at length. After noting that 'the Jewish American community' bears no less responsibility than anybody else for 'the status quo' in the Territories, Benvenisti proceeds to describe this community's ways of influencing US policies. He recalls that 'when the [US] mission headed by Denis Ross came to Jerusalem, a Hebrew paper [*Maariv*] described it as "the mission of four Jews", and gloated with pride while talking about the Jewish and even Israeli roots of all its members.' Other papers did likewise. The 'Israeli roots' of those US diplomats comprising what went under the name of a 'peace mission' included the fact that a son of one of them was said to be studying in a Hesder Yeshiva, to receive military training there. He was also said to be a sympathizer of Gush Emunim and was awaiting the opportunity to serve in the Israeli Army in the Territories. Benvenisti's comment is that 'the ethnic origin of American diplomats sent here to promote peace may be irrelevant, but it is hard to ignore the fact that manipulation of the peace process was entrusted by the US in the first place to American Jews, and that at least one member of the State Department team was selected for the task because he represented the views of American Jewish establishment. The tremendous influence of the Jewish establishment upon the Clinton administration found its clearest manifestation in redefining the "occupied territories" as "territories in dispute". The Palestinians are understandably angry. But lest they be accused of anti-Semitism, they cannot, God forbid, talk about Clinton's "Jewish connection". After all, for its own purposes, the PLO wants anything as much as to keep its lines of communication with the Jewish community in the US open, because it perceives that community as so formidably powerful. Let it be recalled that Arafat chose in 1988 a delegation of American Jews as a channel to publicize his decision to recognize Israel, because he believed that only via them might he gain some legitimacy for himself.' Like the rulers of Third World countries whom I mentioned earlier, Arafat seems to have firmly believed in the myth of the Protocols of the Elders of Zion.

Benvenisti acknowledges that 'Israel benefits from Jewish influence', but he also points to the resultant dangers: 'The uncontrollability of the American Jewish establishment, together with its presumption that it represents Israeli interests "better" than Israel's elected government does, should be a matter for concern because American Jewish leaders tend to be more hawkish than the present leaders of Israel are.' Benvenisti observes that 'their involvement in Israeli politics was recognized long ago as legitimate.' He also discusses their increasing financial support for the Israeli parties and movements as a manifestation of legitimacy. Even more importantly, he indicates the difference between Israeli Jews and organized US Jewry: 'The Jewish community in Israel is a sovereign body, its membership is determined by binding state laws and it bears full responsibility for its fate in every walk of life. US Jewry is a voluntary body, has power only over those who choose to accept its authority and even this power is limited in scope. Whoever wants to bear full responsibility should come and bear it here. Those who prefer to bear only a partial or marginal responsibility are free to choose so, provided they do not demand for themselves a status they do not qualify for.' It is rather curious that after defining the American Jewry as 'a voluntary body', Benvenisti deplores its 'uncontrollability'. But in Zionism such paradoxes abound.

It can be seen that for Benvenisti only Jewish citizens of Israel count as 'the people of the state', as it used to be said when the state religion was a condition for exercise of any political rights. Whatever their legal status, all non-Jewish Israeli citizens are in his eyes entitled to no more than toleration, such as accorded to the Jews before their emancipation. Needless to say, had anyone applied Benvenisti's implicit assumptions about the Israeli non-Jews to the Jews in the US, he would be accused of anti-Semitism. A conclusion to be drawn from Benvenisti's attitude is that the influence of organized US Jews in Israel poses an insoluble problem as long as Israel remains 'a Jewish state'. No palliative measures can have any effect. That influence is going to last no matter how many Israeli generals are sent on propaganda missions to please US Jewish hawks.

The financial support of the US Jews is not distributed equitably among Israeli political parties. The right-wing Tzomet ('Junction') party, for example, does not solicit money abroad as a matter of principle. By paring down its expenses and relying on volunteer labour, it manages to sustain itself only with the allowances that each party with seats in the Knesset has the legal right to receive. By contrast, Likud, the religious parties, Gush Emunim and other extremist groups depend primarily on financial support from Jews living outside Israel. To all appearances, most of that support comes from English-speaking countries, an exception being the Shass party which gets support from France and Morocco. The Hebrew press reported that after Netanyahu was elected as Likud leader, he used to spend most of his weekends on fund-raising tours in the US and other English-speaking countries. But however organizations under his direct control benefit from such tours, Likud gets less such money than the more extreme organizations. For most weathy right-wing diaspora-Jews, Likud is now not extremist enough, as a result of which they now prefer to contribute to other recipients.

Let me quote from a report by the *Jerusalem Post* New York correspondent Sue Fishkoff (1 August), the gist of which also appeared in the Hebrew press. Although her report reads as if borrowed from the Protocols of the Elders of Zion, there is no reason to suspect its accuracy: 'Convinced that mainstream American Jewish organizations, notably the Conference of Presidents and AIPAC, have lost their effectiveness, an international group of powerful, affluent Jews has created a new organization dedicated to preserving Israel's security and territorial integrity.' It is named the World Committee for Israel (WCI) and 'headquartered in New York'. Fishkoff named some of the richest Jews of the world as affiliated with the WCI, including the leaders of the Syrian, Egyptian and Moroccan Jewish communities in the US, as well as some of the wealthiest Jews in Britain and other English-speaking countries.

One of the WCI's founders, Dr Manfred Lehmann of Miami, told Fishkoff that 'we are an affluent group. We are not looking for donations and we won't be doing fundraising.' He added that 'the organization was founded by Sephardic [that is, 'Oriental'] and Ashkenazi leaders, marking the first time that both diaspora communities have joined forces to make a single, united statement to Israel: "We are saying that the Rabin government must understand that any decision about the Land of Israel must have the approval of Jews in the Diaspora. Shimon Peres, Shulamit Aloni, Yossi Sarid - they are falling all over each other in their rush to offer Jerusalem, the Golan Heights and Gaza to the Arabs. But who has given them the legal, moral and historic right to give away Jewish land?"' Indeed, in terms of authentic Zionism, as also reflected in the Israeli 'Law of Return', Lehmann is certainly right. After all, the Zionist doctrine postulates that 'the Land of Israel' belongs to all the Jews, not only to those who happen to live on it. But, for a considerable time Likud has failed to stand by these sacrosanct principles, whether in deed or even in words. I cannot recall in the last 16 years a single speech by Begin, Shamir or Netanyahu that would reaffirm that 'any decision about the Land of Israel must have the approval of Jews in the Diaspora'.

The WCI may thus be said to be a guardian of ideological traditions which in the early 1970s were accepted unquestioningly both in Israel and in the Diaspora. While the bulk of Israelis have explicitly or tacitly transcended those traditions under the impact of the military stalemate of the 1973 war and the Lebanese debacle, many diaspora Jews have stood by them faithfully to this very day. The WCI may be therefore expected to donate money only to those Israeli groups with views according with those dominant in the early 1970s, that is, to religious settlers and assorted Messianists, but not to Likud. It may be mentioned that the Shass Party's spiritual leader, Rabbi Ovadia Yosef, 'has given his stamp of approval to the WCI. He offered a taped statement to them, indicating his growing dismay at the territorial concessions envisaged by the Rabin government, and suggesting that Shass will not agree to them.'

The publication of the Oslo Accord sparked a long-anticipated crisis in the Rabin government's relations with the majority of organized US Jews. This was why on Friday, 10 September, the Hebrew press devoted a huge amount of space to discuss the reactions of the US Jews to the news that the Israeli government violated all the taboos it had upheld until a short while earlier. For reasons of space, let me confine myself to a discussion of three articles published by *Haaretz* on that day. Emmanuel Sivan, a Hebrew University professor and an expert on Islam, who is on good terms with the Israeli establishment, begins his article by recounting two stories from his life which clearly bother him, but which in his view are descriptive of 'the deep strain' existing in the relations between Israel and organized US Jews. Let me quote these stories verbatim: 'In mid-August I received a letter from Mr G. L. Greenberg of Seattle, Washington State, who apparently is a major donor to the institution in which I am employed. He enclosed a clipping from the *New York Times* quoting some criticism of my authorship of certain aspects of the "Accountability Operation". "It is deplorable", wrote Mr Greenberg, "that the Hebrew University is either unwilling or unable to inculcate its employees in an amount of pride and respect for the State of Israel, sufficient to make them

realize that anything they may say might damage Israel. I have
contributed to the Hebrew University for years, but from now I
no longer will give it even ten cents to be used for a salary of
someone petulant enough to besmirch Israel's good name. I hope
you will understand the reason of my decision to discontinue
donations to your employer."

'In the process of replying to Mr Greenberg, I realized that the
right wing [of the US Jewish community] has no monopoly in
resorting to such methods. Years ago, Michael Lerner, the editor
of a Jewish bimonthly journal [*Tikkun*] published in San Francisco,
commissioned from me an article analysing some developments in
the Israeli–Arab conflict. Two weeks after I delivered my work, the
editor phoned to tell me that the article was OK, provided it were
supplemented by two or three paragraphs upbraiding the Shamir
government's response to the described developments. I told him
I disagreed because the article was analytical and already contained
parts critical enough. "But your critism is too tame", argued the
editor. "It must be more direct and emphatic. Do you know what
we might do? You will add just one really juicy paragraph, and I
will double your fee. Can we call it a deal?" I hung up the receiver.'

Digressing for a moment from Sivan's story, I have two
observations. The first is personal: I have the honour to be the first
Hebrew University professor whose 'besmirchings' have provoked
a spate of letters of protest from organized US Jews to the university,
even more hostile in their tone than the letter quoted by Sivan. Many
such letters, or copies of letters written to the university, or vice
versa, were also addressed directly to me. Unlike Sivan, I refused
to answer any of them. I left the job to the university authorities,
who persevered honourably to stand by my right (within the
limitations imposed by Israeli law) to speak my mind, regardless
of the financial losses incurred in their defence of this right of their
employees. When letters from English-speaking countries protesting
my continuing employment by the Hebrew University rose to an
avalanche, the University thoughtfully prepared a form letter to send
to all such protesters in reply. There was only one instance when
I reacted personally. It was when some Jewish chemistry professors
in the US, headed by the Nobel prize winner H. C. Brown, in
addition to objecting to my employment out of their chauvinism,
cast doubt upon my professional competence. I then asked some
West German organic chemists not only to speak up in defence of
my rights, but also to send letters to the Hebrew University and
to H. C. Brown attesting to my qualifications for my job. The
intended effect was achieved: the Jewish professors of chemistry
in the US were thus silenced.

Sivan is undoubtedly right when he says that 'liberals' among
organized US Jews have totalitarian leanings no less strong than

overt chauvinists. In this, my second observation, I would go even further than Sivan and say that, much as I abhor the journal *Commentary*, I abhor *Tikkun* even more for its sanctimonious hypocrisy and for its methodical mendacity about everything that concerns Judaism. I prefer to deal with the overt chauvinism of a Podhoretz who is at least intelligible, than with 'the politics of meaning' of a Lerner devoid of any meaning and therefore more dangerous. Sivan is right in pointing to an attitude shared by nearly the entire organized US Jewish community which most Israeli Jews find increasingly intolerable: namely to the former's conviction that they can buy the latter, or even that they have bought them already. Sivan perceives the financial benefits derived by Israel from the donations of US Jews as 'a necessary evil', acceptable 'during the first years of Israel's existence or during the crisis in the aftermath of 1973. But by now the volume of the United Jewish Appeal (UJA) collections is already smaller, not to mention the fact that about 60 per cent of its revenues are destined for local [Jewish] organizations.' According to news items sporadically appearing in the Hebrew press, far less than the remaining 40 per cent ever reaches Israel. It is difficult to trace what happens to those funds. Sivan hints that 'the sums which do reach Israel should not be downplayed because for the most part they are used to finance the fund-starved sectors of education, welfare and health, with the effect that such [Israeli] budget increments can sometimes determine the survival of an institution. Still, after the American guarantees, the value of the Appeal's funding is declining steadily.' This is at best a half-truth. Since 1975, Israeli governments, especially those of Labor, starve the sectors of education (particularly higher education), welfare and health on purpose, one of their motives being to maintain the discrimination of Palestinians who are Israeli citizens in those sectors. Only Jewish citizens (with a token addition of some Druzes) can benefit from UJA money. When the financing of education, welfare and health is to some extent entrusted to the UJA, the standard-of-living gap between Jews and Arabs in Israel can be preserved. The 'Jewish state' can thus remain 'Jewish', or at least Zionist. But it is true that the funds which Israel has been obtaining from the UJA have since long been paltry when compared to the amounts received from the federal budget of the US. The role of the UJA is political: it helps AIPAC and other bodies of organized US Jewry to force the 97 per cent of the non-Jewish US citizens to contribute to Israel indirectly through the medium of their federal taxes. This method is more efficient than relying on the goodwill of the organized half of 3 per cent of the Jewish citizens for voluntary donations.

Sivan expects peace to be immensely profitable to Israel in financial terms. Accordingly, he thinks that once peace is reached,

Israel could and should dispense with such methods of securing its revenues. This idea has nothing to do with discrimination against non-Jews, which he does not even mention. If anything, his thinking reflects the emotions of the new power elite in Israel. He strongly resents the humiliation, when 'in order to get money from the Appeal, we need to display to them our wounds, our defects and the poorest among us. For that purpose, our most heroic generals need to recount stories of their deeds under personal danger, because otherwise the hearts of American Jewish millionaires won't be warmed enough. And the same goes when they address [Jewish] provincial audiences. We can only hope that those humiliations will be no more. The abolition of the UJA should be one of the dividends of peace.'

Sivan waxes even more emotional about the conflict between the tenets of 'quasi-familial' (his term) Jewish unity and those of the free-market economy. (The latter is the only ideology which now begins to compete with Zionism in the hearts of the new Israeli power elite.) He considers 'egoism, advantage seeking and treating other human beings as objects' as preferential values, to be adhered to in economy and politics, but not in family relations. The latter need to be subordinated to the opposing values of 'affiliation, affinity and unconditional obligations'. To Sivan's sorrow, however, the financial relation between Israel and organized US Jewry rests upon the exploitation of emotions which perceive world Jewry as one big family. This is, according to him, acceptable only in situations of extreme emergency, and should now be dispensed with, 'especially when donors of Mr Greenberg from Seattle's ilk perceive their donations as a means to become our owners'. Sivan supports emotion-based relations of US Jews with Israeli Jews, but not with the State of Israel. He proposes that groups of American Jews contribute to specific institutions or for specific aims, provided they recognize that 'the existence of the State of Israel is a precondition of their pursuit of Jewish secular way of life'. In my view, Sivan's proposals are an instance of having your cake and eating it too. According to his cherished principles of free-market economics, human relations can be based either on pristine egoism or on its absence, but the two cannot be blended together. Relations which in his understanding 'cannot revolve around dollars alone', are by definition tainted by blending emotions with dollars, in dissonance with the principles which he cherishes.

So much about Sivan. I proceed to discussing two other articles published by *Haaretz* on 10 September, one by its Washington correspondent Akiva Eldar and the other by the New York correspondent, Shlomo Shamir. They both deal with developments among US Jews in the immediate aftermath of the publication of the Oslo Accord. They both say that it was easy to persuade the leaders of the organized Jews to toe the new Israeli line, but that their rank and file were less amenable to such persuasions, thereby posing the risk that in spite of all precautions against it, they may yet be able to publicize their views far and wide, thus revealing to Gentiles all their hostility toward the Rabin government. Shamir informs us how Sharon, who happened to be in New York when the Oslo agreement news was published, urged his Jewish friends to organize protest demonstrations before the Israeli consulate in New York and the embassy in Washington. His suggestion evoked utter shock and was rejected. It was in my view the same kind of shock that would have been felt if somebody suggested to some members of the American Communist Party to organize a demonstration before the USSR's embassy in protest against the memorable Khrushchev 1956 speech. Shamir also reports with satisfaction that 'when some rabbis from the Association of Orthodox Rabbis proposed to name the coming Sabbath "a Sabbath of protest" and to make all the Association's rabbis sermonize against the accord, influential rabbis managed to prevent that proposal from even being discussed.' He also says that 'leading Jewish publicists' were afraid to publish their views in opposition of the accord in the American media. To illustrate this information, he has a story, clearly originating from behind the scenes of the *New York Times*. After that paper published 'some reactions of prominent Jewish leaders enthusiastically supporting the Accord', it wanted to publish a Jewish voice with opposite views. Among Jews otherwise acceptable to the *Times*, it could find only Ruth Wisse, a professor of Yiddish literature whose views are more extremist than of Gush Emunim. Sensing that Wisse was not representative enough, the newspaper turned to Norman Podhoretz.

Eldar provides more information. His article contains an interview with Gail Pressberg, the current president of Friends of Peace Now in the US, an organization which has clearly become charged with controlling the organized US Jewish community on behalf of the Clinton administration and the Rabin government: 'Last week Pressberg was asked by the White House to draft a list of influential leaders of Jewish organizations to be invited to the ceremony of signing the Accord. The idea was to exploit their influence in favour of the peace process.' Other Hebrew papers reported that the number of Jewish invitees amounted to over one thousand, out of the total of 3,300. Eldar writes that 'the sympathizers of Friends of Peace Now are now holding many key positions in both regimes', that is, the American and the Israeli. Pressberg told Eldar that donations to her organization have soared, 'reaching the magnitudes received in the good old days when we supported Begin after Camp David'. Parallel with this flow of money and the spectacle of Jewish leaders rapidly changing sides, the advancement of

Pressberg to what could only be described as the post of White House superintendent of Jewish affairs has been achieved. She said with glee that 'many Jewish leaders are leaving the organizations which used to support Likud in order to join us.' But there are no indications that a comparable process of changing sides is occurring among the members of those organizations. On the contrary, other Hebrew papers report that many Likud supporters are now switching to more extremist organizations. Also, the White House's stand has failed to move the US Jewish masses in the direction of Peace Now. Eldar reports that 'a demonstration of support organized by Peace Now on the evening of 8 September in front of the Israeli embassy attracted no more than about two dozen rather bewildered participants.'

In spite of her 'present exultant feelings', Pressberg shares Eldar's assessment of the situation. She told him Israel can expect dangers on the part of organized US Jewry: 'The greatest danger is that the [Israeli] extreme right may be capable of soliciting huge amounts of money from the American Jewish community.' To avert this danger she proposes the same remedy as Nishma's, namely to invite Israeli generals or other 'major figures' to speak in American synagogues. She is sure that 'the majority of ordinary Jews will stop posing problems after hearing correct explanations from [Israeli] military figures and others.' Eldar asked Pressberg to comment about another danger: Jewish columnists in influential papers, 'such as Rosenthal' [in the *New York Times*] who oppose the Accord. Pressberg agreed that 'they are very dangerous.'

The most important part of the interview, which I am going to quote *in extenso*, concerned Peace Now's manipulation of the media, aimed at influencing the White House. Eldar: 'Suppose President Clinton, for whom Jewish support has its weight, comes eventually to the conclusion that the articles by [Jewish] opponents of the Accord do represent the authentic position of the Jewish community. Might it not deter him from persisting in supporting the deal? What are you doing to persuade the administration that its support for the Accord is not going to make the Jewish supporters of Clinton and his campaign contributors change their minds?' Pressberg: 'The President knows that the responsible community leadership has published a declaration of support for the Accord. But we also run a campaign to let thousands of our supporters cable the White House or address it otherwise. We are using all our influence to make the papers accept for publication lots of articles authored by both Israelis and Americans who support the Israeli government. We provide instructions to anyone willing to subsequently write letters to the editor.' It can be presumed that Peace Now influences the papers and to all appearances even more the television, not only in order to publish what it wants to be published, but also in order to conceal what it wants to be concealed from public knowledge. This is, after all, what all US Jewish organizations have done for years, with considerable success.

Two conclusions can, in my view, be drawn from the developments described in this report. The bulk of the organized US Jewish community is totalitarian, chauvinistic and militaristic in its views. This fact remains unnoticed by other Americans due to its control of the media, but is apparent to some Israeli Jews. As long as organized US Jewry remained united, its control over the media and its political power remained unchallenged. But right now, there have appeared clear indications of its vulnerability to splits in its ranks, in addition to a silent protest of many Jews who may not be ready to rebel outwardly, but who already refuse to support actively the Israeli government and its policies. Parallel with that, there have appeared indications of an unease within the Israeli power elite. These two new developments may yet lead to a major change in Israeli policies. Concretely, Israel may yet try to rely more on its own strength and less on the influence of US Jewry upon American politics.

12

The Pro-Israeli Lobby in the US
and the Inman Affair
11 February 1994

After Admiral Inman's announcement that he would not serve as
Clinton's defence Secretary, the Hebrew press devoted a fair
amount of space to the implications of that affair for Israel. The
first responses expressed Israeli satisfaction. A good example is the
comment of *Yediot Ahronot*'s Washington's correspondent Haim
Shibi, who wrote that 'every Israeli in Washington could but sigh
with relief at the news of Inman's resignation' (20 January 1994).
However, after a few days, deeper analyses of that event appeared,
disclosing its implications for Israel, in particular in so far as its
nuclear policies were concerned. Some articles on that subject,
however, also discussed Israeli influence upon the US exerted via
the Jewish lobby in that country. Most important were the articles
by Amir Oren (*Davar*, 28 January) and Yoav Karni, published the
same day in *Shishi*. Oren's article stressed the incompatibility
between Inman's past policy recommendations and Israeli political
aims, especially in regard to nuclear matters. Both authors, usually
mildly critical of Israel's policies but never of its nuclear build-up,
were very hostile toward Inman. Furthermore, Oren discussed in
depth Pollard and Israeli espionage in the US, as having something
to do with Israeli objections to Inman as a person and to his policy
recommendations.

At about the same time the Hebrew press reported on the
contents of the recently published book *Critical Mass* by William
E. Burrows and Robert Windrem. Information contained in that
book about Israeli nuclear power was assessed by Hebrew press
commentators as accurate, even though its publication was
attributed to the viewpoint of the US officials known for their
objections to Israeli nuclear power and contingent policies. At the
same time knowledgeable Hebrew press commentators discussed
Israeli threats against Iran, including those of using nuclear weapons
against that country. After reviewing the Inman affair as perceived
by the Hebrew press, I will discuss other articles discussing Israeli
nuclear policies and the points where they clash with the avowed
(but seldom acually pursued) nuclear policies of the US.

Let me first express my view on the actual scope of 'Jewish influence in the US' and its capability of bending US policies so as to suit Israeli interests, also in matters nuclear. Some of the best informed and most widely read Hebrew press commentators (who are quoted in this book), perceive the scale of that influence as hardly limited by anything and as extending upon large areas of the world. One of the most prestigious of Israeli commentators, Yoel Markus (*Haaretz*, 31 December 1993) recently spoke of the 'courtship' of Israel by various states, concluding that 'this courtship has nothing to do with the peace process: its only reason is the entire world's recognition of the Protocols of the Elders of Zion as true. When the US is being ruled by an administration as favourably disposed to Israel as the present one, conviction spreads in every state that the only way to America's purse leads via Israel. It is as if this accursed book were not written by an anti-Semite, but by a clever and far-sighted Jew.' I myself would perceive the scope of that influence as more restricted. Although it is obviously very considerable, and although Israel is doing its best to sustain and augment it, actual Israeli influence upon the US still falls far short of the mythology of the Protocols of the Elders of Zion. Its scope cannot be measured exactly, but it can be estimated, albeit with the help of guesswork. True, any knowledge, no matter how approximate, of the extent of Jewish influence upon the US policies is hard to obtain. The topic is taboo in the US (although not in Israel), with all major American Jewish organizations exerting themselves to maintain the taboo, often with the help of philosemitic Christians, who delude themselves that by gagging discussion of Jewish affairs, and in particular about Jewish chauvinism and exclusivism, they 'atone' for the Holocaust. Reliable knowledge about Israeli influence, as about any other taboo subject, can be arrived at only after the interdict is lifted and the subject is freely discussed.

Oren mentions a number of reasons why Israel loathed and feared Inman. The main reason he names is Israeli expectation that if Inman would be appointed the US Defense Secretary, he would be able to put into effect independent American inspections of Israeli nuclear armaments and their production process in Dimona. It needs to be recalled that by virtue of a secret agreement with the US reached during the first year of John F. Kennedy's term of office as president, the US to this day receives only such information about Israeli nuclear power as Israel is pleased to convey. After the Bay of Pigs fiasco Kennedy needed the support of the 'Jewish lobby' and in order to get it, he sanctioned this curious agreement. Oren opens his article by drawing two horror scenarios which he regards as perfectly possible if US policies are ever influenced by Inman or somebody with similar views. In the first scenario a hypothetical

US Defense Secretary is, 'in December 1994', gloating to his subordinates, that 'after the US succeeded to force North Korea to limit its nuclear programme, and after its first success in negotiations with Iran concerning the same matter, "we must now concentrate all our attention on India, Pakistan and Israel. Since our dispute with the CIA is not yet resolved, I decided to instruct the Defense Intelligence Agency to begin gathering independent information about advances in Israeli nuclear armaments, so that after subjecting the data to our analysis, we would provide the President with our well-informed assessment of the situation". Then the former Admiral cleaned his glasses, laughing sardonically. "Although the person responsible for the conclusive Intelligence evaluation is their friend, we can at least show the Israelis that we have eyes and ears."' It is fair to assume that had a US paper published such a caricature of a hypothetical Israeli Jewish defence minister, it would be accused, not without reason, of anti-Semitism. It is virtually certain, however, that no press commentator in the US will accuse Oren of being anti-Gentile.

The second horror scenario anticipates an American attempt to use a spy aircraft to photograph the Israeli nuclear installations in Dimona 'in January 1995' and Israeli hesitations over whether to bring it down. If Israel does bring down the plane, it will be sure to antagonize the 'Gentiles' [*Goyim*], even worse than in the *Liberty* affair of 1967, when Israel bombed the US warship *Liberty* inflicting heavy casualties. The scenarios lead Oren to the conclusion that, due to Inman's resignation, 'the ghastly anticipations are not going to materialize'. The first scenario can no longer take place, because 'by the coming December or at any other time the post of the US Defense Secretary can no more be held by the intelligence expert former Admiral Bobby Ray Inman.' More significantly, at the end of his article Oren says that if the US administration ever 'weighs the utility of Dimona against the utility of American support of any other states, the Israeli government is sure to call up a general mobilization of all its friends in Washington. Israel will be pleased at such time about each of its enemies no longer in position to influence the administration or the Congress but also feel sorry about each Pollard and each "*Liberty*" [affair] for which it has ever been responsible. It will not regret Inman's absence, in spite of the fears that the latter may voice his views in the US media.'

Let me proceed to Karni. He says that 'Inman's candidacy for the post of the Defense Secretary has raised the gravest apprehensions of the Israelis and the Jews.' It is reasonable to suppose that when saying 'the Jews' Karni really means only those 'American Jews' whom I defined as 'organized'. It is also reasonable to suppose that the organized American Jews did not remain idle when they had their 'gravest apprehensions', but did something concrete to relieve them, which means that they did play a role in events leading to Inman's resignation. When discussing the role of the *New York Times* columnist, William Safire, whom Inman named his main enemy, Karni says: 'Safire is but one in a group of Jewish columnists and publishers who wield enormous influence over the American media, and who are prepared to automatically defend every Israeli policy measure, except for the peace initiative of the Rabin government which they were quick to condemn and to consign to the grave.'

Both Oren and Karni are nevertheless under no illusion that Inman is the only 'enemy' left in the US Defense and Intelligence establishment. Karni provides a whole list of US Defense Secretaries whom he defines as mischievously hostile to Israel, among whom he names Caspar Weinberger as the most pernicious. He even attempts to draw a 'sociological profile' of an American Gentile who in his view is likely to become an 'enemy'. Apparently Karni is a unaware that in drawing such 'profiles' he follows in the footsteps of anti-Semites (and other xenophobes) who also used to draw 'profiles' of Jews with the same purpose in their minds. It can be nevertheless presumed that his 'profile' originates with sources close to Israeli Intelligence. It reads as follows: 'The personal profile of Inman is from the Israeli point of view unpromising. He is a white Anglo-Saxon Protestant, graduate of the best universities, a member of the elite clubs. He represents the kind of personality more similar to George Bush or James Baker than to Ronald Reagan.'

Oren is more subtle than Karni in his description of Inman's 'personality': 'In spite of the absence of Inman in the future, Washington (and Texas even more) is still saturated with people born in provincial towns during the hard times. Such people tend to be motivated to rise up via the military services, most often via service in the Navy. Inman is merely one of such characters. Ross Perot is another, and one of their allies [he doesn't say who] is similar. Inman and Perot are highly intelligent and sly, but they have inferiority feelings due to their failure to achieve anything of significance. Whenever an individual of this type becomes a candidate for the US presidency or for a position which in the scale of authority almost approaches the presidency, such as the position of Defense Secretary, the problem becomes not just an domestic American one, but a global one. When an incumbent of either post perceives himself as a victim of an Israeli or Jewish plot, Israel cannot treat it as a joke.'

We can see how certain Americans are a *priori* defined by Israel (and by organized American Jews) as 'undesirable', or worse, at least when they occupy positions of authority. For a comparison, it is worthwhile to quote Oren about the biography of a 'desirable'

American, namely William Safire: 'William Safire loyally served an anti-Semitic president, Nixon, because he was free to be most impressed by Israeli military might, long before he became a *New York Times* columnist. Safire's best friend, the CIA Chief, William Casey, was at the beginning of Reagan's administration forced to accept Inman as his Deputy ... Fortunately, Safire didn't regard his *New York Times* columns as equivalent to a monastery. An Israeli who toward the end of the 1970s served in Washington and was then year after year invited to Safire's home for a meal ending the Yom Kippur fast, was surprised to discover that the number of Safire's guests, all Jewish with high standing either in politics or Washigton's media, was increasing each year. There was even talk that no one not born of a Jewish mother or converted to Judaism according to *Halacha* would be admitted to Safire's table, even though it meant that Henry Kissinger, if invited, would have to choose between his wife [who is a Gentile] and Safire. Inman knew that Safire always worked in tandem with Casey and that Casey always worked in tandem with Israel. Casey's relatively authoritative biography informs us that in the spring of 1981 he met Yitzhak Hofi, then Mossad Chief, for the purpose of making a deal. Casey undertook to provide [Israel] with satellite-derived information about the Iraqi nuclear reactor, in return for Hofi's undertaking to restrain AIPAC in its opposition against the sale of AWACS planes to Saudi Arabia. Some time later Safire vociferously denounced the restrictions imposed by Inman on automatic transmission [to Israel] of American intelligence information about Iraq and Libya.' Incidentally, the terms of the deal between Casey and Hofi conclusively prove that AIPAC (and presumably other American Jewish organizations as well) operates under the command of Mossad, and that it could be used by the Israeli government just as it uses Mossad.

Yediot Ahronot's correspondents Tzadok Yehezkeli and Danny Sadeh (30 January), write in their review of the previously mentioned book *Critical Mass* that 'Israel solicits money from wealthy Jews from all over the world for financing its nuclear weapons programs. This fundraising drive is directed by a committee comprised of 30 Jewish millionaires.' As usual, Jewish exclusivism and chauvinism are here exploited by Israel as a major tool of its policies. The impact of this practice can be a matter for discussion, but denials of its very existence, let alone denials of the right to discuss this matter, are in my view not only intellectually and morally offensive, but also preclude any informed inquiry into both Middle Eastern and American politics.

Karni clarifies that the mentioned restrictions imposed by Inman applied only to automatic sharing of all information. Israel could still make specific requests for information, however, which could be either approved or rejected, but which seem to have in most cases been approved. What apparently irked Safire and his Jewish pals, was the very fact that Israel had to request information from the US. Karni nevertheless says that information about what was going on 'within the radius of 250 miles from the Israeli borders continued to be automatically shared with Israel'. According to him, a problem appeared 'in 1982 when Yasser Arafat moved his residence from Beirut to Tunis, thus leaving the area within which all information from the American [satellite] cameras was to be instantly passed on to Israel'. This was the reason for Israel's displeasure with the 250-mile limitation. In all probability, this limitation was eventually rectified. Still, as long as it existed, the 250-mile radius meant that information was automatically conveyed to Israel about goings on in all of Jordan, hefty chunks of Syria, Lebanon, Iraq and Egypt, and part of Saudi Arabia. Nevertheless, countries like Libya or Pakistan lay outside the area in question, which worried the Israelis, especially since automatic transmission of intelligence from outside of the radius was discontinued after the Israelis destroyed the Iraqi nuclear reactor. Karni informs us, I believe accurately, that 'what particularly worried Jerusalem was that Inman didn't convey to Israel any information about the nuclear projects of Iran and Pakistan.' In my view the anti-Iraqi posture of Israel was a momentary deviation from the consistent pattern of seeking to maintain good relations with Saddam Hussein, in recognition that Israel's main enemies have been first Iran and, next in line, Pakistan, for the simple reason that both states are bigger and stronger than Iraq.

Let me again quote in this context Tzadok Yehezkeli's and Danny Sadeh's review of *Critical Mass* in Yediot Ahronot (30 January 1994). They write that 'Israel is ever ready to launch its nuclear missiles on 60 to 80 targets. Those targets include sites in the Gulf, the capitals of all Arab states, some nuclear bases on the territory of the former USSR and some sites in Pakistan.' (I am convinced this is accurate.) It means that Israel must very much want to obtain US satellite information about the targeted area, a not-so-negligible part of the earth's surface. The existence of so formidable a nuclear power in Israel's hands cannot be convincingly attributed to its own research and development efforts nor to its role as a tool of American policies. On the contrary, a nuclear power of that magnitude must be presumed to run counter to US imperial interests. It is also doubtful, to say the least, if Israel by itself ever had the money for constructing nuclear power of this size, even when US financial help is taken into consideration. Nor can nuclear power of this extent be explained away by the usual excuse of 'guarding against threats to Israel's very existence' or by nauseating misuse of the memories of the Holocaust. The only plausible explanation of the extent of Israeli nuclear power is that

Israel acquired it with at least some help of its 'Jewish friends' in the US and of some Jewish millionaires all over the world. Yehezkeli's and Sadeh's information about 'the nuclear bases on the territory of the former USSR' fits well with what Geoffrey Aronson, relying on US State Department sources, reveals about the Pollard affair in the *Christian Science Monitor* (27 January). He writes that according to 'unanimous response' from these sources, what Pollard had betrayed were 'this country's most important secrets', namely 'information relating to the US targeting of Soviet nuclear and military installations and the capabilities and defences of these sites'. This seems in accord with Israel's global aspirations based on the extent of its nuclear power. Aronson's sources say that much of the intelligence passed on by Pollard 'was unusable by the Israelis except as bargaining chips and leverage against the United States and other countries' interests'. In view of this fact Aronson conjectures that Pollard's intelligence was used by Israel for deals with Moscow consisting of 'trading nuclear secrets for Soviet Jews'.

Oren, who is a firm believer in Jewish influence on US policies (even if perhaps not as firm as Markus), provides some examples of its exercise that have to do with the person of Inman. Here, I quote him verbatim, interspersing the quotes with my own comments. 'Although Inman behaved with fairness and propriety towards Mossad and the Central Gathering Unit of Military Intelligence [of the Israeli Army], the shadow of the *Liberty* affair could always be sensed in the background. In the early 1960s, Inman had been a research and operation officer serving on behalf of [US] Navy Intelligence in the NSA [National Security Agency], which ran *Liberty* and its sister ships. The NSA was subordinated to the Pentagon and not to the CIA. It dealt with tactical intelligence, including the trailing of Soviet ships, but not with strategic intelligence. The US Navy has never reconciled itself to the closure of the *Liberty* file after its destruction by the Israeli Air Force, and has always perceived the timing of the Israeli attack as evidence that Israel did it deliberately, in order to conceal from the Americans its decision to conquer the Golan Heights before a cease-fire could be put into effect through an American–Soviet agreement.' (This appraisal of Israeli intentions strikes me as perfectly accurate.) 'True, Rabin, the then [Israeli] Chief of Staff, learned about this decision only after Dayan suddenly changed his mind from opposing to supporting the plan of that conquest, and issued orders to this effect directly to the Commander of the Northern Command, passing Rabin by. But Inman also recalls how three years later [in 1970] Dayan didn't hesitate to threaten the Americans openly and directly, telling them that if they ever dared to send a photo-taking aircraft over the Israeli bank of the Suez Canal, he was going to order to down it.' Let me comment, first, that I find Oren's information's perfectly accurate, and second, that I find it most significant that the US, possibly due to the influence of Safire and Kissinger over Nixon, then gave in to Dayan's threats so supinely.

'During the *Liberty* affair and thereafter, including the time when the CIA ship *Pueblo* was captured (but not destroyed) by the North Koreans, Inman was chief of the Department of Current Intelligence of the Navy's Pacific Command. He learned a lot there, enough to disbelieve in coincidences or at least in their frequent occurrence. This is why, while serving as a NSA chief during Carter's administration he refused to attribute to coincidence two other facts he then learned about. He first learned that the Carter administration had agreed under pressure to the appointment of Colonel Shlomo Inbar as the Israeli military attaché in Washington. That Inbar – previously the head of Research and Development in the [Israeli] Security System, then Commander of Communication Division [of the Israeli Army] and finally Commander of the Central Gathering Unit of the Military Intelligence [of the Israeli Army] – told directly his American visitors that providing Israel with any secret information it requests would lie in the best American interest because "anything you would refuse to share with us we will steal anyway."'

'The pig-headed Americans didn't then grasp the Israeli sense of humour. They understood it only when a Navy Intelligence employee, Jonathan Pollard, was caught red-handed while passing on to Israel precisely this kind of information which Inman had decided to withhold from Israel. Nevertheless, some Americans interpreted the link [between Inbar's words and Pollard's deeds] as purely coincidental. And interpreted likewise as coincidental were the links connecting Rafi Eitan, then the chief of the Office for Scientific Contacts (LEKEM), who employed Pollard, with the [Israeli] Defence Minister, Ariel Sharon, who had appointed Eitan and who rushed to Washington in order to complain against Inman and his orders.'

Karni recounts two more curious coincidences. The first is that among those to whom Sharon 'complained' against Inman was no one else but Safire. The second is that shortly afterwards 'Lieutenant-Colonel Aviam Selah was sent to the US for a lecture tour sponsored by the United Jewish Appeal and the Israeli Bonds organization. He turned out to be one of the pilots who destroyed the Iraqi nuclear reactor, relying on American satellite information in the process. Selah once delivered a lecture to a group of stock-market brokers, all of them Jewish, in the office of one such broker, William Stern. Stern was very impressed by Selah, in a way in which the American Jews typically tend to be impressed by Israelis who posture as war heroes and have photogenic cheeks. He was so impressed by Selah, that he rushed in great excitement to tell his

cousin all about him. That cousin happened to be a junior officer
in the US Naval Intelligence and his name was Jonathan Pollard.
Pollard shared the excitement and asked to meet Selah.' Karni is
biased in favour of Pollard and willing to twist evidence accordingly,
due to which the sequel of his story brings nothing new. Nevertheless
his story of a quickly arranged meeting between an Israeli lieutenant-
colonel on a busy tour and an American Jew working for US
Intelligence bears in my view all the marks of truth.

Oren continues: 'But Eitan ran Pollard with the explicit approval
of four Defence Ministers and Prime Ministers, concretely Arens,
Rabin, Shamir and Peres. The details of this affair must be known,
among others, to General Danny Yatom [now the Commander of
the Central Command], who at that time served as military secretary
to Arens and Rabin and who in that capacity was drafting the
minutes of their conversations with Eitan. All such individuals
know how to use the rhetoric of the importance of the US support
for Israel, but they also know what to do in order to risk the loss
of that support. Of course, owing only to another fortunate
coincidence, the [secret Israeli] Inquiry Committee headed by
[the former Mossad Chief] Tzvi Tzur and Yehoshua Rotenstreich
found it possible to absolve all [Israeli] politicians of all responsibility
for the Pollard affair and to put all the blame on LEKEM
functionaries.' Tzur was subsequently appointed as the Chairman
of the Directors of the [Israeli] 'Aviation Industries', owned by the
Israeli government, and considered one of the most desirable
government jobs in Israel. Rotenstreich already then held the post
of the Chairman of the Censorship Committee, where he always
was siding with the government. Rafi Eitan was not forgotten
either. After helping sell Iraqi oil all over the world, he now oversees
Israeli trade with Cuba and some of its agricultural development.

This story shows that Israel, by skilfully exploiting its influence
within the US, manages to steer very far from becoming an
American satellite. Sure, the fact that Israel has its value for
American imperial interests also contributes to the same effect. This
explains why, in spite of Israel's financial, and now lesser political
dependence on the US, Israel can often afford to provoke the US
in a manner that may be crude and arrogant. Oren understands
that Israel's relative independence should not be undermined by
crass displays of Israel's brashness but only because avoidance of
such displays helps Israel maintain its independence more effectively.
In his view, which, as will be shown below, is shared by the entire
Israeli establishment, the extent of Israeli independence can be
tested, indeed has already been demonstrated above: that if the US
administration ever 'weighs the utility of Dimona as against the
utility of American support of any other states, the Israeli
government is sure to call up a general mobilization of all its friends

in Washington'. The two crucial areas which Israel wants to maintain its independence from the US are its nuclear power and its influence within the US itself.

The Inman affair and the publication of *Critical Mass* has brought the issue of Israeli's relative independence from the US into sharp focus. It would be instructive to review some past manifestations of this independence together with their impact upon regional politics. Let me begin with some quotations from what the Hebrew press wrote about Israeli nuclear power in 1991. Even then, boasts about Israeli nuclear power could be seen as a response to Bush's attempts to somehow limit Israel's options in nuclear, and perhaps also missile, development. That response was described by the chief political commentator of *Haaretz* Uzi Benziman (31 May 1992). He attributed it, though, not straight to Shamir or Arens, but only to their 'underlings', who 'vented all their wrath at [Bush's] plan without even bothering to get acquainted with all its details ... [They] saw Bush's initiative as dangerous, amateurish, reflecting [Bush's] arrogance ... Laborites such as Rabin, were unanimous in unconditionally rejecting Bush's initiative, differing at best over how their rejection should be phrased.' Benziman explains it: 'The fierceness with which the entire power elite of the State of Israel reacted to the new ideas of Bush cannot come as a surprise. Bush hit our softest spot. When he proposes to freeze the proliferation of weapons he is interpreted as trying to deprive us of our soul, of the last asset we have. When he proposes to prohibit installation of long-range ground-to-ground missiles he is perceived as threatening our very survival.'

Out of the important articles published in mid-October 1991 in *Haaretz* let me quote from those by Ze'ev Shiff (15 October) and the nuclear expert Avner Yaniv (16 October). Shiff, admitting that he reflected the official Israeli viewpoint wrote: 'Whoever believes that Israel ever will sign the [UN] Convention prohibiting the proliferation of nuclear weapons ... is daydreaming. There are no misgivings in Israel about the need to reject this convention with all firmness.' Yaniv substantiated the same conclusion by recounting the history of nuclear negotiations between the US and Israel from Kennedy's time. He wrote, 'in so far as this subject matter is concerned the past is quite a reliable guide to prospects for the future.' According to Yaniv, 'Kennedy was no less determined to prevent Israel from acquiring nuclear weapons than Bush is now.' But 'both Kennedy and Johnson failed in all they wanted, to the point that in the end they found themselves, against their will helping lay foundations for the subsequent close and amicable cooperation between the US and Israel.' He concluded that as long as Israel follows the precedents of the past, the US, far from imposing any nuclear limitations on Israel, would be in the end bound to contribute to Israel's nuclear strength.

Israel's insistence on the independent use of its nuclear weapons can be seen as the foundation on which Israeli grand strategy rests. The Oslo process changed nothing in this respect. Yoel Markus (*Haaretz*, 1 February 1994) quotes Rabin's first open reference to the putative Iranian threat 'made on 20 January 1993, while answering in the Knesset a question of MK Efraim Sneh (Labor). Rabin said that "we are following with concern the Iranian nuclearization and attempts to develop long-range ground-to-ground missiles." His operational conclusion was that "we should precipitate the peace process in order to create an international machinery capable of responding to the Iranian threat."' Markus disapproves of what he interprets as Israeli threats to use Israeli nuclear weapons against Iran in the relatively near future. Obviously relying on the best Israeli Army and Intelligence sources rather than on his own understanding, he provides an estimate of 'Iranian political aims [which] can be assumed to be ordered in importance as follows: A. Systematic conquest of oilfields. B. Undermining the present Arab regimes in Egypt, Lebanon, Iraq, Algeria, Saudi Arabia, Jordan and of course, the subjugation of the Palestinian entity to itself with help of Hamas. [The absence of the Syrian regime from this list is conspicuous.] C. The ultimate unification of 900 million Muslims of the world under its command, with a single theology imposed on all of them.' The difference between Markus' views and the policies Israel is now said by him to pursue is timing. In his view the time to fight Iran will come if and when the above-estimated Iranian aims are achieved: 'In the long range, if Iran ever comes close to fulfilment of its dreams to turn all Islamic states, from Algeria to Turkestan, into a single Khomeinistic empire, Israel would have good reasons to feel keenly concerned.'

There are good reasons for assuming that for the Israeli Security System in general and for Shimon Peres in particular the 'peace process' is conceived of primarily as a tool to promote such mad strategies. The best recent summary of Peres' policies has been provided by Aluf Ben writing in *Haaretz* (23 January 1994). According to Ben, Peres agrees with 'the heads of the Security System' that 'at present there exist two main threats to Israeli and Middle Eastern security', namely 'fundamentalist Islam and nuclear weaponry, in particular when held by Iran. But', continues Ben, 'unlike the heads of the Security System, Peres does not want Israel to rely on the defensive, deterrent and offensive power of the Israeli Army alone, but wants to overhaul the [Israeli] concept of security'. His idea is that in the coming era of peace 'Israel should be recognized as a legitimate player on the Middle Eastern playground', in the position to exploit its legitimacy for the sake of promoting its grand strategy. According to Peres, in the Middle East there is no room for nuclear deterrence as it was used in the Cold War, because 'the enemies of Israel are not as rational as the rulers of the US and the USSR were, to the point that under the influence of the Ayatollahs they may court disasters for the entire world.' Let me recall in this context how in 1984 Peres saved the career of that paragon of rationality, Ariel Sharon, and how he was sustaining for years that ultra-rational movement, the Gush Emunim. And he still maintains fairly good relations with both.

According to Ben, Peres proposes that Israel establishes 'a regional alliance system which will operate as a single political entity', and which 'will be powerful'. But 'in contrast to NATO, which limited its aims to defending its members against the external Soviet threat, Peres' regional alliance system is meant to defend the countries of the Middle East from themselves, that is from the internal seeds of destruction, instability, religious and ethnic zealotry and the economic competition between its constituent parts.' Although Ben tends to agree with Peres' ideas, still, for the sake of clarity he comments: 'Only one question Peres let remain unanswered: what will be the future of the Israeli nuclear arsenal which Peres has so often boasted he helped create?' In my view there are many questions which 'Peres let remain unanswered', for example the obvious question about the geographical boundaries of the area to be included in his 'regional alliance system'. Obviously, the states listed by Markus as threatened by Iran are planned to be included. But what about Syria and Iran, even after the 'regional alliance system' settles its accounts with them? And what about Pakistan on which, as mentioned above, Israel's nuclear missiles are now targeted? It would be instructive to recall in this context that toward the end of 1981, Sharon made a public speech in which he cheerfully proposed that Israel's influence extend 'from Mauritania to Afghanistan'. When so defined, the area may include Pakistan. In my view it can be reliably assumed that strategic aims which Sharon defined in so brutal a manner are the same as those pursued by Peres though the 'peace process'.

Ben doesn't try to answer the question about 'the future of the Israeli nuclear arsenal'. He says that in Peres' view 'the "fog" enveloping the [Israeli] nuclear plans is a factor strengthening Israeli deterrence.' In my view there cannot be any doubt that plans for 'Peres' regional alliance system' rest on the Israeli monopoly of nuclear weapons and has two aims, one offensive and the other defensive. The former is to fight Iran and its allies such as Syria, unless it passes over to the pro-Israeli camp. The latter is to preserve the status quo in the Middle East by protecting all regimes not labeled 'fundamentalist'. Incidentally, since according to Peres, Israel's strategic aim is to maintain the existing regimes intact, 'the abolition of the economic competition' as envisaged by Peres can be presumed to be effected not through the mechanism of referendums and parliamentary elections, but through a diktat, in all probability backed by the Israeli nuclear monopoly.

The plans of Peres imply a considerable Israeli emancipation from its dependence on the US (and marginally on Europe). In that respect they differ from the views of 'the heads of the Security System' and from Israeli foreign relations as pursued to date. Some implications of Peres' views and of his disagreements with the Israeli commanders are clarified in another article by Amir Oren (*Davar*, 4 February 1994). Oren claims that 'by choosing the channel of Oslo' as top priority for the pursuit of Israeli policies 'Peres gambled by staking a lot on the PLO' as 'against staking on the US', because he expected the PLO to help establish the 'regional alliance system'. According to Oren, this explains Peres' indifference to the progress of peace negotiations with Syria, in defiance of US pressures to advance them. But the order of priorities of 'the chiefs of the [Israeli] Security' is quite different. Their top priority is 'to sever Syria's connection with all too many threats [to Israel] originating from Iran'. Oren quotes the commander of the Air Force, General Budinger, who last week said that the F-15-A warplanes which Israel recently obtained from the US, in addition to 'their ability to fly to Iran and back without refuelling', could also 'operate efficiently within 50 per cent of the radius of their maximal outreach'. As Oren admits, this means the F-15-A warplanes 'will be able to penetrate deep into Syrian territory, and cruise there for quite a while in search of their targets, whereas lower quality warplanes could at best bomb a target upon reaching it and then be forced to quickly return to Israel'. But, continues Oren, 'this capability, though important, is still not as important as the capability of a F-15-A warplane to reach Tehran and rain on it bombs which can improve the hearing of Iranian decision-makers.' The Israeli generals, whose views Oren can be presumed to echo also 'rely on security arrangements agreed upon with Jordan more than on any deals which could be made with a Palestinian entity'. Their criticism of Peres (described by Oren in detail but omitted here) and of his way of negotiating with Arafat is according to Oren attributable to much deeper differences over strategy, such as described here.

The idea of a 'regional alliance system' implies the exclusion of the US from it and Israel's supremacy within it, backed by the latter's nuclear monopoly. Its avowed goal 'to secure peace in the region' resembles all too closely similar claims of the imperial powers of the past, made for the consumption of the gullible. This is why Peres' plan can be viewed as an extreme version of Israeli imperialism. The nature of the relations between Israel and other states of the 'regional alliance system' is described in another article by Aluf Ben

(*Haaretz*, 11 February 1994). Ben quotes the first director of the Israeli Institute for Development of Weaponry [RAFAEL], Munya Mardoch, that 'the moral and political meaning of nuclear weapons is that states which renounce their use are acquiescing to the status of vassal states. All those states which feel satisfied with possessing conventional weapons alone are fated to become vassal states.' A transparent implication of that view is that by insisting on its nuclear monopoly, Israel aims at reducing all other Middle Eastern states to the status of its vassals, probably hoping for approval of such a state of affairs by the US.

Apart from the question of whether all existing Arab regimes would want to join 'an alliance' so transparently stewarded by Israel, one can also ask about the survivability of any Arab regime joining that 'alliance'. I feel unable to answer this question. I am concerned, however, more with a third question: whether the US would be pleased by a unification of the Middle East under Israel's command – it could then influence this unified region only via its influence on Israel. Let me recall that through such unification, entailing an Israeli hegemony, Israeli financial dependence on the US and thereby the US's chances to influence Israel would be diminished. It seems also doubtful whether the US (or indeed Europe) would be pleased with the abolition of 'economic competition' between states under 'an alliance system' powerful enough to accomplish it. This is why Peres' plan can only be interpreted as assuming that Israeli influence upon the US, exerted through the medium of organized American Jews, is sufficient to outweigh US imperial interests. As I mentioned above, I do recognize the power of organized American Jews as quite formidable. But contrary to some Hebrew press commentators, I don't believe that it is sufficient to justify that tacit assumption of Peres. The organized American Jewish community may, as Oren hopes, succeed in protecting the independence of Israeli nuclear policies but I doubt if they are capable of accomplishing much more.

I hope I have succeeded in showing that the role of 'organized' Jews in the US in the affair of Inman's resignation touches on the deepest issues of Israeli grand strategy. I also hope I make it clear that the Peres' plans are in my view not only immoral and crudely imperialist, but also downright unrealistic, no matter how enthusiastic western commentators are about him. They represent an Israeli expansionist's utopia. In my view the plans of Peres are more morally reprehensible than the plans of the Israeli Security System: more nauseously hypocritical, and more pregnant with more disastrous consequences for the entire Middle East if any attempt is ever made to bring them about. I consider the imperial plans of the Israeli generals to be at least implementable, primarily because they pose less of a threat to the imperial interests of the US. Still, those plans are also symptomatic in that they reflect two most cherished Israeli ambitions: the ambition to reduce its dependence on the US, especially in the nuclear domain, and the ambition to exploit their thus enhanced independence for the pursuance of Israeli grand strategies. Peres' plans articulate those two ambitions in the most extremist manner possible. But what is most dangerous are the ambitions themselves rather than any of their articulations.

Part V

OSLO AND AFTER

13

The Real Significance of the Oslo Accord
10 September 1993

The Oslo Accord between Israel and the PLO has to be understood first of all in the context of the more than 26 years of Israeli conquest of the Territories. This conquest can be divided into two periods: before and after the outbreak of the Intifada in December 1987. From the point of view of the Israeli establishment the first period can be defined as 'an easy conquest'. During this time the average number of soldiers and other armed forces which Israel kept in the Territories was small, between 10–15,000. During the heyday of the Intifada, in mid-1988, the number of troops was 180,000. After the Gulf War the number of troops declined and in spring 1993 the number rose again to about 100,000. The increase in the number of Israeli officials in the Military and Civil Administrations and of Shabak agents is unknown to me, but must have been proportionally much greater; much of the routine work of the Civil Administration which before the Intifada used to be performed by Palestinian clerks was afterward done by soldiers.

Equally important are two further changes which the Intifada introduced and which in spite of its decline, persist and impair Israel's ability to rule the Territories easily. Before the Intifada the single instance of resistance which swept through all Palestinian society in the Territories occurred in 1969 in protest of the arson of al-Aqsa mosque. All other protests were either geographically or socially limited. Many of them were limited only to the Gaza Strip refugee camps. Calls for strikes or other forms of protest were not widely observed. Many villages, which Israeli authorities described as 'loyal', never participated in protests before the inception of the Intifada. Although the Intifada as an active force has declined dramatically, a considerable demonstration of national unity, as seen in joint actions, persists.

More important is the second change which has continued since the inception of the Intifada, since it is more visible to the Israeli Jewish public. Before the Intifada Israeli Jews enjoyed full freedom of movement within the Territories, including places such as the Gaza Strip refugee camps where no Israeli will venture now, except on the rare invitation from an activist and accompanied by

Palestinian guides. Stone throwing was infrequent and quite unknown in most villages. It is hard to recall now, but before the Intifada Israeli Reserve soldiers would frequently celebrate the end of their service in the Gaza Strip by holding a party in a restaurant, even in a refugee camp. Obviously, many of the effects of the Intifada remain and cannot be eradicated by Israel.

The reason for the change is that before the Intifada Israel could always find Palestinian collaborators who could rule the Territories on its behalf. When using the term 'collaborator' in this context, I do not mean a spy. I mean, on the contrary, a person who was publicly known as one who has good relations with the Israeli authorities, and who could be employed by other Palestinians to obtain favours for them. In return, he used his social and political influence in Israel's interest. The method operated best in Dayan's time, from 1967 to 1974, when the 'notables', that is the figures influential in Palestinian society even before the conquest, were used in this role. The efficiency of the method declined to some extent under Sharon in 1981–83, who demolished the power of the notables and put in their place his 'Village Leagues', often composed of the dregs of the society. But since the start of the Intifada this method has proved impossible to implement. The consequence is that Israel had to undertake the task of ruling the Palestinians on every level by its own manpower. This form of direct rule is much less efficient, and also more corrupt and burdensome. The Israeli establishment wanted for quite some time to restore the old method of indirect rule, especially in the Gaza Strip on Israeli terms. This is the meaning of the Oslo Accord as Israel perceives it: the PLO, or rather a part of Fatah with an absolute loyalty to Yasser Arafat is intended to fulfil the role which the notables performed under Dayan and Village Leagues, under Sharon, but more efficiently. It will be rewarded by a lot of money, by a much greater degree of honour than the notables enjoyed and by some verbal concessions, vaguely formulated so as to lead to further stalemates in negotiations. Neither side to the Accord intends to realize it as it stands.

Therefore, in order to explain in detail the real meaning of the Oslo Accord, as perceived by Israel and tacitly accepted by the PLO, I will not quote its text, which is purposely vague on issues of Palestinian rights while precise on issues of what powers Israel will retain. Rather I will quote the interpretations of the real Israeli intentions made by the most knowledgeable Hebrew press correspondents. Their opinions clearly come from the highest sources in the government and were not contradicted by anyone in Israel. (The fact that their opinions were not mentioned by the self-censored Arabic press in East Jerusalem and the Territories appears to me equally significant.) The most important of them were made by the chief political correspondents of *Yediot Ahronot* and *Haaretz*, Shimon Shiffer and Uzi Benziman respectively. Both enjoy excellent connections with Rabin and Peres and can be considered as reliable informants. While *Yediot Ahronot* is the Hebrew paper with the largest circulation, *Haaretz* is the most prestigious.

Shiffer reports from Washington (2 September 1993) that 'in meetings held between Israeli delegates and personalities in the PLO it was decided to form a joint committee, comprising Shabak and PLO figures. The purpose of setting a joint committee is to reach cooperation in all matters concerning domestic security in the Gaza Strip ... Israel and the PLO, in recognition of their present interest in ensuring success of the peace process, will try to prevent all attempts by Hamas to sabotage it, also after the autonomy is in force.' Shiffer then adds on his own, so that his readers will have no doubt about the nature of the cooperation, that 'most of Shabak's activities take place in the Territories, where it prevents sabotage and captures wanted Palestinians.' It can be safely assumed that Shabak is already helped to a considerable extent in those activities by the cooperation of the PLO, or of such forces within it which accepted this task.

The real purpose of the cooperation and of the Oslo Accord itself, is clearly indicated by Benziman in two articles, published on 3 and 5 September respectively. In the first article Benziman wrote, 'A tacit understanding exists between Israelis and Palestinians who attended the secret negotiations [in Oslo] to the effect that no autonomy in the West Bank and the Gaza Strip can possibly materialize even if the Oslo Accord mandates it. Instead of the autonomy as mandated by the Oslo Accord, the PLO may at once begin to rule over the Gaza Strip and Jericho, exercising there the full authority of the Civil and Military Administrations except in foreign affairs, and thus be freed from the need to hold any elections and to compete over the votes with Hamas ... In spite of the fact that the Accord stipulates that elections to the Autonomy Council are to be held in June 1994, it is quite likely that negotiations preliminary to carrying out the elections may fail. This may happen due to a disAccord [*sic*] over the Council's authority or, even more likely, just because the PLO will prefer to have no elections. Instead of holding elections, the PLO is expected to make all the efforts to obtain in the remainder of the Territories the same authority it will have in the Gaza Strip and Jericho. The expected result is that PLO jurisdiction in the Gaza Strip and Jericho as determined by the Oslo Accord, will gradually diminish the authority of the Military Administration over the Palestinians in the remainder of the West Bank. Israel may agree to this, provided the PLO jurisdiction does not ever extend to Jewish settlements, the Security Zone and Jerusalem. During the five years after signing the Oslo

Accord, the interim Accord which defines the status of the PLO in the Gaza Strip and Jericho (the authority to administer domestic affairs, including the police) may yet turn into a permanent arrangement for the entire West Bank and Gaza Strip.'

While the above quoted passages occurred in an article whose first part was devoted to the praise of Rabin and Peres for this achievement, in his second article of 5 September, Benziman repeated the quoted argument independently of it. He first compared the deception involved on the Israeli side in the Oslo Accord, to the deception involved in the 1982 invasion of Lebanon and recorded that even the defenders of the Oslo Accord agree that it was achieved by the use of deceit. Benziman then admits that the distinction made by the defenders of the Oslo Accord, namely, that the first deception was intended to enlarge the war while the second to bring peace, is not really valid, since 'the opponents of the 1993 peace can claim that the 1982 war was intended to bring lasting peace ... [While] negotiations in Oslo may bring about a result causing many victims in the future.' Benziman's opinion is that deceptions are permitted in a democracy, but he is uneasy with the deception underlying the Oslo Accord. His predictions deserve to be extensively quoted: 'There is something in the peace of 1993 which disturbs also those who support it entirely, and which concerns the tacit meanings involved in it. There are indications that the Accord is built on a tacit assumption that it will never be carried into effect. Even now, before it was signed it is clear to its initiators (at least to the Israeli side) that the probability within nine months, of establishing the Autonomy Council to be elected by the Palestinians living in the West Bank and the Gaza Strip is very small.

'Even today all knowledgeable people in Jerusalem talk about a system of rule in which the interim settlement will be based on an increase of the authority which the PLO will be granted in the Gaza [Strip] and Jericho over the entire West Bank, not as a result of any elections but by an Israeli decree. The elections, if any, will come after this decree. Thus, the regime in the Territories will not be an elected autonomy but a PLO-appointed administration. If this happens, Israel supports a process which is intended to prevent any chance to form by its side a democratic Palestinian entity (or a state), and establishes instead an autocratic form of regime, similar to those existing in the Arab states. This is in spite of the Israeli claims that the democratization of its Arab neighbours is a basic condition for Israeli-Arab peace-making and for Israel's readiness to make sacrifices for its sake. The probability that it is this autocratic regime which will be the outcome of Oslo Accord (and it was not I who invented this outcome) is the logical conclusion from the gap existing between the text of the many paragraphs in the Accord and the ability to realize the aims formulated in them.

Those gaps will be expressed in difficulties in carrying out the Accord and also in other issues (the permanent Accord, for example). When this estimate is made by those who formulated the Accord, the question of whether it is based on deception is valid.'

Let me first discuss the sanctimonious acceptance by Benziman of the official thesis that Israel is interested in a democratization of Arab societies. In my view it is just one of those sacrifices which I suppose an Israeli correspondent of his standing must make from time to time to appease his high-placed informants. (It reminds me of Voltaire attending a Mass occasionally for the same reason.) The easily ascertained fact is that Israel (and the Zionist movement) vigorously oppose democratization of Arab societies, and are mortally afraid of such a process. The more undemocratic, unpopular and corrupt an Arab regime, group or leader is, the more likely it is that Israel will either ally itself with it or support it. This could easily be seen during the period of the intense Israeli involvement in Lebanese affairs. In this policy Israel enjoys the full support of the US, whose customary policy is to oppose democracy in the Middle East. There are several reasons for following this policy. The most important is that the Israeli establishment knows that an Arab democracy will be much stronger than any Arab autocratic regime, even if such a regime happens to be temporarily popular. This is also true of the Palestinians. When the Intifada was more democratic it was also stronger. Its strength declined when its democratic character waned. It can be assumed that the reason why Israel is trying to prevent formation of 'a democratic Palestinian entity' and 'will try to establish instead an autocratic form of regime', as Benziman says, is because democracy will strengthen the Palestinians while Israel wants to keep them weak.

In addition to the greater social strength of an Arab democracy of which Israel is afraid, it should be recalled that an Arab democratic state will be able to form a much more efficient army than 'an autocratic form of regime'. One reason for the weakness in numbers and training of all Arab armies is that dictatorship is always afraid of its own people. It therefore either does not arm them or, as in Iraq, it forms two armies, a big, badly trained, army augmented by well-paid and well-armed but small 'guard units'. (The situation in this respect in Saudi Arabia is rather similar.) The ignominious Iraqi military defeat in the Gulf War was due, first of all, to the dictatorial nature of the Iraqi regime. It may be safely assumed that the US opposition to the democratization of Arab states is also due primarily to the fact that it wants to keep them weak.

While a basic Israeli opposition to the democratization of Arab societies is common to all Zionist parties, it has been and is still, strongest among the Zionist 'left', that is the Labor Party and the groups to its left. The Zionist right wing, now represented mainly by Likud, is basically uninterested in Arabs. It wants to keep the Arabs outside the Land of Israel behind the 'iron wall' of Israeli power (as Jabotinsky expressed it in the mid-1920s); those within the Land of Israel should be quiet and apathetic. In contrast, the 'left' wants to 'cultivate' (to use its own expression) Arabs who will support Israeli policies. 'Cultivation' of pro-Israeli Arabs involves a greater degree of manipulation of Arab society and requires therefore stronger opposition to its democratization than a policy of simple domination and exploitation. During the period in which Labor was 'in charge of Arab affairs' (until 1977, 1984–90 and since 1992), it has invariably supported the most feudal elements in Arab society and shown enmity to all progressive Arab groups, for example, to Palestinian feminists. This was the principle applied by Rabin as Defence Minister in 1984–90 when he 'cultivated' Hamas. This is why Rabin and his henchmen consistently praise Mubarak for not allowing any democracy in Egypt, and for ruling the country by emergency regulations. A few months ago Rabin said that Egypt is actually superior to Israel in this respect, citing this example: when new roads are being constructed in Israel people may appeal against them on the grounds of environmental damage, even up to the Supreme Court, 'while in Egypt Mubarak just goes ahead and does not allow any appeals to courts'. There is no reason to suppose that Rabin has now changed his approach. It can be assumed that his present 'cultivation' of Arafat is based on a similar approach.

The explanation of this crucial point, namely that Palestinians are to be given only strictly limited power in order to use it on Israel's behalf is important in order to sway the Israeli Jewish public in favour of the Accord. For this reason, Rabin took good care to often reiterate this point. Let me quote one of his explanations, expressed with his customary vulgarity. After attacking Likud (*Yediot Ahronot*, 7 September), he stated that 'the four crucial issues around which negotiations with the Palestinians had revolved are: united Jerusalem, the fate of the settlements, the redeployment of the Israeli Army and the enforcement of domestic security in the Gaza Strip.' He then boasted of his victories regarding all of them: 'The entire united Jerusalem will be outside the autonomy. We ourselves obtained this concession from the Palestinians – from those with whom one should make such deals – without any American promises, as in the Camp David Accords. Jewish settlements will be placed under an exclusive Israeli jurisdiction; the Autonomy Council will have no authority over them. The forces of the Israeli Army will be redeployed on locations determined only by us, unlike in the Camp David Accords which mandated a withdrawal of the Israeli Army forces. In the Accord we reached we didn't consent to use the formula "withdrawal of Israeli Army forces" except when it applied to the Gaza Strip. In application to all other places the only term used is "redeployment".'

'Discussing the issue of "Gaza [Strip] and Jericho first", Rabin said: "I prefer the Palestinians to cope with the problem of enforcing order in the Gaza [Strip]. The Palestinians will be better at it than we were, because they will allow no appeals to the Supreme Court and will prevent the [Israeli] Association for Civil Rights from criticizing the conditions there by denying it access to the area. They will rule there by their own methods, freeing – and this is most important – the Israeli soldiers from having to do what they will do. All Gaza Strip settlements will remain where they are. The Israeli Army will remain in the Gaza Strip to defend them, and to guard all confrontation lines. It will also control the Jordan River end to end, and all the bridges on it".' It is quite clear that the most important point for Rabin is that Arafat's faction in the PLO will become, or already is, a part of Shabak in order to perform its work better than Israel can by itself. The main point is that the PLO is expected to be more immune to criticism than Israel. The parallel with the methods employed by the US in countries dependent on it, such as El Salvador or Guatemala, in which the worst kinds of oppression are entrusted to local forces, is inescapable.

But if Arafat and his henchmen really hope that in recompense for doing efficiently the job which Rabin assigned to them they will get the same formal recognition as the rulers of El Salvador or of similar countries do, they are deluding themselves and their people. On this point, as on Israeli intentions in general, one can trust the countless declarations of Rabin, Peres and other Israeli figures of lesser importance, to the effect that Israel will never allow a formation of a Palestinian state, but only of 'an entity' which will lack all outward signs of sovereignty. Rabin had boasted of his superiority to Begin in his respect: while Begin allowed the Autonomy Council to sit in Bethlehem, close to Jerusalem and to other centres of Palestinian population, Rabin insisted on moving the Council to Jericho, the smallest and the most backward of all Palestinian towns. The express condition that 'the Palestinian police will not have powers to detain any Israeli citizen' in any part of the autonomy will remain as a visible sign of the inferiority of the autonomy's powers compared with those of a nominally sovereign state. The police of El Salvador or even Antigua have the power, which they use in cases of American drug users or drunken drivers, to detain US citizens. Arafat's police will not have such powers. As Uzi Benziman put it in *Haaretz* (3 September), 'if Arafat wants to call the resulting entity "a state" it is his own business', but it will not be a state. He may not be prevented from using stationery headed by empty titles, and people of the autonomy may be allowed to call him 'His Excellency', but he will not receive the formal recognition granted to a President of Panama or of Antigua in his relations with Israel.

Another advantage which Israel will get from the Oslo Accord is lucidly explained by Danny Rubinstein in *Haaretz* (8 September). He points to the fact that under the present conditions the Israeli authorities are responsible, at least formally, for the living conditions and welfare of the Territories' population. They have to worry about the increase in population which is 'one of the greatest in the world', and has increased even more because of 'the influence of the Intifada and the recent closure, which limit the freedom of movement of the inhabitants'. Once the Territories were separated from Israel such issues will not concern it. In Rubinstein's view – with which I concur – the separation had already occurred with the imposition of closure, which can be assumed to continue under the autonomy: 'Of course, Israel should make all effort to procure maximum international aid to flow to the Gaza Strip and other autonomous areas, so as to eradicate poverty, unemployment and despondency. Otherwise, unrest will be inevitable, with outbursts bound to affect Israel's security adversely.' This is why Israel is prepared to allow some of the 'Palestinians wishing to settle in the autonomous territories rather than in any other Arab country' to do so, since 'their problems will be theirs alone: to be solved by themselves or by the Palestinian Council to be set in the Territories.' The deeper intention of the Accord is to create an apartheid regime in which the Autonomy Council in the Territories will in effect relieve Israel from any duties towards the population. The efficiency of this apartheid regime will be assured by the PLO, on the one hand, and by the international financial aid which will be given it, on the other.

14

Analysis of Israeli Policies: The Priority of the Ideological Factor

12 May 1995

At the time of this writing it can be seen that the Israeli government did nothing to make the majority of the Palestinians in the Territories support the peace process, although it could have obtained their support without sacrificing any major imperial Israeli interests. Commentators, including some well-intentioned ones, are wringing their hands imploring Rabin to refrain from taking another provocative step, for example, the further confiscation of land in East Jerusalem as decided on 30 April 1995. Those commentators fail to perceive that Rabin's policies have an internal logic and consistency based on the consensus of Labor Zionism as formed already in the 1920s. It can be concluded that the analysis and prediction of those policies are very easy to make on the assumption that they constitute an application of the Zionist ideology which tends to override pragmatic considerations. The apparent exceptions to this rule, for example Israeli withdrawals from formerly conquered territories, are also explicable in terms of ideological factors, in this instance in terms of the loss of Jewish lives in unsuccessful or inconclusive wars and of the wish to avoid further losses of Jewish lives.

For instance, as pointed out by Tanya Reinhart in *Yediot Ahronot* (1 May 1995), in all Rabin's interviews to the Hebrew press published on the Passover Eve, 14 April, he reiterated his ideological commitment to the principle that only the Jews 'have the right over the entire Land of Israel'. Rabin didn't bother to specify the exact borders of the Land in question: he only admitted that 'it is also inhabited by two million Palestinians' who constitute 'a problem' which only the Labor Party knows how to solve. This is a standard formula of Labor and centre Zionism which hasn't changed for more than 75 years. On the same day 'a senior officer of the Central Command of the Israeli Army', which is in charge of the West Bank, was interviewed by Nahum Barnea for *Yediot Ahronot*. The officer defined 'the official policy of the Israeli Army as providing every Jew in every settlement, whether of the West Bank or the Gaza Strip, with exactly the same degree of security and well-being as Jews of

Haifa and Tel Aviv have during all stages of the peace process and afterwards'. Needless to say, nothing was said about the security of the Palestinians who, more than before Oslo, are harassed by the settlers backed by the Army and by Arafat's secret police forces backed by the Shabak.

The plan which the Israeli Army already implements in the Territories (known as 'Rainbow of Colours') was published in the Hebrew press in November 1994, but its crucial feature, the 'bypassing roads' on which only the Jewish settlers, their visitors and the Israeli Army will be permitted to drive, was discussed by the press already in September. Reinhart notes that the plan had been 'formulated already in the early 1980s' by the settlers, but under Likud and 'national unity' governments nothing much was done to implement it: 'It is "the peace government" which opened new vistas for the plan's implementation.' The annual cost of the plan is one billion shekels [$330 million], to be continued for three years. Most of the cost, as noted by Meir Shteglitz (*Yediot Ahronot*, 9 April) Israel expects to be covered by the US. Relying on an interview given by the commander of the Central Command, General Biran, to *Haaretz* on 28 April, Reinhart described the plan as 'envisaging the maximal defence of all existing Jewish settlements and the partition of the West Bank into enclaves containing Arab localities. Each enclave is to be surrounded by bypassing roads, settlements and Israeli Army fortresses. The situation will be then the same as in the Gaza Strip. If Israel ever decides to withdraw its troops from any downtown area of an Arab city [of the West Bank], the plan is to guarantee that the Israeli Army will continue to rule that city from outside.' Indeed, 'control from outside' is a favourite term of Rabin and other Labor stalwarts, in use from before the June 1992 elections.

Actually the plan was formulated in 1977 by Ariel Sharon and it was then described in the Hebrew press in detail. At that time Sharon was still 'only' an Agriculture Minister. Rabin and Peres, fresh from their defeat in the 1977 elections didn't object to the plan, but Begin and Weizman (Defence Minister 1977–80) did, since they assigned a higher priority to making peace with Egypt. When Begin began to lose his sanity in 1981 and Sharon became Defence Minister, the highest priority was assigned to the invasion of Lebanon. To the best of my knowledge, the plan under current implementation has since remained the Israeli Security System's 'preferable solution' to 'the problem' of Palestinians in the Territories. According to information available in the Hebrew press, the plan began to be implemented in the Gaza Strip right after Oslo. Reinhart quotes press sources showing that in the West Bank the beginnings of its implementation date from July 1994 when, in an amicable meeting, Rabin agreed with Gush Emunim leaders 'who explained to him that construction of the bypassing roads lay in the common interest of both the government and the Jewish settlers. At the same time Rabin was told the same by [the then Chief of Staff] Barak'. The plan was welcomed by Gush Emunim leaders in internal writings, but attacked in public. According to General Biran the plan 'was intended to give the settlers the full opportunity to live a normal life. I take this occasion to stress that no Jewish settlement whatsover will ever be removed from its place. In order to achieve this goal the Israeli Army is now implementing a number of plans, such as the construction of the bypassing roads and of separate electricity and water networks intended to guarantee that each Jewish settlement will have maximum security and welfare.'

Reinhart provides sophisticated but in my view insufficient explanation of why the apartheid-like 'Rainbow of Colours' plan was welcomed by most of the Jewish and Palestinian 'peace camp'. All too clearly, the plan favoured the settlers and was intended to perpetuate the Israeli conquest of the Territories more effectually than before, by using 'control from outside'. Yet Peace Now extolled this racist plan as 'a positive sign of implementation of the peace process', and its leaders rushed to convince Arafat in Gaza about its virtues. Noting that the settlers and the right wing censured the 'Rainbow of Colours' plan as 'selling out the Land to the Gentiles', Reinhart observes that 'the religious settlers and Likud had long ago discovered the panacea for neutralizing the left. As soon as they attack the government, the doves of various persuasions stand to attention ready to help the government pursue the "peace process". The result is that the supporters of a plan devised by the settlers can pass for "peace lovers". The more one insists that the government speeds up carrying out this plan in the whole of the West Bank, the more reputation for "peace loving" he acquires. And whoever dares to oppose this plan is instantly censured by the doves for "sabotaging the peace" and branded as one of those "extremists from both sides" who by virtue of opposing Rabin's policies is "objectively against peace".'

This explanation is correct on a tactical level. It points out how the Oslo process in effect advanced the cause of the Israeli apartheid, by virtue of making it possible to brand Jewish or Palestinian opponents of racism as 'enemies of peace'. Yet in my view Reinhart, like other Jewish leftists misses the main point. I agree with her prognosis of the effects of the 'Rainbow of Colours' upon the Palestinians. She writes, 'The meaning of the plan is that we will solve the problem of two million Palestinians in the Territories by imprisoning them in ghettoes, starving them and turning them into beggars. But instead of calling it "an occupation", we will present it as a step toward a Palestinian state. We will crush Palestinian throats with our boots while smiling to them nicely,' [a clear allusion to Shimon Peres]. But the point which Reinhart misses is that not only has Labor's version of Jewish racism always been much more hypocritical and hence more dangerous than Likud's, but it is also more noxious in terms of the actual oppression of its victims. I will return to this point below.

Meron Benvenisti's presentation in *Haaretz* (27 April) is similar to Reinhart's. He also derides the Zionist doves who support Israeli brutalities committed after Oslo in general and the 'Rainbow of Colours' in particular, while reassuring the Palestinians that these are means conducive to the Palestinian state, 'at first only in the Gaza Strip'. Benvenisti says that 'far from promoting justice, peace or progress, a world-view reduced to establishing a state as its single goal cannot but be empty, deceitful and conforming to Israeli interests. Now, when the Palestinian Authority has an autonomous authority in domestic affairs, its corruption and arbitrariness in the Gaza Strip forms a contrast to the ideals of human freedom and dignity, and the struggle against deprivation. Hence, even if Israel grants Arafat a semblance of a state, no relief can be expected in the conditions of oppression, control and exploitation. Such conditions were dictated by Israel to Arafat in the Oslo and Cairo Accords. This is why no conceivable change of labels may prompt the Palestinian population to identify ideologically with Arafat's regime.' Benvenisti says that Israel may agree to Arafat's statehood, but only in order to present it as a 'seeming concession enabling Israel to demand from the Palestinians in return "more flexibility", in acquiescing to the perpetuation of the Israeli colonial rule over the Territories'. I don't think the Labor government will agree to an independent Palestinian state, even in the Gaza Strip alone. The talk about such a prospect was no more than a typical ploy by Shimon Peres, intended to extract from Arafat more compliance with Israeli demands. Had Labor intended to establish a Palestinian state, it would have exploited it in the fast-approaching Israeli election campaign. Moreover, Rabin would have sought to justify it in his numerous Passover Eve interviews. Yet the Israeli government has done nothing in order to explain and justify such a policy change to the Israeli public.

To describe the aims of the 'Rainbow of Colours' apartheid, Benvenisti speaks, in my view cogently, of 'conceptual ethnic cleansing, i.e. of erasing the others from one's consciousness. It cannot be attributed only to chance that the so-called "peace process" with the Palestinians is in Jewish society accompanied by a high incidence of ethnocentrism approaching racism, of tribal forms of morality and of the failure to distinguish between the moral right to exist and the moral obligation to behave decently.' Among Benvenisti's examples of such 'incidence', a particularly outrageous act (at least in my view) was the imposition of a round-the-clock curfew on Palestinians of Hebron so as to let the visitors of Jewish settlers 'hold a picnic', and roam around the city in perfect safety. For a single day during the Passover week the city was for this purpose filled with troops: a circumstance which let the picnickers exult over Palestinians confined in their houses and throw stones at them, especially if they dared to look out from their windows. The whole thing was intended as a concession of Rabin to Gush Emunim. It nevertheless failed to prevent the latter to use the day for the grossest forms of abuse of what they call 'the government of wickedness', including public prayers to God to 'abolish it quickly'.

Benvenisti concludes, rightly in my view, that 'the Oslo process, the resultant ideology of segregation and the resultant security considerations are intended to cloak [Israeli] ethnic cleansing with an aura of respectability. Sure, my use of that term may be viewed as a manifestation of extremism compared to its usual use as an elegant term for expulsions and mass murders. But in my view ethnic cleansing may also be more limited in time. A closure of the Territories or a curfew intended to cleanse the public space from the presence of "others" are perfect examples of such conceptual ethnic cleansing limited in time.'

Those developments could have been predicted by those who took the trouble to analyse the actual Zionist policies pursued since the 1920s, and after 1967 in the Territories. Let me begin with Israel itself. The laws of the State of Israel pertaining to the use of land are based on the principle of discrimination against all non-Jews. The State of Israel has turned most of the land in Israel (about 92 per cent) into 'state land'. After those lands are defined as owned by the State of Israel they can be leased for long periods only to Jews. The right to a long-term lease of such land is denied to all non-Jews without a single exception. This denial is enforced by placing all state lands under the administration by the Jewish National Fund, a branch of the World Zionist Organization, whose racist statutes forbid their long-term lease, or any other use, to non-Jews. Their lease to Jews, conditioned upon the prohibition of sub-lease to non-Jews, is granted for the period of 49-years with an automatic renewal for another 49-year period. Consequently, they are treated as property and are bought, sold and mortgaged, provided the party to the deal is Jewish. The small and decreasing number of cases of leasing state land to non-Jews for grazing is never for more than eleven months. A Jewish leasee of state land is allowed, often subsidized or otherwise encouraged, to develop the land and especially to build a house for himself there, but non-Jewish leasee is strictly prohibited to do so. Leasing state land to a non-Jew is accompanied by restrictive conditions, such as the prohibition of construction or development, or of sub-leasing it to somebody else. By the way, membership of all kibbutzim and moshavim (whose supposed 'socialist' or 'utopian' character is so stridently advertised outside Israel) is strictly limited to Jews by virtue of their being all located on state land. Non-Jews who desire to become members of a kibbutz, even a kibbutz whose Jewish members are atheists, must convert to Judaism. The kibbutz movements, in cooperation with the Israeli Chief Rabbinate, keep special training facilities for preparing 'easy', (that is, in most cases fake) conversions to Judaism for such people.

As a consequence the Galilee can be described as the land of apartheid. Palestinian localities are bursting with population growth but are surrounded by state land which they cannot use it in order to expand. The town of Sakhnin in the Galilee, inhabited by about 25,000 Palestinians, is surrounded by state land allotted to three kibbutzim founded in the 1970s for the express purpose to 'guard state land' from 'Arab encroachment'. Those kibbutzim are in every respect failures. The original members had long ago left them and so did their successors, but new Jewish volunteers (mostly from the 'peace camp') are being sent there all the time. Those kibbutzim receive huge subsidies from the Israeli government and from the Jewish Agency, that is, ultimately from tax-free contributions of Jews all around the world. No one proposes, even for the sake of efficiency or winning support of the Palestinians for the peace process, that even the tiniest part of state land around Sakhnin be allotted to non-Jews of that town. Obviously, an ideological consideration overrides all political considerations, as in religion the sacred always overrides the profane.

There are many states which in the past were systematically engaged in land robbery. The US, for example, robbed the Indians of their land, transforming most of it into state land. Nevertheless, this land is now available for use by any US citizen. If a Jew were in the US prohibited to lease land belonging to the state only because he were Jewish, this would be rightly interpreted as anti-Semitism. But anti-Semitism is already considered in the US disreputable, whereas in Israel 'Zionism' is the official state ideology and is indoctrinated as a goal of public education. Of course, the land issue is no more than a single example of official discrimination against the non-Jews which pervades all walks of life in Israel, victimizing mainly the Palestinians. Some Zionists recently want to alleviate its effects, but no Zionist party nor Zionist politician has ever proposed to abolish it or had second thoughts about its underlying ideology. The whole discriminatory system is obviously intended to be practised in the foreseeable future.

It is easy to see that by the rigorous enforcement of such laws, also against the most loyal supporters of the state, Israel is undermining its own imperial and military power. Let me give two instances of this. The first concerns the Druzes who serve in the Israeli Army, Police and Intelligence, often reaching high ranks in those services. They are nevertheless legally barred from use of the state land and as non-Jews they suffer from other discriminatory laws as well. The same can be said about other Palestinians who either serve in the above-mentioned security services or reach high ranks in various branches of civil service, for example as judges. Israel had appointed Palestinians to be consuls and other diplomatic representatives. It is now contemplating appointing the first Palestinian ambassador. But a Palestinian general, ambassador or judge is still subject to the discussed discriminatory laws. He still does not have the right to lease even a small plot of state land, whereas any released Jewish murderer has this right as matter of course.

Right now, Palestinians may or may not perceive themselves as victims of Israeli discrimination. Many of them are too mystified by their feudal mindset to perceive it clearly. If anything, that mindset dictates to them an almost exclusive concern with the loss of ancestral property. But their eventual modernization is inevitable. It is anticipated even by the Israeli 'Arabist experts' who are no fools. As soon as it comes, the Palestinians are bound to perceive themselves first and foremost as victims of Israeli legal discrimination, applied against them by virtue of their being non-Jews. When this occurs, Israel's domestic and international position can be expected to become highly unstable. Some Israeli decision-makers can be presumed to be aware of it. It can even be presumed that a major reason of the Oslo process was the hope (common to both Israel and Arafat) to arrest the process of Palestinian society's change by using force to refeudalize it. But the Israeli experts must know that the probability of arresting social change is very low, at least within Israel. In other words, Israel as an imperial power is not even contemplating adapting itself to changing circumstances in a way other than the way previous imperial powers did with success. To return to the Druze case: even if Brigadier-General (Reserves) Muhammad Kana'an, who performed to perfection the duties of military commander of the Gaza Strip during the Intifada and who yet, as a non-Jew is as discriminated against by Israel as any other non-Jew, is not aware of this fact, his sons and sons of other Druze are sure to be aware of it in a not-so-distant future.

The second example concerns the two Arab villages in Galilee, Bir'am and Ikrit. The inhabitants of both are Christians who didn't resist Israeli forces in 1948, and who surrendered as soon as the Israeli Army was approaching. Their inhabitants were evacuated 'for two weeks only', as was solemnly promised in the capitulation accord signed by the Israeli Army. After two weeks, however, the Army reneged on its promise. In 1951 the Supreme Court ruled in favour of the villagers' return, but its verdict was soon overruled on the basis of the 'Defence Regulations 1945'. These regulations had originally been passed by the British to be used against the Jews. Before the creation of the State of Israel they were described by some of the most respected Jewish legal authorities in Palestine as 'Nazi-like laws', or as 'even worse than the Nazi laws', because they provided the government with almost unlimited powers on the condition of exercising them through the Army. Begin's Deputy Prime Minister, Simha Erlich, quipped that 'these Regulations let a general commanding the Jerusalem district or a Defence Minister surround the Knesset by tanks and arrest its members with perfect legality.' The State of Israel nevertheless kept them in force, applying them, however, almost exclusively against non-Jews. In the case of Bir'am and Ikrit, Ben Gurion's administration was able to respond to the Supreme Court's verdict by using the Defence Regulations 1945 to confiscate land belonging to the two villages and by ordering the Air Force to bomb both villages on Christmas Eve 1951; the adult male villagers were rounded up and forced to watch from the nearby hill how their houses were being demolished. Only the churches were spared from destruction: they serve to this day as destinations for pilgrimage for the former villagers who retain their Israeli citizenship. The remainder of the land was allocated to kibbutzim and moshavim, with a 'left-wing' kibbutz (which even adopted Bir'am's name) receiving the lion's share. The Supreme Court ruled that these confiscations and demolition orders had been perfectly legal.

Nevertheless, the inhabitants of the two villages have been campaigning up to this very day: particularly those of Bir'am who are all of Maronite religion and many quite right-wing politically. Rationally speaking, their campaign could have a good chance in succeeding, especially after they solemnly and repeatedly declared that they weren't demanding their farmlands, but only the church, the neighbouring cemetery and a tiny plot nearby to be used as a museum. All pragmatic considerations would be in favour of accepting their modest request. After all, many of them serve in the Israeli Police. They have close connections with Maronites in Lebanon which Israel had exploited before and during its invasion of Lebanon. Their case is supported by the Catholic Church and other important international bodies. Yet there is no chance that their request may be accepted, least so by the current 'peace government'.

For the analysis of Israeli policies in the era of the 'peace process', it is even more important to recall that by the time the Oslo Accord was signed Israel had already turned about 70 per cent of West Bank land into 'state land' which, like in Israel, could be leased only to Jews. (By further confiscations this percentage has after Oslo risen to 72 or 73 per cent but for the purpose of this report I will use the round figure 70 per cent.) All the West Bank settlements being built on this land, are intended only for Jews, who don't even need to be Israeli. Jews from all over the world are entitled to settle on this land. Hence the Western media are wrong (possibly even deliberately) in their persistent use of the term 'Israeli settlements'. The fact is that a non-Jewish Israeli citizen, like Brigadier-General (Reserves) Muhammad Kana'an, is denied the legal right to settle in these settlements; and so are Christians who fervently support 'Greater Israel'. If we suppose that one day the Spirit will command the Reverend Jerry Falwell or the Reverend Pat Robertson to leave their holy work in the US in order to settle in Kiryat Arba, they won't be allowed to as non-Jews. But if we suppose that the Spirit will command them to convert to Judaism, they will become legally eligible to settle in any Jewish settlement right from the moment their conversion is finalized. This is not just a theoretical possibility, as groups of converts to Judaism from some obscure tribes in Peru and India have actually been brought and settled in the Territories.

On the other hand, Druze veterans (some of whom profess very hawkish views) have made several attempts of to apply for an allotment of West Bank state land in order to establish a Druze settlement there. All such requests were firmly denied, against best Israeli interest. Moreover, especially since the inception of the Intifada, Palestinian collaborators living in fear of death have persistently requested the Israeli authorities to let them settle in Jewish settlements of the West Bank, even temporarily. As some of them argued, this would be highly advantageous to Israeli Intelligence since they could live close to their former homes and be able to maintain to some extent their former contacts. Yet again, all such requests were firmly denied. After Oslo, Israel had to remove some collaborators from the West Bank and settle them in Israel. But even then, instead of allotting them any state land, it rented private land or private housing for the purpose.

Let me return to the West Bank land issue. Of the 70 per cent of its land which became state land, only 16 per cent has actually been allocated to Jewish settlements. The remaining 54 per cent stands empty. It needs to be acknowledged that removing Jewish settlements, perhaps even a single one of them, may well give rise to grave political problems, including the risk of armed clashes which may even escalate into a civil war. But the prospect of returning some of the 54 per cent of empty state land back to Palestinian peasants carries only minimal risks. It could have been done easily during the first months after Oslo. Since the attachment of the Palestinians (not only the peasants but of the entire nation) to the land is profound, and the well-justified fear of being driven away from it palpable, one can easily imagine the effect of a partial restitution of the empty 54 per cent of the West Bank land on the Palestinian masses. A better way of binding Palestinian public opinion to Israeli interests served by the Oslo and Cairo Accords could hardly be imagined.

The same is true for the Gaza Strip. If anything, its case is more glaring because the number of Jewish settlers there – 5,000 when the Oslo Accord was signed and since increased to about 8,000 – is incommensurably smaller than the number of Jewish settlers in the West Bank – 130,000 when the Oslo Accord was signed, since increased to about 160,000, East Jerusalem excluded. Also, the proportion of Jewish settlers to Palestinians in the Gaza Strip (officially 800,000, in reality about million) is completely different in scale than the proportion of the West Bank Jewish settlers to West Bank Palestinians (officially about 1,200,000, in reality about 1,300,000 excluding East Jerusalem). Yet about 28 per cent of the Strip's area duly converted to state land, was allotted to Jewish settlers long before Oslo and after Oslo withheld from the autonomy's jurisdiction. Also in the Strip no empty state land was restored to Palestinian ownership. In the case of the Gaza Strip I don't know the proportion of the empty to the settled state lands, but I know that the former exist. In the case of settlement of Netzarim (whose residents are for the most part engaged in studying Talmud), detailed maps have been published in the Hebrew press (for example, *Haaretz*, 10 April). The maps show a large land area attached to that settlement, necessarily empty but of course denied to the Palestinians.

Nevertheless, Rabin hasn't contemplated giving back to Palestinian peasants, or even to the Palestinian Authority, a few symbolic dunums of the state land around Netzarim. True, some Zionist 'peaceniks' are advocating the removal of the whole Jewish settlement of Netzarim saying that if they remain, they may be killed by Palestinians. As mentioned above, this is regarded as a factor which may temporarily override ideological considerations. But no Zionist 'peace lover' has as yet advocated the return of an empty state land for the sake of a political advantage. This can be generalized. The peace process was 'sold' to Israeli Jews not only as an effective means of guaranteeing their security, but also as potentially profitable from the trade with Arab states expected to expand in its wake. Nevertheless, no Zionist has ever proposed that the sacred ideology of discriminating against non-Jews be for once sacrificed for the sake of advancing the Oslo process and thus enhancing Israel's power and wealth. To the best of my recollection, Israel (or the Zionist Movement before its inception) has never sacrificed its ideology on the altar of merely political considerations or economic interests.

In other words, empirical evidence (valid as anything in politics can be valid) shows that Israeli policies are primarily ideologically motivated and the ideology by which they are motivated is totalitarian in nature. This ideology can be easily known since it is enshrined in the writings of the founders of Labor Zionism, and it can be easily inferred from Israeli laws, regulations and pursued policies. Those who, like Arafat, his henchmen and most Palestinian intellectuals, have through all these years failed to make an intellectual effort to study seriously this ideology, have only themselves to blame for being stunned by all the developments in the 20 months after Oslo. Whoever after Oslo stopped denouncing Israeli 'imperialism' for the sake of a meaningless 'peace of the brave' slogan, showed that he learned nothing and forgot nothing. Their blunder is the greater since Israel is by no means unique in pursuing ideologically determined policies. Strict ideological considerations determine policies in plenty of other past and present states. In other cases an ideology underlying a given policy, however, is not only openly admitted by a state concerned, but also well-known and discussed beyond its borders. Israel is indeed unique in that the discriminatory Jewish ideology dictating its policies is hardly ever discussed beyond its borders, due to the fear of offending the Jews of the Diaspora and of being labelled by their powerful organizations as an 'anti-Semite' or 'Jewish self-hater'. At the same time in Israel the ideology of discriminating against all non-Jews is not only openly admitted but also advocated as guaranteeing the character of Israel as a 'Jewish state' mandated to preserve its 'Jewish character'. The Jewish supporters of Israeli discriminatory practices admit that they thus want to preserve the 'Jewish character' of Israel, conceived of by them and by the majority of Israeli Jews, as the legacy of historical Judaism. Indeed, if we overlook modern times, there is sufficient truth in this claim. Until the advent of modern times all Jews firmly believed that non-Jews should be discriminated against whenever possible. It now turns out that the Jewish Enlightenment failed to change the attitudes of most Jews in this respect. Many irreligious Jews still believe that for the sake of Jewish religious law and tradition which commanded the discrimination of the non-Jews, the latter should be discriminated in the 'Jewish state' forever. This is professed in spite, or perhaps even because of the undeniable fact that this discrimination has the same character as that which the anti-Semites want to apply against the Jews.

In the light of the ideological impact upon actual Israeli policies, the critiques of the latter by the pragmatists of the Israeli left are valid, yet in one crucial respect inadequate. For all their superiority to the 'experts in Israeli affairs' from the Western press, the Israeli leftists always seem puzzled by the policies Israel is pursuing. They never cease to offer the Israeli government 'good advice' on how it can gain in its relations with the Arabs by 'being moderate'. Analysis and experience show that offering such advice amounts to an exercise in futility. Numerous historical analogies, including the recent collapse of communist regimes in Europe, show conclusively that a real change is impossible as long as a party representing no matter how flexibly a state ideology stays in power. In Israel, power is firmly in the hand of the Security System and of the Zionist parties whose deep commitment to Zionist ideology has not been challenged. On the other hand, those analogies show that once the power of a state ideology is challenged in public, it means that a real change is on its way. Eventually, such a change may materialize in a sudden disintegration of the state ideology and the state apparatus supporting it. This happened since the late 1970s in Poland. KOR and Solidarity, which challenged the ideological basis of the state, were the true harbingers of the fall of European communism; whereas the plethora of reforms imposed by the Polish Communist Party from above amounted to no more than palliatives which changed nothing. The Israeli ideology, which had been only slightly undermined in the period of 1974–93, has been again revitalized in the aftermath of Oslo. Due to its great social cohesiveness, military and particularly nuclear power and the increasing support of the US Israel feels at present too strong to offer even palliative concessions to Palestinians. Under those conditions ideological considerations can remain to be predominant, except when Jewish lives are lost.

From high abstraction let me again pass to matters more concrete and show how the actual Israeli policies in the Gaza Strip and the West Bank draw from the ideology of continuous discrimination by means more effectual than beforehand. Let me first deal with the Gaza Strip. Detailed maps of the Strip often published by the Hebrew press (but never by the Palestinian press!) show how it is criss-crossed by 'military roads' which according to the Cairo Accords remain under Israeli jurisdiction. Those roads are constantly patrolled by the Israeli Army, either separately or jointly with the Palestinian police. The Israeli Army has the right to close any such road to all Palestinian traffic, even if it runs deep within the autonomy, and it actually uses this right after any Palestinian assault. For example, *Haaretz* (11 April) reported that the Israeli Army closed 'until further notice' two road sections deep inside the autonomy 'to all Palestinian vehicles' after two assaults which occurred two days earlier. Appended to the report was a map showing the Strip's roads. One of them, called 'Gaza city bypassing road', traverses the entire length of the Strip, carefully bypassing the cities and refugee camps. A military road and a narrow strip of land not included in the autonomy cuts it off from Egypt. A number of parallel roads traverse the Strip's autonomous area from the Israeli border on its east side to the sea or a Jewish settlement block on the west. One such road is the Netzarim road. It begins at an authorized entry point to the autonomy at Nahal Oz. From there it runs westward, skirting all Palestinian localities. After crossing the 'Gaza city bypassing road' it reaches Netzarim. It does not end there, however, but continues to a military fortress on the sea. It thus cuts the Gaza Strip into two parts. All authorized entry points to the autonomy are located at the beginning of military roads.

The overall effect is that the autonomous part of the Gaza Strip is sliced into enclaves controlled by the bypassing roads. The role of the Jewish settlements is not only to guard state land, but also to serve as pivots of the road grid devised to ensure a perpetual Israeli control of the Strip under a new and more effective form. This 'control from outside' allows the Army to dominate the Strip (and to reconquer it with a minimum effort if need be) without having to commit a large number of personnel for constant patrolling and pacifying the Strip's towns and refugee camps 'from inside'. The latter task is now being undertaken on Israel's behalf by various uniformed and secret polices under Arafat's command.

Turning to the West Bank, the task of the 'Rainbow of Colours' is to produce results similar to those already existing in the Gaza Strip. The conditions there may turn out even worse, due to a much larger number of settlers and to the extensive construction of the separate networks of roads, electricity and water supplies for the settlers which cannot but pass near or through the Palestinian enclaves. Moreover, the West Bank includes the 'Greater Jerusalem' area in which the apartheid is practised more strictly than elsewhere. 'Greater Jerusalem' officially extends from Ramallah to the south of Bethlehem, but in the future it can be assumed to grow. To make the matters worse, the Palestinians from the Territories are to be forever barred from crossing to Israel. Their labour force is to be employed in 'industrial parks' exporting mostly to the US. Even at its worst, South African apartheid was not as all-inclusive as what is planned for the West Bank and what already exists in the Gaza Strip.

Why do the experts of the Israeli government expect acquiescence to this situation on the part of the Palestinians (including the Israeli citizens among them, whose influence in Knesset can be considerable) and on the part of international public opinion? Israeli experts and the government apparently anticipate to make those realities palatable for both parties as long as Israel confines itself only to 'control from outside', while leaving 'control from

inside' (that is, the job of actually enforcing order) in the hands of
Israel's Palestinian proxies who will be granted a semblance of an
independent authority. (I am not going to discuss international
public opinion because Latin American and African precedents
make me convinced that the response of the world at large to the
'control from inside' will be as acquiescent as in Palestine.) Much
as I abhor the Israeli government's plans on moral grounds, this
anticipation strikes me as well-grounded. After all, a large majority
of Palestinians have tamely acquiesced to the numerous violations
of human rights committed directly by Arafat's regime in the Gaza
Strip and by his secret police in the West Bank. The potentially
violent dispute between Arafat and Hamas is about power rather
than about human or any other rights.

This is the place to recall that the standard of life in the Strip
has decreased by about 60 per cent since Arafat arrived there. Of
course, the main responsibility for this state of affairs is Israel's,
although Arafat's contribution to it through his corruption and
inefficiency shouldn't be overlooked. But the point I am trying to
make is not at all economic. To keep the Palestinians as poor as
possible has always been an aim of Israeli policy, in my view also
in order to arrest social change in their society. With Arafat's
complicity Israel now can achieve this aim without eliciting any
strong protests, and without spending much of its manpower on
suppressing such protests. In other words, it can impoverish the
Palestinians cheaply and effectively. Bureaucracies tend to believe
that their successes can be stretched indefinitely, and the Israeli
Security System is no exception. No wonder it believes that if a
solution tested in the Gaza Strip has worked well there, it would
also work well when the 'Rainbow of Colours' is implemented in
the West Bank. Likewise, the Security System probably believes
that if the Palestinian uniformed and secret police obey Arafat's
orders so faithfully, they will continue to do so when commanded
by somebody else.

Those hypotheses about the Israeli Security System's modes of
thinking can be confirmed by facts. For example, while much land
is now being confiscated in the West Bank for the purpose of
constructing the bypassing roads, there have been few if any popular
protests against those confiscations. The protests of the Palestinian
Authority against the recent confiscations of land in East Jerusalem
stand in glaring contrast to its silence in cases of the much more
massive land confiscations currently going on elsewhere in the
West Bank. Danny Rubinstein, writing in *Haaretz* (12 May),
explains that in the case of Jerusalem Arafat is constrained to
protest by the leaders of Arab and Muslim states, for whose publics
Jerusalem is a particularly sensitive religious issue. The same
leaders, however, couldn't care less about the West Bank. Rubinstein

reports that 'many delegations from West Bank localities came recently to Arafat. Their grievances were many, but they particularly emphasized that their lands were being confiscated. Arafat did his best to mollify those delegations. For example, a delegation of inhabitants of [the town of] Al-Birah, located near Ramallah, who received land confiscation orders from Israeli authorities intending to build a road bypassing their town to serve the needs of the settlement of Psagot, recently requested Arafat to intervene to have these orders annulled. One delegate told me how stunned he was by Arafat's response. Arafat told them: "Forget this matter. This is only a minor confiscation. It is preferable to have this land confiscated than Psagot settlers driving through your town and causing trouble. Owing to this confiscation, the settlers will at least be able to bypass your town."' Rubinstein says that Arafat is giving such 'advice whenever he fears that his opposition to an Israeli measure may result in cancellation of his negotiations with Israel'. I can confirm Rubinstein's view by information from my own sources, both Israeli and Palestinian. Moreover, Arafat's 'advice' works, because it is backed by the people's fear of his thugs. This is why most attempts to organize popular protests against the confiscation of land have been stifled. Israel could not expect a more effective support for its apartheid policies than Arafat's.

Yet in two factual points I differ from the Israeli Security System's assessments of Arafat's role. First, they ignore the impact of Arafat's behaviour on the Jewish public in Israel. In order to let Arafat serve Israeli interests effectively, Israel must salvage his dwindling prestige among the Palestinians, and for that purpose leaves him a considerable freedom of expression, never granted to Palestinian collaborators before. Arafat takes advantage of this privilege to indulge in the most outrageous lies and to make the most provocative attacks on Israel. As an example of the former, one can give his oft-repeated assertion that Israel (or Israeli Army officers, or Shabak's agents) conspired with Hamas to carry out the Beit-Lid terror assault. As an example of the latter, one can give his frequent assertion that all of Jerusalem (not only its Eastern part) belongs to the Arabs or to the Muslims. While neither Rabin nor Peres dare to expose Arafat as a liar or to denounce his position on Jerusalem as incompatible with that of all Zionist parties (even Meretz supports the so-called 'unification of Jerusalem'), the Hebrew press often does so, and so do the opposition's politicians. Rabin's dwindling credibility and popularity can be attributed to the Jewish public's outrage at his condonement of Arafat's lies and antics. To a much greater degree the same is the case of Peres and the entire Israeli 'peace camp' which seem to be losing whatever political clout they once had. In other words, the advantages of the 'control from outside' are being neutralized by the domestic drawbacks of using

Arafat. As the 1996 elections are approaching, the latter factor can be assumed to increasingly outweigh the former in importance.

The second point where I differ from the Israeli Security System's assessments concerns the 'Rainbow of Colours'. The Israeli experts assume it can last forever, whereas I think it is bound to collapse eventually. Even if Arafat succeeds in smashing all opposition to his rule, I doubt if he can keep the Palestinian population inside their enclaves forever under his control. After all, the facts on the ground, including the deterioration of the economy and the increased apartheid will be all too tangible for the Palestinians and will be bound to undermine Arafat's standing. At present it is mainly Arafat's vestigial prestige and his use of brute force which keeps the 'control from outside' functioning. Once all his credibility is gone the Israeli alternative for exercising 'control from outside' would be by a naked Palestinian dictatorship, Arafat's or somebody else's. The oppression then unleashed is bound to surpass anything experienced in the period of 'control from inside'.

I am fully conscious of the immense human suffering which such an oppression is bound to cause. Yet I do not attribute much political importance to the question of whether it can succeed and for how long. In any event, it will mark the failure of the 'control from outside' scheme as an easy and cheap method of domination, which can be 'sold', Peres-style, to the international public. In the last analysis the failure of the 'control from outside' cannot but mark the end of Israeli policies based on the absolute priority of Zionist ideology.

Index

Abdullah, King, of Jordan, 80
Abramovitz, Amnon, 35
Abud, Bob, Hammer oil
  company, 52–3
Admon, Telem, *Maariv*
  journalist, 56
Afghanistan, 86
Africa, Israeli contacts in, 70
Africa, Horn of, Islamic
  fundamentalism in, 67–8
Agrexco, agricultural exports,
  108, 109, 111
agriculture: exports, 107–8,
  111–12; racist principles in
  Israeli, 112
Aharonson, Professor Shlomo,
  56–7
AIPAC (American Israeli Political
  Action Committee), 121, 128,
  129, 132, 135, 144
air raids, 49, 55
Al Birah, land confiscations in,
  179
Al-Ahram (Egyptian newspaper),
  Peres interview, 67
al-Aqsa mosque, arson attack on,
  157
Al-Hamishmar (former kibbutz
  movement newspaper), 9, 20,
  54–5, 56; Ein-Dor's article in,
  99, 100, 106
Aleppo, Israeli threat to, 46, 48
Algeria, 72, 86, 106
Alon, Azarya, *Davar* journalist, 80
Alon, Yigal, former Foreign
  Minister, 49
Aloni, Shulamit, 132
Amin El-Haj, Lebanese merchant,
  110–11

Amit, Yosef, Military Intelligence
  officer, drugs trial of, 113–14
apartheid, Israeli policy for
  Occupied Territories, 164, 167,
  177
Arab citizens of Israel, 17, 112,
  131–2, 135; in Army, 1, 120;
  and land laws, 169–70, *see also*
  Druzes; Occupied Territories;
  Palestinians
Arab states, 39, 100, 122; direct
  trade with Israel, 103–6, 107,
  174; Israeli fear of democracy
  in, 76, 106, 122, 160–1; Israeli
  relations with, 71–2; Israeli
  strategy against, 33, 151–2;
  nuclearization of, 34, 37, 54,
  150; trade boycott of Israel, 99,
  100, 101, 107; weakness of
  armies, 161, *see also* individual
  states, especially Iran; Iraq;
  Syria
Arafat, Yasser, x, xii, 69, 131,
  145; and control of Occupied
  Territories, 158, 163–4, 166,
  179–80; corruption of, 178–9;
  'cultivated' by Rabin, 162;
  ignorance of Israeli ideology,
  175; and Saddam Hussein, 89
Arap Moi, Daniel, of Kenya, 68
Arens, Moshe, Defence Minister,
  24, 46, 101, 148
Argentina: state terrorism of, 85,
  86, *see also* Buenos Aires
armed forces *see* Israeli Army
Armenian nationalism, Turkey,
  76
arms sales: by Israel, 68, 71,
  103–4; from US to Israel, 25,
  26, 64, 94–5, 96